STRUCTURED FORTRAN 77 for Engineers and Scientists

STRUCTURED FORTRAN 77

for Engineers and Scientists

D. M. Etter
University of New Mexico, Albuquerque

The Benjamin/Cummings Publishing Company, Inc.
Menlo Park, California · Reading, Massachusetts · London ·
Amsterdam · Don Mills, Ontario · Sydney

To my family, Amy Marie and Jerry Richard.

Sponsoring Editors: S.A. Newman, John Noon
Production Editor: Greg Hubit
Book Designer: Marilyn Langfeld
Cover Designer: Henry Breuer

Library of Congress Cataloging in Publication Data

Etter, D. M.
  Structured FORTRAN 77 for engineers and scientists.

  Includes index.
  1. FORTRAN (Computer program language)
2. Structured programming.   I. Title.
QA76.73.F25E85   001.64′24   82-4400
ISBN 0-8053-2520-4   AACR2

BCDEFGHIJ-HA-89876543

The Benjamin/Cummings Publishing Company, Inc.
2727 Sand Hill Road
Menlo Park, California 94025

The Benjamin/Cummings Series in
Computing and Information Sciences

G. Booch
Software Engineering with Ada (1983)

H. L. Capron, B. K. Williams
Computers and Data Processing (1982)

D. M. Etter
Structured FORTRAN 77 for Engineers and Scientists (1983)

P. Linz
Programming Concepts and Problem Solving: An Introduction to Computer Science Using PASCAL (1983)

PREFACE

The techniques, examples, and problems in this book were developed with the following objectives:

1 To acquaint students with the capabilities of computers and the types of problems that computers can solve.

2 To teach the fundamentals of FORTRAN 77 so that students can use the computer to solve problems they encounter in both academic and nonacademic environments.

3 To establish good problem-solving techniques that can be applied to any problem, whether computer-related or not.

4 To use practical, real-world engineering and science problems while accomplishing the first three objectives.

This book assumes no prior experience with computers; it therefore begins with an introductory chapter that explains many terms associated with them. This chapter also introduces the process of converting a problem solution described in English into a solution understandable by a computer. The presentation of FORTRAN statements begins with Chapter 2, using the language version established in 1977 (and thus called FORTRAN 77). By the end of Chapter 3, simple, yet complete, programs have been written.

It is recommended that the material in this book be covered sequentially, and it is reasonable to expect to cover all nine chapters in one semester or two quarters. Typically, this material is presented at the freshman level in a university curriculum, and, although calculus is not required, a knowledge of basic algebra and trigonometry is assumed.

A number of features distinguish this from other FORTRAN books:

Engineering and Science Applications   Over 300 examples and problems represent a wide range of engineering and science applications. Such topics as laser mirror alignment, radioactive decay, economics of timber management, and solar energy data analysis are included. Many of the solved problems contain sample data and corresponding output from an actual computer run.

Complete FORTRAN 77 Coverage   Complete coverage of FORTRAN 77 makes this not only a suitable book for the first-time computer user but also one that can be a valuable reference for the sophisticated user. In addition, only standard FORTRAN 77 statements and structures are used so that all programs and statements are compatible with FORTRAN 77 compilers.

Motivational Problems as Chapter Openers   Each chapter is opened with a specific problem that cannot reasonably be solved with the FORTRAN statements presented up to that point. Hence, motivation is established to develop new elements of the language in order to solve the described problem. After the new topics are covered, the introductory problem is then solved.

Structured Programming Approach   The most important new feature of FORTRAN 77 is the addition of a new control structure (IF-THEN-ELSE) that allows us to write structured programs—programs that flow smoothly from top to bottom. The importance of this top-down flow is emphasized repeatedly. All program loops are implemented as iteration loops (DO loops) or WHILE loops, thus avoiding the stray GO TO statements that defeat the objectives of structured programming.

Stepwise Refinement   As we develop algorithms (the ordered steps to solve a problem), we start with a general solution and refine it until we arrive at an algorithm detailed enough to convert into FORTRAN 77. Both flowcharts and pseudocode are used to describe the algorithms.

Style/Technique Guide   Each chapter after the introductory chapter contains a "Style/Technique Guide" to promote good programming habits that stress readability and simplicity. Although there are entire books devoted to programming style and technique, this topic is included in each chapter with the premise that developing good style and technique is an integral part of learning the language.

In addition to this special section at the end of each chapter, a number of examples in the text have multiple solutions, thereby exposing the student to different approaches for solving the same problem. If one of the solutions has better style or technique than the others, this is pointed out in the accompanying discussion.

Debugging Aids   Each chapter after the introductory chapter also contains "Debugging Aids," a section which outlines efficient methods for locating and correcting program errors that are relevant to the programming techniques described in the chapter. With guidance from this section, the student learns consistent methods for spotting and avoiding the common errors associated with each new FORTRAN statement.

In addition to this special section at the end of each chapter, a number of examples in the text include an incorrect solution to a problem, along with the correct solution. The incorrect solution is used to highlight the more common errors, thus helping the student avoid making the same mistakes.

Large Number of End-of-Chapter Problems   Over 250 problems are included for end-of-chapter review and practice. These problems vary in degree of difficulty, with the more challenging problems marked with an asterisk. Solutions to nearly half of the problems are included at the end of the text. These problems are identified by printing the problem number in color. Many of the problems include data to use when testing the programs on the computer.

Emphasis on Interactive Processing   While both batch processing and time-sharing processing are discussed, emphasis is placed on time-sharing processing with interactive terminals. The use of data files is presented in Chapter 3 and included in many examples in the remainder of the book. Conversational computing is also presented in several examples and problems.

I/O Flexibility   List-directed I/O is presented first, immediately followed by a complete description of formatted I/O. Instructors can have the student skip the formatted I/O sections entirely if they want to use only list-directed I/O. However, if a good understanding of formatted I/O is desired, it is important to present it early so that it can be reinforced in the remainder of the book. While I/O is formatted in the examples and problems, students using list-directed I/O need only ignore the FORMAT statements.

Use of a Second Color   Few computer language books have had the opportunity to use an additional color for emphasis and clarity. Pedagogically, the use of color in emphasizing certain statements within a computer program is especially significant. Without using arrows or lines or other distracting symbols, we can clearly emphasize every use of a new statement or point out the differences in two similar program segments.

New Computer Print Characters   This is one of the first computer language textbooks to use the new typeface that duplicates the dot matrix characters of computer printouts. This special typeface allows us to identify each line that represents a complete FORTRAN statement or computer output with a clarity that is not possible when merely photocopying actual computer output.

Student Aids   Several features of this book were designed specifically to aid the student. Each chapter summary is followed by a list of key words from the chapter. In all, over 200 key words have been selected to assist in identifying important terms. Appendix A contains a summary of all FORTRAN 77 statements along with references to the location in the text of the initial presentation of each statement. Appendix B contains a table of all FORTRAN 77 intrinsic functions, their definitions, and their input arguments. A Glossary contains the definitions of over 100 common computer-related terms in addition to the index references.

Instructor Aids   An Instructor's Supplement is available to instructors by request to the publisher. This supplement contains class notes, viewgraphs that use new examples, sample test questions and solutions, new computer projects, and complete solutions to the end-of-chapter problems.

ACKNOWLEDGMENTS

This book is the product of many semesters of teaching and incorporates many creative thoughts from my students. I would especially like to express my appreciation to Barbara Johnston, Jim Krone, Donna O'Shay, Bernie Clifford, Richard Owen, and Rick Nichols for their contributions. I would also like to thank the following reviewers who provided helpful suggestions: Ronald Danielson, University of Santa Clara; William Holley, Oregon State University; John Goda, Georgia Institute of Technology; Lee Maxwell, Colorado State University; Joyce Blair, Eastern Kentucky University; John R. Zimmerman, University of Delaware; Susanne M. Shelley, Sacramento State University; Ted Wagstaff, Georgia Institute of Technology; Glen Williams, Texas A&M; Edward T. Ordman, New England College (Henniker, NH); Elizabeth Unger, Kansas State University; Joe Jefferis, Wright State University (OH); Robert Aiken, University of Tennessee; Enrique A. Gonzales, University of Lowell (MA); William Harlow, University of Cincinnati. Most of all, I would like to thank my sponsoring editor, Susan Newman, for her support, encouragement, and confidence in me. Finally, I must also thank Barbara Myers and Donna Kelly for the meticulous typing and retyping of the several drafts of this book.

D. M. ETTER

BRIEF CONTENTS

DETAILED CONTENTS

Chapter 1 ends with a Summary and Key Words; Chapters 2–9 end with a Summary, Key Words, Debugging Aids, Style/Technique Guides, and Problems.

STRUCTURED FORTRAN 77 for Engineers and Scientists

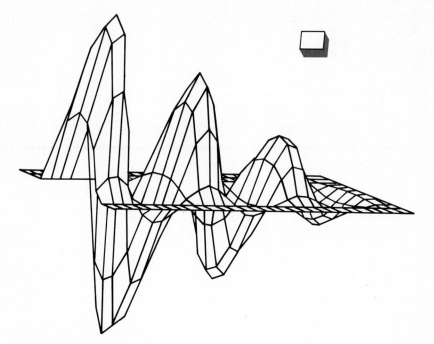

COMPUTER GRAPHICS

Most FORTRAN programs are used to compute numerical values. While the values could be printed in a table, they could also be displayed graphically, as shown above. The graph represents a damped sinusoid, a three-dimensional sine function that decays to zero as time increases. Trying to visualize such a function from a list of numbers would be difficult, but as you can see, *computer graphics* provide one way of displaying data in a clear and simple form.

INTRODUCTION TO COMPUTING

INTRODUCTION

Computers are evident in nearly every aspect of life today. As we understand more about computers and their capabilities, we will be able to use them more effectively and creatively in both our professional and personal endeavors. One objective of this text is to teach you the capabilities and the limitations of computers—what they can and cannot do. Another objective is to teach you how to logically solve problems by breaking them into a series of sequentially executed steps. These two objectives will be interwoven with the primary objective of teaching you how to use the FORTRAN computer language to solve typical problems encountered in engineering and science.

1-1 GENERAL INTRODUCTION TO THE COMPUTER

Computers come in many forms, from the large multi-purpose computer system shown in Figure 1-1 to the integrated circuit chips shown in Figure 1-2. The size and complexity needed in a computer system depend on the functions required of the computer. If the computer is to be part of a specialized piece of electronic equipment, such as a fuel-injection system for a car engine or an oscilloscope with a memory component, a *minicomputer* or *microprocessor* is sufficient. However, if a computer system is to perform many

FIGURE 1-1   Large computer system. (Courtesy of Cray Research, Inc.)

functions and accept many different computer languages, a larger system is often necessary.

Nearly all forms of computers, large or small, can be represented by the block diagram of Figure 1-3. In large computer systems, each part is physically distinguishable from the others. In a microprocessor or minicomputer, all the parts within the dotted line may be combined in a single integrated circuit chip.

The *processing unit* or *processor* is the part of the computer that controls all the other parts. The processor accepts *input* values and stores them in the *memory*. It also interprets the instructions in a computer program. If we want to add two values, the processor will retrieve them from the memory and send them to the *arithmetic logic unit* or *ALU*. The ALU performs the desired addition, and the processor will then store the result in the memory. If we desire, we may also direct the processor to *output* the result on printed paper.

FIGURE 1-2 Microprocessor and integrated circuit chips. (Courtesy of Digital Equipment Corporation)

A small amount of memory, the *internal memory*, is used by the processing unit and the ALU in their processing, while most data is stored in *external memory*. The processor, internal memory, and ALU are collectively referred to as the *central processing unit* or *CPU*.

When working with computers, you will often hear the terms *software* and *hardware*. Software refers to the programs that direct computers to perform operations, compute new values, and manipulate data. Hardware refers to the actual components of the computer, such as the memory unit, the processor, and the ALU. Thus, a person who works with software would write computer programs, while a person who works with hardware would design new components or connect devices together. For example, a hardware engineer might design the *interface* equipment necessary to connect a microprocessor to an input terminal.

It is very advantageous to know both software and hardware when working with computers. Even if you will be emphasizing only one of the areas in your use of the computer, it would benefit you to learn more about the other area. The two disciplines must obviously be used together to be productive. Therefore, the better you understand the requirements, capabilities, and limitations of the other area, the better you will be able to perform in your own area.

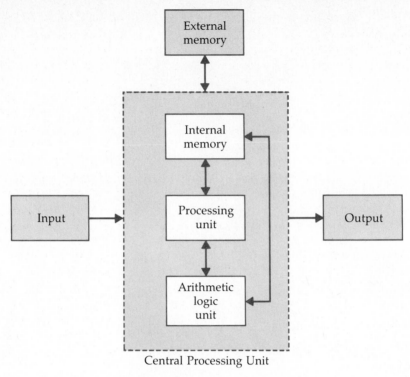

External
memory

Internal
memory

Processing
unit

Input

Output

Arithmetic
logic
unit

Central Processing Unit

FIGURE 1-3 Block diagram of a computer.

1-2   COMPUTER LANGUAGES

Computer hardware is based on two-state (*binary*) technology; that is, computers are built from components that have two values, such as open or
closed, on or off, plus or minus, high or low. These two values can represent
the numbers 0 and 1, and hence computers are often defined to be machines
capable of interpreting and understanding sequences of 0's and 1's called
binary strings. Since the human mind has been trained to think in terms of
English-like phrases and formulas, we use languages such as FORTRAN to
tell the computer the steps we want to perform. Then a special program called
a *compiler* will translate the FORTRAN program into binary strings that the
computer can understand. This compilation procedure will be discussed in
the next section.

FORTRAN (*FOR*mula *TRAN*slation) is a language commonly used by
engineers and scientists because of its orientation toward technical applications. FORTRAN 77 is a specific version of FORTRAN based on a set of
standards established in 1977. It contains essentially all the statements of
older versions, along with new features that enhance the language. When we
refer to FORTRAN, we will be referring to the FORTRAN 77 version. Besides

FORTRAN, there are many other *high-level* languages, such as BASIC, COBOL, Pascal, PL/I, ALGOL, and Ada. These languages are called high-level languages because they are English-like and reasonably easy for us to understand, as opposed to a low-level language such as the binary strings that computers understand. Given a specific problem, its solution could generally be programmed into any computer language. However, some languages were designed with specific types of problems in mind. Thus, while FORTRAN is technically oriented, COBOL was designed to handle more business-related problems. BASIC, a language similar to FORTRAN, is commonly used with minicomputers. ALGOL and Pascal are structured languages, which means that they were designed to yield programs easier to follow and correct than programs in an unstructured language. PL/I is a language that combines many features of FORTRAN, COBOL, and ALGOL. Ada is a structured language designed for the government to be used in technical applications.

Learning a computer language has many similarities to learning a foreign language. Each step that you want the computer to perform must be translated into the computer language you are using. Fortunately, computer languages have a small vocabulary and no verb conjugations. However, computers are unforgiving in punctuation and spelling. A comma or letter in the wrong place will cause errors that keep your program from working. Thus, you will discover that you must pay close attention to many such details.

We have discussed high-level languages (such as FORTRAN) and low-level languages (binary or *machine language*). Another level of computer languages is *assembly languages*. Assembly languages are between high-level and low-level languages and do not require a compiler to translate them into binary. A smaller program, called an *assembler,* translates the assembly language into machine language. Most assembly languages do not have many statements, making them inconvenient to use. For example, you might have to do a series of additions to perform a single multiplication. Also, you have to understand certain elements of the design of the computer in order to use an assembly language. For these reasons, when given a choice, most people prefer to write programs in a high-level language. However, with microprocessors and some minicomputers, you may not have a high-level language capability because a high-level language compiler may require more memory than is available.

Some of the statements in various high-level languages are illustrated in Table 1-1. Each section of code represents the calculation of an employee's salary based on the hours worked and the hourly pay rate. If the number of hours worked is less than or equal to 40, the salary to be paid is computed by multiplying the number of hours worked by the hourly pay rate. If the number of hours worked is greater than 40, then time-and-a-half is paid for the hours over 40. The different names used to represent hours worked, pay rate, and salary reflect the various rules within the individual languages. Also note the differences in punctuation among the various languages.

TABLE 1-1 Examples of High-Level Languages

Language	Example Statements
FORTRAN	``` IF(HOURS.LE.40.0)THEN SALARY = HOURS*PAYRTE ELSE SALARY = 40.0*PAYRTE + (HOURS - 40.0)*PAYRTE*1.5 ENDIF ```
COBOL	``` IF HOURS IS LESS THAN 40.0 OR HOURS IS EQUAL TO 40.0, COMPUTE SALARY = HOURS*PAYRATE ELSE COMPUTE SALARY = 40.0*PAYRATE + (HOURS - 40.0)*PAYRATE*1.5, ```
BASIC	``` IF H > 40.0 THEN 200 LET S = H*P GO TO 250 200 LET S = 40.0*P + (H - 40.0)*P*1.5 250 . . . ```
PL/I	``` IF HOURS <= 40.0 THEN SALARY = HOURS*PAYRATE; ELSE SALARY = 40.0*PAYRATE + (HOURS - 40.0)*PAYRATE*1.5; ```
ALGOL	``` IF HOURS ≦ 40.0 THEN SALARY := HOURS X PAYRATE ELSE SALARY := 40.0 X PAYRATE + (HOURS - 40.0) X PAYRATE X 1.5; ```
Pascal	``` IF HOURS <= 40.0 THEN SALARY := HOURS*PAYRATE ELSE SALARY := 40.0*PAYRATE + (HOURS - 40.0)*PAYRATE*1.5; ```
Ada	``` IF HOURS <= 40.0 THEN SALARY := HOURS*PAYRATE; ELSE SALARY := 40.0*PAYRATE + (HOURS - 40.0)*PAYRATE*1.5; ```

1-3 COMPILING AND EXECUTING A PROGRAM

In the previous section, we defined the compiler as a program that translates a high-level language to machine language. This compilation step is the first step in running a program on the computer. As the compiler translates statements, it also checks for *syntax* errors. Syntax errors, also called *compiler* errors, are errors in the statements themselves, such as misspellings and punctuation errors. If syntax errors are found, the compiler will print error messages or *diagnostics* for you. After making corrections (called *debugging*, because you are removing the *bugs* in your program), you can rerun your program, again starting with the compilation step. Once your program has compiled without errors, it is then submitted to the second step, *execution*. It is in the execution step that the statements are actually performed. Errors can also arise in the execution step; they are called *logic* errors, run-time errors, or execution errors. These errors are not in the syntax of the statement, but are errors in the logic of the statement that are detected only when the computer attempts to execute the statement. For example, the statement

$$X = A/B$$

is a valid FORTRAN statement that directs the computer to divide A by B and call the result X. The statement contains no syntax errors. Suppose, though, that the value of B is zero. Then, as we try to divide A by B, we are attempting to divide by zero, which is an invalid computer operation. Hence, we will get an execution error.

It is uncommon for a program to correctly compile and execute on the first run. Therefore, do not become discouraged if it takes several runs to finally get answers. When you do get answers from your program, do not assume that they are correct. If possible, check your answer with a calculator or check to see if the answer makes sense. For example, if the answer represents the weight of a boxcar, then 5 pounds is not reasonable and suggests that you have not given the computer a correct program to execute.

The FORTRAN program, which is the input to the compilation step, is sometimes referred to as the *source program,* while the output of the compilation step, the machine language translation, is referred to as the *object program.* There are two types of FORTRAN statements in a program, *executable* and *nonexecutable* statements. Executable statements cause some action during execution of the program. Nonexecutable statements generally affect the way that memory is used by the program. In the remaining chapters, we identify statements as executable or nonexecutable as they are introduced.

1-4 INPUT AND OUTPUT DEVICES

Input and output devices, usually called *I/O* devices, form our communication link to the computer. Computer cards can be used for entering programs or data into the computer. In Figure 1-4, we see that a computer card has 80

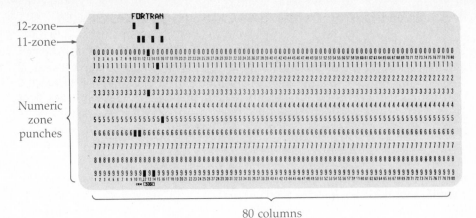

12-zone
11-zone

Numeric
zone
punches

80 columns

FIGURE 1-4   Typical computer card.

FIGURE 1-5   Computer terminals. (Courtesy of Digital Equipment Corporation)

columns for storing information. Each column can have none, one, two, or three holes punched in it to represent different characters. A keypunch machine has a keyboard similar to a typewriter and the holes in the card are punched for an individual character at the same time that the character is printed at the top of the column. For example, in Figure 1-4, we can see that column 10 contains the letter F. The punches that comprise an F are the 12-zone punch and the 6-zone punch. The computer will only read the holes punched in the card. The printing at the top is for your convenience.

The primary output device used by computers typically has been the line printer, which uses computer paper. Usually a computer paper sheet is 11 inches by 14⅞ inches with alternating bars of white and another color. One line of output on this size paper contains 132 characters. Most line printers can also print on forms such as checks, telephone bills, and university grade reports.

The device most commonly used now in industry and universities is the terminal. This device is used for both input and output. It can be a *hard-copy* terminal that prints on paper or a *CRT (cathode ray tube)* terminal that uses a screen. Figure 1-5 contains pictures of these two types of terminals. Ideally, you should use a CRT terminal to do all your initial programming. Then use a hard-copy terminal to get a printed copy of your finished program.

Another common output device is a plotter. Several types of plotters are shown in Figure 1-6. Plotters can be used not only to plot mathematical functions but also to draw items such as electrical circuits or topographical maps. The sinusoidal graph shown at the beginning of the chapter was drawn by a pen plotter.

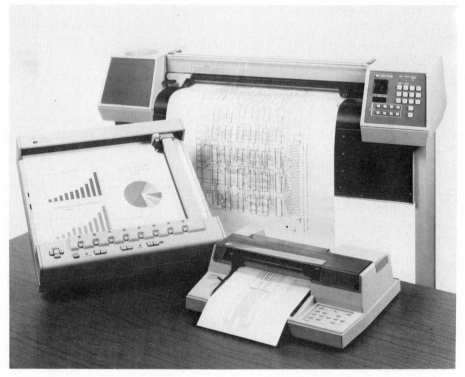

FIGURE 1-6 Pen plotters. (Courtesy of Hewlett-Packard Corporation)

There are many ways to communicate with computers. We have mentioned a few ways, but you have probably seen other examples. Many grocery stores use a light pen to read the bar code on grocery items as you go through the check-out line. A computer then determines the price of the item that is displayed on the cash register screen. The computer can also adjust the inventory totals at the same time it is computing the grocery bill, so that it can print at the end of the day a list of items to restock. Making airline reservations is done almost completely through computer terminals. Computers even control the temperature and humidity in many new buildings.

When using an input device, there are rules about entering the data values or computer programs. With computer cards, data can usually be keypunched in any of the 80 columns. We must, however, be very specific about the columns used in keypunching FORTRAN statements (illustrated in Figure 1-7):

1 Columns 1–5 are reserved for statement numbers, which must be nonzero positive integers. You do not have to number every statement, but, as you will see in later chapters, some statements do need numbers. If column 1 contains the letter C or an *, the card is a *comment card*. The information on comment cards is printed in your program listings but is not converted into machine language.

2 Column 6 is used to indicate that a statement has been continued from the previous card. Any nonblank character except a zero can be punched in column 6 of the second card to indicate continuation. A FORTRAN statement may have several continuation cards if needed.

3 FORTRAN statements cannot start before column 7 nor go beyond column 72.

4 Columns 73–80 are ignored by the computer and can be used for program identification or sequence numbers.

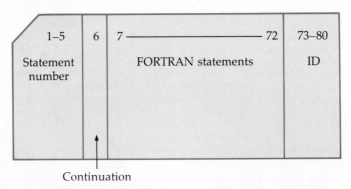

FIGURE 1-7   Keypunch guide for FORTRAN statements.

Blanks may be inserted in FORTRAN statements to improve readability without affecting the way a program executes. For example, the following two statements are exactly the same as far as a FORTRAN compiler is concerned, but the second statement is clearly more readable.

```
A=B+C*6.0-D
A = B + C*6.0 - D
```

The only time that the compiler attaches significance to blanks is within *literals* and character strings, which will be discussed in later chapters.

1-5   BATCH PROCESSING AND TIME-SHARING

There are two methods for running computer programs—*batch processing* and *time-sharing*. In most batch processing systems, your program is entered on cards using a card reader. The computer stores the program in its memory and will compile and execute it when it is next in line. The output of a batch processing system is usually printed on a line printer. Time-sharing systems, however, usually use terminals for entering programs. The program is typed into the terminal, followed by a command such as RUN, which immediately begins the compilation and execution of the program. This technique is called time-sharing because the computer does one step of a program from one terminal, one step of a program from another terminal, and so on until it is back to the first terminal. The computer then performs the next step in each program. We usually do not notice the time between steps because the computer executes a statement so fast. We seem to have the undivided attention of the computer, although we are actually sharing it with many other terminal users. Thus, the main difference between batch processing and time-sharing is the degree of interaction with the computer. The FORTRAN statements used for both systems, however, are virtually the same.

Most time-sharing systems allot each user a specified amount of memory to be used as a *workspace* in the computer. This workspace is usually divided into a *temporary workspace* and a *permanent workspace*. As you enter programs or data into the temporary workspace, you can *edit* the information, which means you can add to it, delete portions of it, or modify it, with the use of a program called an *editor*. When you have the program or data in the form that you want, you can then *save* it in the permanent workspace. You can then *clear* the temporary workspace and begin entering new information, or *log off* the terminal. The next time you *log on* the terminal, you can *load* any information that was previously saved in your permanent workspace into your temporary workspace.

A diagram of a computer system that supports both time-sharing and batch processing is shown in Figure 1-8. The additional memory is used by the time-sharing system.

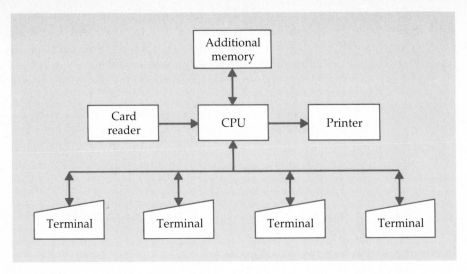

FIGURE 1-8 Computer system with batch processing and time-sharing.

1-6 ALGORITHMIC APPROACH TO PROBLEM SOLVING

We have discussed hardware and software in general terms and are now ready to begin looking at the process of solving problems with computers. This process begins with the development of an *algorithm*, a step-wise procedure for solving a problem. We have used this technique when solving mathematical word problems or physics problems, but probably did not use the term algorithm. We are developing algorithms when solving problems, though, every time we determine the steps to be performed and their sequence. This experience will be invaluable when learning to write programs in FORTRAN. To solve a problem using the computer, first determine the steps that need to be performed and the order in which they are to be performed. These steps can then be translated into FORTRAN statements. Cartoons lead us to believe that computers are capable of solving large complex problems at the touch of a button, but in reality the computer can only perform simple steps in the order directed. The great advantage that computers offer, however, is that they can perform these steps extremely rapidly without errors.

We will develop two tools to aid in developing algorithms: *flowcharts* and *pseudocode*. Flowcharts present a graphical flow diagram of the solution to a problem, while pseudocode presents an English-like description of the problem solution. Both techniques are commonly used, and will be illustrated in Section 1-7. Chapter 4 contains the formal presentation of these techniques.

In addition to using flowcharts and pseudocode, we must also be sure to define the problem solution carefully. *Stepwise refinement* is a technique for developing an algorithm to solve a problem by first looking at the solution in general terms, then successively refining the solution in more detail until the algorithm is specific enough to convert into computer instructions. For simple problems, the transition from a general flowchart to a refined flowchart may take one step, while the transition for a complex problem may take several steps. The advantage of stepwise refinement is that we can initially think of the overall processes required in the algorithm without getting lost in the details. The details of the solution are introduced only as we refine our algorithm. The application in the next section illustrates the use of stepwise refinement, along with flowcharts and pseudocode.

1-7 APPLICATION – UNIVERSITY GRADE POINT AVERAGE

To illustrate the procedure of developing and refining an algorithm, we will present a simple problem and discuss the steps necessary to solve it. These steps will then be shown in flowcharts and in pseudocode to give you an idea of the usefulness of these tools. The significance of the shape of the symbols in the flowcharts and the capitalized words in the pseudocode will be explained in Chapter 4.

EXAMPLE 1-1   Grade Point Average

Assume that you have just received the grades for your university courses. Compute your grade point average, using a 4.0 system.

Solution

To compute your grade point average, you must first convert the letter grade to a numerical grade, using the following table:

LETTER GRADE		NUMERICAL GRADE
A	⟷	4.0
B	⟷	3.0
C	⟷	2.0
D	⟷	1.0
F	⟷	0.0

You then multiply the numerical grade by the number of credit hours for that course. Thus, an A in a 3-hour course yields 12 points.

Finally, you add the points for all the courses and divide that sum by the total number of credit hours to obtain the final average. The following is an example of the procedure:

COURSE	HOURS	GRADE	POINTS
INTRO TO ENGINEERING	4	A	16
CALCULUS I	3	B	9
PHYSICS I	4	B	12
ENGLISH I	3	B	9
AMERICAN HISTORY	3	C	6
	17		52

Grade point average = 52/17 = 3.06.

The general flowchart on the left side of page 17 shows the order of the steps involved—convert letter grade to number grade, multiply number grade by the hours to get points, add points and divide by total hours, and print final answer. The refinement of the general flowchart to a refined flowchart involves defining each step in more detail and adding steps to clarify the process. For instance, the conversion, multiplication, and addition steps in the refined flowchart on the right are repeated for each class; so we can combine them into a *loop*—a set of operations that is repeated. We then need a way to exit the loop, and hence need to ask the question, "Are there more classes?" If there are more classes, we repeat the conversion, multiplication, and addition steps. If there are not more classes, we exit the loop and finish the computation of the grade point average. After printing this final value, the program is completed.

The process of refining pseudocode, as shown on page 18, is essentially the same as refining a flowchart. The general pseudocode for this problem also starts with the steps involved—convert letter grade to number grade, multiply number grade by the hours to get points, add points and divide by total hours, and print final answer. However, these steps are written in a list instead of a flowchart. The refinement of the pseudocode is again the process of defining the steps in more detail. If you compare the refined flowchart to the refined pseudocode, you will see that both define the same steps to the problem solution.   ◇

The purpose of this example was to illustrate refinement of an algorithm with both flowcharts and pseudocode. Typically, you will use flowcharts or pseudocode in developing your solutions, but not both. We will use both methods frequently in the following chapters and discuss in more detail the significance of the symbols used in the flowcharts and the terminology of the pseudocode. A flowchart or pseudocode must ultimately be translated into a computer language in order to be understood by a computer. The discussion of how we make that translation, using FORTRAN, begins in the next chapter.

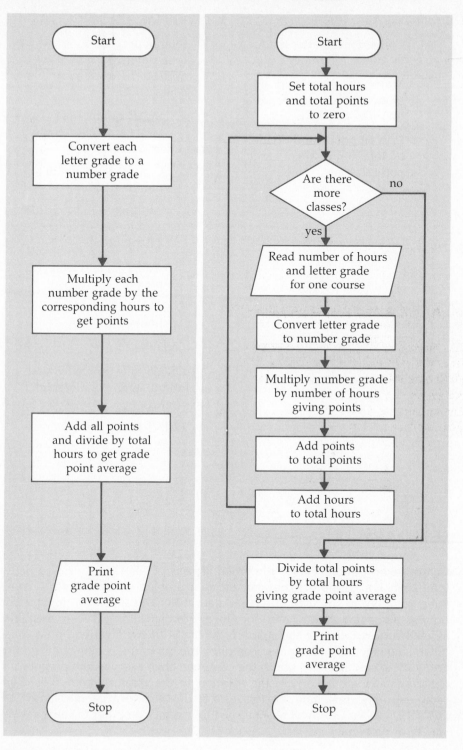

PROGRAM GPA

    Convert each letter grade to numerical grade.

    Multiply each numerical grade by the corresponding hours to get points.

    Add all points and divide by total hours to get grade point average.

STOP

PROGRAM GPA

    total hours ←0
    total points ←0
    WHILE there are more courses DO

        READ number of hours and letter grade for a course

        Convert letter grade to number grade

        Multiply number grade by number of hours, giving points

        Add points to total points

        Add hours to total hours

    ENDWHILE

    Divide total points by total hours, giving grade point average

    PRINT grade point average

STOP

SUMMARY

Chapter 1 introduced you to the broad aspects of computing using a high-level language. The process of converting a problem statement into a computer solution begins with a general algorithm. This algorithm is typically expressed in a flowchart or pseudocode, and is then successively refined into a detailed description of the solution, which is then converted into a computer language. The computer compiles the program, looking for syntax errors. If no syntax errors occur, the computer then executes the program. If the program logic is correct, the solution to the original problem is then computed. The remainder of this text is devoted to a detailed study of FORTRAN so that you will be equipped to use the computer to solve a wide variety of problems.

KEY WORDS

algorithm
arithmetic logic unit (ALU)
assembler
assembly language
batch processing
binary
bug
central processing unit (CPU)
comment statement
compilation
compiler
CRT terminal
data
debugging
diagnostic
editor
executable statement
execution
flowchart
FORTRAN 77
hard-copy terminal
hardware

high-level language
input/output (I/O)
interface
logic error
machine language
memory
microprocessor
minicomputer
nonexecutable statement
object program
pen plotter
permanent workspace
processor
program
pseudocode
software
source program
stepwise refinement
syntax error
temporary workspace
time-sharing

Courtesy of New Mexico Tourism and Travel Division

SAMPLE PROBLEM – Railroad Track Design

When a train travels over a straight section of track, it exerts a downward force on the rails, but when it rounds a level curve, it also exerts a horizontal force outward on the rails. Both these forces must be considered when designing the track. The downward force is equivalent to the weight of the train, while the horizontal force, called *centrifugal force*, is a function of the weight of the train, the speed of the train as it rounds the curve, and the radius of the curve. The equation to compute the horizontal force, in pounds, is:

$$\text{FORCE} = \left[\frac{\text{WEIGHT} \cdot 2000}{32}\right] \cdot \frac{[\text{MPH} \cdot 1.4667]^2}{\text{RADIUS}}$$

where WEIGHT is the weight of the train in tons,
     MPH is the speed of the train in miles per hour, and
     RADIUS is the radius of the curve in feet.

The computation of this horizontal force for a given set of values for WEIGHT, MPH, and RADIUS, using FORTRAN, is given in Example 2-1, page 32.

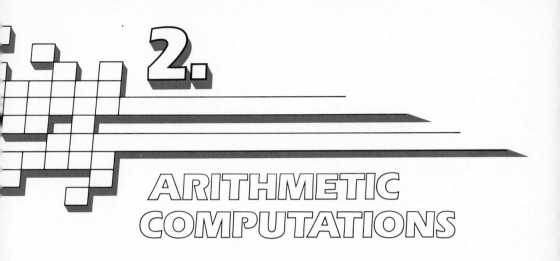

2. ARITHMETIC COMPUTATIONS

INTRODUCTION

The most fundamental operations that are performed by computers are arithmetic operations, such as adding, subtracting, multiplying, and dividing. Engineers and scientists also need other routine operations, such as raising a number to a power, taking the logarithm of a number, or computing the sine of an angle. This chapter discusses the methods of storing data in computers and develops the statements for performing arithmetic calculations with the stored data.

2-1 CONSTANTS AND VARIABLES

Numbers are introduced into computer calculations with *constants* and *variables*. Constants are numbers used directly in computations, such as -7, 3.141593, and 32.0. Constants may contain plus or minus signs and decimal points, but they may not contain commas. Thus 3147.6 is a valid FORTRAN constant but 3,147.6 is not. Variables are memory locations with names that store numeric values. The value of a constant does not change, but operations performed on a variable can change its value.

When working with a high-level language such as FORTRAN, we can visualize the storage of variables in the computer memory as shown below:

SUM	36.84	VOLUME	183.0
INCR	−40	TOTAL	−6.37
AREA	.0005	NUMBER	0

A name is first given to each storage location to identify it uniquely; then each storage location is assigned a numerical value. Hence, in the examples shown, the storage location named TOTAL contains the value −6.37.

Each variable must have a different name, which you provide as you write your program. The names may contain one to six characters consisting of both alphabetic characters and digits; however, the first character of a name must be an alphabetic character. The following are examples of both valid and invalid variable names:

VELOCITY	Invalid name—too long
π	Invalid name—illegal character (π)
TEMP	Valid name
X2	Valid name
2X	Invalid name—first character must be alphabetic character
VOL	Valid name
PI	Valid name
V*2Z	Invalid name—illegal character (*)

Numerical values in FORTRAN can be one of four types: integer, real, double precision, or complex. *Integer*-type values are those with no fractional portion, such as 16, −7, 186, and 0. Since these values have no decimal portion or decimal point, they are also called *fixed-point* values. *Real*-type values, on the other hand, contain a decimal point and may or may not have digits past the decimal point, such as 13.86, 13., .0076, −14.1, 36.0, and −3.1. These real values are also called *floating-point* values. Double-precision values and complex values will be discussed in Chapter 9.

A storage location can contain only one type of value. The type of value stored in a variable can be specified by one of two methods: *implicit* typing or *explicit* typing. With implicit typing, the first letter of a variable name determines the type of value that can be stored in it. Variable names beginning with letters I, J, K, L, M, or N are used to store integers. Variable names beginning with one of the other letters, A→H and O→Z, are used to store real values. Thus, VEL represents a real value and MASS represents an integer value. An easy way to remember which letters are used for integers is to observe that the range of letters is I→N, the first two letters of the word *int*eger itself.

With explicit typing, a special statement is used to specify the type of a variable. For example, the statements

```
INTEGER  WIDTH
REAL  NUM, K
```

specify that WIDTH is a variable that will contain an integer value and that NUM and K are variables that will contain real values. These *specification* statements have the following general forms:

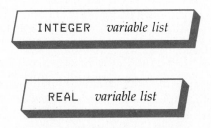

The variable list is the list of variable names which are being designated as integer names or real names. Specification statements are nonexecutable because they are used by the compiler to specify the nature of variables, but are not translated into machine language. Specification statements must be placed at the beginning of the program, before any executable statements.

It is very helpful to select a variable name that is descriptive of the value being stored. For example, if a value represents an area, call it AREA. If the implicit typing of the variable name does not match the type of value to be stored in it, then use a REAL or INTEGER statement at the beginning of your program to specify the desired type of value.

2-2   SCIENTIFIC NOTATION AND MAGNITUDE LIMITATIONS

When a real number is very large or very small, decimal notation does not work satisfactorily. For example, a value used frequently in chemistry is Avogadro's constant, whose value to four significant places is: 602,300,000,000,000,000,000,000. Obviously, we need a more manageable notation for very large values like Avogadro's constant or for very small values like .00000000042. A notation commonly used in science, called *scientific notation*, expresses a value as a number between 1 and 10 multiplied by an appropriate power of 10. Hence, in scientific form, Avogadro's constant becomes 6.023×10^{23}. This form is sometimes referred to as a *mantissa* (6.023) and an *exponent* (23). The FORTRAN form of scientific notation, called *exponential notation*, expresses a value as a number between 0 and 1 multiplied by an appropriate power of 10. Exponential notation uses only the letter E between the mantissa and exponent. Thus, in exponential form, Avogadro's constant becomes 0.6023E24. Other examples of decimal values in scientific and exponential notation are given below:

Decimal Value	Scientific Notation	Exponential Notation
3,876,000,000	3.876×10^9	0.3876E10
.0000010053	1.0053×10^{-6}	0.10053E−05
−8,030,000.	-8.03×10^6	−0.803E07
−.000157	-1.57×10^{-4}	−0.157E−03

Although FORTRAN uses an exponential form with a mantissa between zero and one, it will accept mantissas outside that range. For instance, the constant 0.16E03 would also be valid in the forms 1.6E02 or 0.016E04.

There are limitations on the magnitude and precision of values that can be stored in a computer. For instance, π is an *irrational* number and thus cannot be written with a finite number of decimal positions. In a computer with seven digits of accuracy, π could be stored as 3.141593. For real values, such as π, we have limits on the number of significant positions in the mantissa and on the size of the exponent. These limitations on the values in a computer depend on the specific computer itself. Table 2-1 compares the approximate range of values that can be stored in several large computers. Check a reference manual to find the ranges of real and integer values for the computer you will be using for your classwork.

TABLE 2-1 Typical Ranges for FORTRAN Data Values

Computer	Real Value Ranges	Maximum Integer
IBM 360/370	Mantissa: 6 significant digits Exponent: −77 to 75	2,147,483,647
VAX	Mantissa: 7 significant digits Exponent: −38 to 38	2,147,483,647
CRAY-1	Mantissa: 13 significant digits Exponent: −2465 to 2465	2.8×10^{14}
CDC 6000/7000	Mantissa: 14 significant digits Exponent: −293 to 322	9.2×10^{18}

2-3 ARITHMETIC CALCULATIONS

All computations in FORTRAN are specified with the *assignment* statement, whose general form is:

> *variable name = expression*

The simplest form of an *arithmetic expression* is a constant. Hence, if the value of π is needed frequently in a program, we might choose to define a variable PI with the value 3.141593. Afterwards, we could refer to the variable PI each time we needed the constant. An assignment statement that assigns a value to PI, and thus *initializes* PI, is:

```
PI = 3.141593
```

The name of the variable receiving a new value must always be on the left side of the equal sign. In FORTRAN, the equal sign can be read as "is assigned the value of." Thus, the statement above could be read "PI is assigned the value 3.141593."

It is important to recognize the fact that a variable can store only one value at a time. For example, suppose the following two statements were executed one after another.

```
WIDTH = 36.7
WIDTH = 105.2
```

The value 36.7 is stored in the variable WIDTH after the first statement is executed. The second statement, however, replaces that value with the new value 105.2, and the first value is lost.

Consider these two statements:

```
TEMP1 = -52.6
TEMP2 = TEMP1
```

The first statement stores the value −52.6 in TEMP1. The second statement stores in TEMP2 the same value that is stored in TEMP1. Note that the value in TEMP1 is not lost; both TEMP1 and TEMP2 now contain the value −52.6.

Often we will want to calculate a new value using arithmetic operations with other variables and constants. For instance, assume that the variable RADIUS has been assigned a value, and we now want to calculate the area of a circle having that radius. To do so, we need to square the radius and then multiply by the value of π. Table 2-2 shows the FORTRAN expressions for the basic arithmetic operations. Note that an asterisk instead of an X is used to represent multiplication to avoid confusion since AXB (commonly used in algebra to indicate the product of A and B) represents a single variable name

Table 2-2 Arithmetic Operations in Algebraic Form and FORTRAN

Operation	Algebraic Form	FORTRAN
Addition	A + B	A + B
Subtraction	A − B	A − B
Multiplication	A × B	A*B
Division	$\dfrac{A}{B}$	A/B
Exponentiation	A^3	A**3

in FORTRAN. Division and exponentiation also have new symbols since we do not have a method for raising or lowering characters on a keypunch or terminal line.

Since several operations can be combined in one arithmetic expression, it is important to determine priorities of the operations. For instance, consider the following assignment statement that calculates the area of a circle:

```
AREA = PI*RADIUS**2
```

If the exponentiation is done first, we compute $\pi \cdot (\text{RADIUS})^2$, but if multiplication is done first, we compute $(\pi \cdot \text{RADIUS})^2$. Note that the two computations yield different results. The order of priorities for computations in FORTRAN is given in Table 2-3 and follows the standard algebraic priorities. Note that operations in parentheses are performed first. When executing the previous FORTRAN statement, the radius would be squared first and the result then multiplied by PI, thus correctly determining the area of the circle. Remember that we are assuming that PI and RADIUS have been initialized. The following statements also correctly compute the area of the circle:

```
AREA = PI*RADIUS*RADIUS
```

or

```
AREA = 3.141593*RADIUS*RADIUS
```

From Table 2-3, we see that the negation of a single variable has a higher priority than addition. Thus, −B + C would be evaluated as (−B) + C instead of −(B + C).

When there are two operations on the same priority level, as in addition and subtraction, all operations except exponentiation are performed from left to right as they are encountered in an expression. Thus, B − C + D would be evaluated as (B − C) + D. If two exponentiations occur sequentially in FOR-

Table 2-3 Priorities of Arithmetic Operations

PRIORITY	OPERATION
First	Parentheses
Second	Negation of a single value
Third	Exponentiation
Fourth	Multiplication and division
Fifth	Addition and subtraction

TRAN, as in A**B**C, they will be evaluated right to left, as in A**(B**C). Thus, 2**3**2 is 2^9 or 512 as opposed to (2**3)**2, which is 8^2 or 64.

A more complex arrangement is represented by the following expression for one of the real roots of a quadratic equation:

$$X1 = \frac{-B + \sqrt{B^2 - 4AC}}{2A}$$

where A, B, and C are coefficients of the quadratic equation. Since division by zero is not possible on a computer, we will assume $A \neq 0$. The value of X1 can then be computed in FORTRAN with the following statement, assuming that the variables A, B, and C have been previously initialized:

```
X1 = (-B + (B**2 - 4.0*A*C)**0.5)/(2.0*A)
```

To check the order of operations in a long expression, it is best to start with the operations inside parentheses. That is, find the operation done first, then second, and so on. The following diagram outlines this procedure, using underline braces to show the steps of operations. Beneath each brace is the value that has been calculated in that step.

$$X1 = \underbrace{(-B}_{-B} + \underbrace{(B**2 - 4.0*A*C)}_{B^2 - 4AC}**0.5)/\underbrace{(2.0*A)}_{2A}$$

$$\underbrace{-B + \sqrt{B^2 - 4AC}}$$

$$\frac{-B + \sqrt{B^2 - 4AC}}{2A}$$

As shown in the final brace, the desired value is computed by this expression. The placement of the parentheses is very important in this statement. If the outside set of parentheses on the numerator were omitted, our assignment statement becomes:

```
X1 = -B + (B**2 - 4.0*A*C)**0.5/(2.0*A)
```

$$\underbrace{-B} \qquad \underbrace{B^2 - 4AC} \qquad \qquad 2A$$

$$\underbrace{\sqrt{B^2 - 4AC}}$$

$$\underbrace{\frac{\sqrt{B^2 - 4AC}}{2A}}$$

$$-B + \frac{\sqrt{B^2 - 4AC}}{2A}$$

As you can see, omission of the outside set of parentheses would cause the wrong value to be calculated as a root of the original quadratic equation. Omission of a different set of parentheses would result in the following expression:

```
X1 = (-B + B**2 - 4.0*A*C**0.5)/(2.0*A)
```

$$\underbrace{-B + B^2 - 4A\sqrt{C}} \qquad \qquad 2A$$

$$\frac{-B + B^2 - 4A\sqrt{C}}{2A}$$

Again, the wrong value has been calculated. If all parentheses were omitted, the expression becomes:

```
X1 = -B + B**2 - 4.0*A*C**0.5/2.0*A
```

$$\underbrace{-B} \qquad \underbrace{B^2} \qquad \underbrace{\sqrt{C}}$$

$$\underbrace{\frac{4A\sqrt{C}A}{2}}$$

$$-B + B^2 - \frac{4A^2\sqrt{C}}{2}$$

Still another incorrect value has been computed.

As shown in the previous examples, omitting necessary parentheses results in incorrect calculations. Using extra parentheses to emphasize the order of calculations is permissible. In fact, it is advisable to insert extra parentheses in a statement if it makes the statement more readable.

You may also want to break a long statement into several smaller statements. For example, the solution to the quadratic equation could be calculated with the following equations after initialization of A, B, and C:

```
DISCR  =   B**2 - 4.0*A*C
X1 = (-B + DISCR**0.5)/(2.0*A)
X2 = (-B - DISCR**0.5)/(2.0*A)
```

In the above statements, we assume that the discriminant, DISCR, is positive, thus enabling us to obtain the two real roots to the equation, X1 and X2. If the discriminant were negative, an execution error would occur if we attempted to take the square root of the negative value. Also, if the value of A were zero, we would get an execution error for attempting to divide by zero. In later chapters we will learn techniques for handling both these situations.

We often use variables as *counters* in our FORTRAN programs. We first initialize the counter to a certain value and then later, under certain conditions, change it to another value. An example of a statement to increment by 1 the counter COUNTR, which we will assume was explicitly declared with an INTEGER statement, is given below:

```
COUNTR = COUNTR + 1
```

At first, this statement may look invalid because, algebraically, COUNTR cannot be equal to COUNTR + 1. But remember, in FORTRAN, this statement means "COUNTR is assigned the value of COUNTR plus 1." Hence, if the old value of COUNTR is 0, the new value of COUNTR after executing this statement will be 1.

2-4   TRUNCATION AND MIXED MODE

When an arithmetic operation is performed using two real numbers, the *intermediate result* of the operation is a real value. For example, the circumference of a circle can be calculated as

```
CIRCUM = PI*DIAM
```

or

```
CIRCUM = 3.141593*DIAM
```

In both statements, we have multiplied two real values, giving a real intermediate result, which is then stored in the real variable CIRCUM.

Similarly, arithmetic operations between two integers yield an intermediate integer. For instance, if I and J represent two integers such that $I \leq J$, then the number of integers in the interval I through J can be calculated with the following statement:

```
INTERV = J - I + 1
```

Thus, if I = 6 and J = 11, then INTERV will contain 6, the number of integers in the set {6, 7, 8, 9, 10, 11}.

Now consider the statement:

```
LENGTH = SIDE*3.5
```

Assuming implicit typing of the variables, we know that the multiplication between the two real values yields a real intermediate result. In this case, however, the real intermediate result is stored in an integer variable. When the computer stores a real number as an integer variable, it ignores the fractional portion and stores only the whole number portion of the real number. The loss of the fractional portion of a real value when it is stored in an integer variable is called *truncation*.

There are also computations with integers that give unexpected results. Consider the following statement that computes the average or mean of two integers, N1 and N2.

$$\text{MEAN} = (\text{N1} + \text{N2})/2$$

Since all the variables involved in the arithmetic operations are integers, the result of evaluating the expression will be an integer. Thus, if $\text{N1} = 2$ and $\text{N2} = 4$, the mean value is the expected value, 3. But if $\text{N1} = 2$ and $\text{N2} = 1$, the result of the division of 3 by 2 will be 1, instead of 1.5 because the division involves two integers and, hence, the intermediate result must be an integer. At first glance it might seem that we can solve this problem if we call the average by the real variable name AVE, instead of MEAN, and use this statement:

$$\text{AVE} = (\text{N1} + \text{N2})/2$$

Unfortunately, this does not correct our answer. The result of integer arithmetic is still an integer, and all we have done is move the integer result into a real variable. Thus, if $\text{N1} = 2$ and $\text{N2} = 1$, then $(\text{N1} + \text{N2})/2 = 1$, and $\text{AVE} = 1.0$, not 1.5. One way of correcting this problem is to explicitly declare N1 and N2 to be real values and use the following statement to calculate the average:

$$\text{AVE} = (\text{N1} + \text{N2})/2.0$$

Note that there is a difference between rounding and truncation. With rounding, the result is the integer closest to the real number. Truncation, however, causes any decimal portion to be dropped. Thus, if we divide the integer 15 by the integer 8, the truncated result is 1, the integer portion of 1.875.

The effects of truncation can also be seen in the next statement, which appears to be calculating the square root of NUM.

$$\text{ROOT} = \text{NUM}**(1/2)$$

However, since 1/2 is truncated to 0, we are really raising NUM to the zero power. Hence, ROOT will always contain the value 1.0, no matter what value is in NUM.

We have seen that an operation involving only real values yields a real intermediate result, and an operation involving only integer values yields an integer intermediate result. Computers also accept a *mixed-mode* operation, which is an operation involving an integer value and a real value. The intermediate result of a mixed operation is always a real value. The final result depends on the type of the variable that is used to store the result of the mixed-mode operation. Consider the following arithmetic statement for computing the perimeter of a square whose sides are real values.

$$PERI = 4*SIDE$$

The above multiplication is a mixed operation between the integer constant 4 and the real variable SIDE. The intermediate result is real and is correctly stored in the real result PERI.

Using mixed mode, we can now calculate correctly the square root of NUM, using this statement:

$$ROOT = NUM**0.5$$

The mixed-mode exponentiation yields a real result, which is stored in ROOT.

To compute the area of a square with real sides, we could use the mixed-mode expression,

$$AREA = SIDE**2$$

or the real mode expression

$$AREA = SIDE**2.0$$

The result in both cases is real, but the mixed-mode form is preferable in this case. Exponentiation to an integer power is done internally in the computer with a series of multiplications such as SIDE times SIDE. If an exponent is real, however, the operation is performed by the arithmetic logic unit using logarithms. Thus, SIDE**2.0 is actually computed as antilog(2.0 × log(SIDE)). Using logarithms can introduce a small error into the calculations. While 5.0**2 is always 25.0, 5.0**2.0 is often computed to be 24.99999. Also, note that(−2.0)**2 is a valid operation while (−2.0)**2.0 is an invalid operation because the logarithm of a negative value does not exist and, hence, an execution error occurs. As a general guide when raising numbers to an integer power, use an integer exponent, even though the base number is real.

Mixed-mode expressions may still lose accuracy through truncation if there are operations between integers embedded in the expression. For instance, assume that we want to calculate the volume of a sphere with radius R. The volume is computed by multiplying 4/3 times π times the radius cubed. Hence, the following mixed-mode statement at first appears correct.

$$VOL = (4/3)*3.141593*R**3$$

The expression contains integer and real values, so the result will be a real value. However, the division of 4 by 3 will yield the intermediate value of 1, not 1.333333, and thus the final answer will be incorrect.

EXAMPLE 2-1   Centrifugal Force

The horizontal force against the rails (centrifugal force) exerted by a train as it rounds a level curve can be computed, in pounds, with the following equation:

$$FORCE = \left[\frac{WEIGHT \cdot 2000}{32} \right] \cdot \frac{[MPH \cdot 1.4667]^2}{RADIUS}$$

where WEIGHT is the weight of the train in tons,
       MPH is the speed of the train in miles per hour, and
       RADIUS is the radius of the curve in feet.

Give assignment statements to compute the horizontal force against the rails if the weight of the train is 405.7 tons, the speed of the train is 30.5 miles per hour, and the radius of the curve is 2005.33 feet.

Solution

```
REAL   MPH
WEIGHT = 405.7
MPH = 30.5
RADIUS = 2005.33
FORCE = (WEIGHT*2000.0/32.0)*(MPH*1.4667)**2/RADIUS   ◊
```

2-5   INTRODUCTION TO INTRINSIC FUNCTIONS

There are many simple operations commonly performed in engineering or scientific applications. Some examples include computing the square root of a value, computing the absolute value of a number, or computing the sine of an angle. Because these operations are so common, built-in functions called *intrinsic functions* are available to handle all these computations for us. Thus, instead of using the arithmetic expression X**0.5, we can use the intrinsic function SQRT(X). Similarly, we can refer to the absolute value of B by ABS(B). A list of some common intrinsic functions appears in Table 2-4, and a complete list of the intrinsic functions in the FORTRAN 77 language is contained in Appendix B.

Note that the name of the function determines the type (real or integer) of value that is being computed. Thus, the SQRT and ABS functions compute a real value, while the IABS function computes an integer value. The *argument*, or input to the function, is enclosed in parentheses and follows the name of the function. This argument can be any arithmetic expression, but must be the proper type. The input to the functions SQRT and ABS must be real (see Table 2-4), and the input to the function IABS must be integer. There are a few exceptions, but generally a function with real input has real output while a function with integer input has an integer output. Intrinsic functions will be discussed in more detail in Chapter 7.

TABLE 2-4 Common Intrinsic Functions

Function Name and Argument	Function Value	Comment
SQRT(X)	$\sqrt{X}$	square root of X
ABS(X)	$|X|$	absolute value of a REAL number
IABS(I)	$|I|$	absolute value of an INTEGER number
SIN(X)	sine of angle X	X must be in radians
COS(X)	cosine of angle X	X must be in radians
TAN(X)	tangent of angle X	X must be in radians
EXP(X)	e^X	e raised to the X power
ALOG(X)	$\log_e X$	natural log of X
ALOG10(X)	$\log_{10} X$	common log of X
INT(X)	integer portion of X	converts a REAL value to an INTEGER value
REAL(I)	real value of I	converts an INTEGER value to a REAL value
MOD(I,J)	integer remainder of I/J	remainder function

Suppose the variable ANGLE contains the value of an angle in degrees, and we want to store the cosine of ANGLE in the variable COSA. From Table 2-4, we see that the cosine function COS assumes that its argument is in radians. We can change the degrees to radians (1 degree = $\pi/180$ radians) and compute the cosine of the angle in the following statement:

```
COSA = COS(A*(3.141593/180.0))
```

The inside set of parentheses is not required, but serves to emphasize the conversion factor.

It is also acceptable to use one intrinsic function as the argument of another one. For example, we can compute $e^{|A|}$ with the expression EXP(ABS(A)). When *nesting* functions, as done here, be sure to enclose the argument of each function in its own set of parentheses.

It is important to observe that an intrinsic function and its argument represent a value. This value can be used in other computations or stored in other memory locations. It does not in itself, however, represent a storage location and thus a function can never appear on the left of an equal sign; it must always be on the right side of an equal sign. For example, to compute the square root of X, we can use the statement

```
ROOT = SQRT(X)
```

but we cannot reverse the order and begin the statement with SQRT(X).

2-6 APPLICATION – RADIOACTIVE DECAY

The rate of decomposition of a radioactive substance is dependent on the amount of radioactive material present. The growth of a bacteria culture depends on the amount of bacteria. These are examples of the exponential laws of growth and decay for some materials. These rates of change of substances can be represented mathematically with exponential functions.

EXAMPLE 2-2 Radioactive Decay of Thorium

The radioactive decay of thorium is given by

$$N = N_0 \cdot e^{\left[-0.693\frac{t}{1.65 \times 10^{16}}\right]}$$

where N_0 represents the initial amount of thorium and t represents the time elapsed. When $t = 0$, N is equal to N_0, and no decay has occurred. As t increases, the amount of thorium is decreased. If THOR contains the initial amount of thorium, give an assignment statement to find the residual amount of thorium left after TSEC seconds have elapsed.

Solution

Since the result will be a real value, we will call it RESID for residual.

```
RESID = THOR*EXP(-0.693*TSEC/1.65E16)   ◇
```

2-7 APPLICATION – GAUSSIAN DISTRIBUTION

Suppose you needed to know the accuracy of a large number of 100-ohm resistors you planned to use in an experiment. Since the actual resistance of an individual 100-ohm resistor is seldom precisely 100 ohms because of variations in materials and manufacturing processes, you would expect, in a box of 1000 such resistors, that a large number of them would be very close to 100 ohms, some of them would not be quite so close, and a small number would be significantly different from 100 ohms. To estimate the accuracies of the resistors you plan to use, you decide to do a statistical analysis by randomly selecting 100 resistors from the box and precisely measuring to the nearest 1/2 ohm, the resistance of each one. Having completed that task, you record your results as shown in Table 2-5. The data set in Table 2-5 is then used to construct the *histogram*, which is shown in Figure 2-1. Histograms are

TABLE 2-5 Resistor Frequency Distribution

Resistance	Frequency
95.0	0
95.5	1
96.0	1
96.5	2
97.0	3
97.5	5
98.0	6
98.5	8
99.0	9
99.5	10
100.0	12
100.5	11
101.0	10
101.5	7
102.0	6
102.5	4
103.0	2
103.5	2
104.0	1
104.5	0
105.0	0
Total	100

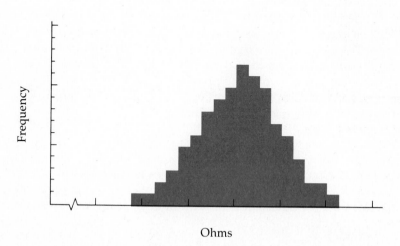

FIGURE 2-1 Histogram of resistor frequency distribution.

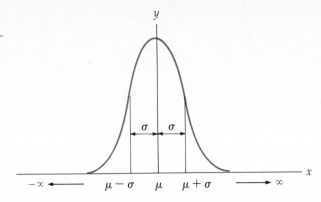

FIGURE 2-2 Gaussian distribution.

used to provide a visual "feel" for certain qualities of a set of random observations, such as the overall average or mean of the group, and relative dispersion or *deviation* of values. By looking at Figure 2-1, you could conclude, based on your random sample of 100 resistance measurements, that the average resistance of the entire box of 1000 resistors is likely to be very close to 100 ohms and most values will be somewhere between 98 and 102 ohms.

If you had the time and patience to continue to choose resistors from the box and measure their resistance in ever finer intervals (.1 ohm, .01 ohm, etc.), your histogram would become more continuous in its appearance and begin to approach the *Gaussian* or *normal* distribution curve shown in Figure 2-2. The average value is represented by μ. The dispersion or *standard deviation* of the values is represented by σ, where approximately two-thirds of the values are between the values $\mu - \sigma$ and $\mu + \sigma$.

The Gaussian distribution has played an important role in the study of random phenomena primarily because experience has shown that many physical processes closely approximate a Gaussian distribution. Another reason for its popularity is that it can be expressed mathematically, thus making it easily adaptable to analytical or computational uses.

A Gaussian curve is often "normalized" such that the area under the curve is equal to 1. The mathematical expression for the normal Gaussian curve is given by the following equation:

$$y = \frac{1}{\sqrt{2\pi\sigma^2}} \cdot e^{-\frac{(x-\mu)^2}{2\sigma^2}}$$

EXAMPLE 2-3   Gaussian Distribution of Resistor Values

Assume that the resistances of a group of 1000 resistors are distributed normally, and that the average resistance, μ, is 100.0 ohms and the standard deviation, σ, is 2.0. Give assignment statements to compute the values Y1, Y2, and Y3 on the normalized

Gaussian curve that correspond to the resistance values stored in variables X1, X2, and X3.

Solution

The intrinsic function EXP will be used to compute powers of e. As you look at the equation for the normal Gaussian curve, you will note that two terms in the expression, $1/\sqrt{2\pi\sigma^2}$ and $2\sigma^2$, depend only on the standard deviation. Hence, we can compute these constants first and store them in variables CONST1 and CONST2. The arithmetic statements for computing Y1, Y2, and Y3 are then simplified.

```
AVE = 100.0
STDEV = 2.0
CONST1 = 1.0/SQRT(2.0*3.141593*STDEV**2)
CONST2 = 2.0*STDEV**2
Y1 = CONST1*EXP(-(X1 - AVE)**2/CONST2)
Y2 = CONST1*EXP(-(X2 - AVE)**2/CONST2)
Y3 = CONST1*EXP(-(X3 - AVE)**2/CONST2)   ◊
```

SUMMARY

This chapter has introduced you to your first executable FORTRAN statement—the assignment statement. This statement can be used to initialize a variable or to compute a new value for a variable. It can also be used with both integer and real constants or variables. The priority of arithmetic operations has been outlined and the effects of truncation have been discussed. The use of intrinsic functions such as SQRT, EXP, and ABS has also been explained. You now have the tools to perform practically any arithmetic calculation in FORTRAN.

KEY WORDS

argument	intermediate result
arithmetic expression	intrinsic function
assignment statement	mixed-mode operation
constant	nesting
counter	operation
explicit typing	REAL statement
exponential notation	real value
fixed-point	rounding
floating-point	scientific notation
implicit typing	specification statement
initialize	truncation
INTEGER statement	variable
integer value	

DEBUGGING AIDS

The following steps will help you correct assignment statements that are not working properly.

1 If the assignment statement is long, break it up into several smaller statements.

2 Double-check your placement of parentheses. Add parentheses if you are not sure what order the computer will use to compute the operations involved. Be sure that you always have the same number of left parentheses as right parentheses.

3 Review each variable name on the right side of the equal sign to be sure you have spelled it exactly as previously used. (Did you use V when you should have used VEL?)

4 Make sure all variables on the right side of the assignment statement have been previously initialized.

5 Be sure that arguments to intrinsic functions are in the correct units (i.e., trigonometric functions use angles in radians instead of degrees).

6 If you have mixed-mode operations for operations other than exponentiation, use the functions INT and REAL so that operations use all integer or all real values.

7 Finally, remember that explicit typing always overrides the implicit typing rules.

If these steps do not help you isolate your error, ask your instructor or a classmate to check the statement. If no one is available to check your statement and you cannot find the error, start over on a clean sheet of paper. Sometimes it is very hard to spot your own errors because you know what you want the statement to do, and you read that into the statement when searching for errors.

STYLE/TECHNIQUE GUIDES

The first requirement for any computer program is that it work correctly. In addition, it should be written so that another person competent in FORTRAN could readily understand the statements and interpret the procedures. This is especially important since the person updating a program is not always the person who originally wrote it. These are challenging requirements to meet, and necessitate building good habits from the beginning when learning a language. The following guides will help you develop a style and technique that will enable you to meet these requirements.

1 Use variable names that indicate something about the values being stored in the variable. For instance, represent velocity by

VEL instead of A, or X1, or something obscure. Use the speci-fication statements if needed to specify the correct type for your variable names.

2 Use a consistent number of significant digits in constants. Do not use 3.14 as a value for PI in the beginning of your program and later use 3.141593 as the value at the end. Accomplish this con-sistency by initializing variables that will be used frequently in the program, such as

```
PI = 3.141593
```

and subsequently using PI instead of a constant as you need the value.

3 Break long expressions into smaller expressions and recombine them in another statement. A complicated fraction can be com-puted by first calculating a numerator, then calculating a denomi-nator, and finally dividing in a separate statement.

4 Insert extra parentheses for readability. It is never wrong to insert extra pairs of parentheses, as long as they are properly located. Extra parentheses often make arithmetic expressions much more readable.

5 Do not mix modes except when beneficial, as in the case of exponents. For example, use B*3.0 instead of B*3, but use B**2 instead of B**2.0.

6 Do not use exponential notation for constants unless the absolute value is greater than 1000 or less than .0001.

7 Use intrinsic functions where possible.

8 Explicit typing is an aid in program clarity as well as in error detection. Some programmers prefer to list all variables on specification statements, including those correctly typed by the implicit rules.

PROBLEMS

Problems 1 through 10 contain both valid and invalid variable names. Explain why the invalid names are unacceptable. Identify the valid names as either real or integer type.

1	AREA	2	PERIMETER
3	VOLUME	4	LENGTH
5	TAX-RT	6	MASS
7	F(X)	8	2TIME
9	TIME2	10	$AMT

In problems 11 through 16, tell whether or not the pair of real constants represents the same number. If not, explain.

11 2300; 2.3E04

12 0.000007; .7E04

13 1.0; 1.

14 110.0; 11.01E01

15 −34.7; −0.34E02

16 −0.76; 7.60E−01

In problems 17 through 24, convert the equations into FORTRAN assignment statements. Use the same variable names as shown in the algebraic equation. Avoid mixed-mode where possible. Assume all variables represent real values and have been explicitly typed if necessary.

17 Slope of straight line given two points, (X1,Y1) and (X2,Y2), on the line:

$$SL = \frac{Y2 - Y1}{X2 - X1}$$

18 Correction factor in pressure calculation:

$$CF = 1 + \frac{B}{V} + \frac{C}{V^2}$$

19 Coefficient of friction between tires and pavement:

$$FR = \frac{V^2}{30S}$$

20 Distance of center of gravity from reference plane in a hollow cylinder sector:

$$DIS = \frac{38.1972(R^3 - S^3)\sin A}{(R^2 - S^2)A}$$

21 Pressure loss from pipe friction:

$$P = F{\cdot}P{\cdot}\frac{L}{D}{\cdot}\frac{V^2}{2}$$

22 Equivalent resistance of a parallel circuit:

$$REQ = \frac{1}{\dfrac{1}{X1} + \dfrac{1}{X2} + \dfrac{1}{X3} + \dfrac{1}{X4}}$$

23 Heat transfer analysis equation:

$$AMU = 0.023(X)^8 {\cdot} \sqrt[3]{Y}$$

24 Mass flow rate through a nozzle:

$$X = 2\pi(X1)\sqrt{\frac{G{\cdot}32.2}{(X2)(Y1)}}{\cdot}\left(\frac{Y2}{Y1}\right)\left[1 + \frac{G - 1.0}{2.0}\left(\frac{Y2}{Y1}\right)^2\right]^{\frac{G+1}{2-2G}}$$

where G = 1.4.

In problems 25 through 32, convert the FORTRAN statements into algebraic form.

25 Uniformly accelerated motion:

```
V = (VI*VI + 2.0*A*X)**0.5
```

26 Electrical oscillation frequency:

```
F = 1.0/(2.0*3.141593)*(1.0/XL*C)**0.5
```

27 Range for a theoretical projectile:

```
R = 2.0*VI**2*SIN(B)*COS(B)/G
```

28 Flow of an ideal, compressible gas:

```
FLOW = (1.0 + (K - 1.0)/(2.0*M**2))**(K/(K - 1.0))
```

29 Length contraction:

```
L = LI*(1.0 - (V/C)**2)**0.5
```

30 Volume of a fillet ring:

```
PI = 3.141593
VFR = 2*PI*X**2*((1.0 - PI/4.0)*Y - (0.8333 - PI/4.0)*X)
```

31 Flow over a dam:

```
F = 0.35E-04*(X/Y)*SQRT(2.0*G)*(Y2 - Y)**2.5
```

32 Mass energy:

```
C = 2.99E10
E = 1.6747E-24*C**2
```

In problems 33 through 41, compute the value that will be stored in the variable on the left side of the equation if the following values have been initialized.

$$R = 1.1 \qquad J = 2$$
$$I = 5 \qquad X = 6.1$$

(Show your answers in the correct form—real or integer type.)

33 `K = R`

34 `N1 = X`

35 `T = I`

36 `RJ = J`

37 `MASS = (I + 7)/5`

38 `TIME = X + 2.2/R`

39 `VOL = R + I/J + 13.5`

40 `TEMP = (X - R)**2/J`

41 `IBASE = R*J + J*X`

In problems 42 and 43, tell what the segment of code accomplishes.

42
```
A = B
B = A
```

43
```
C = A
A = B
B = C
```

In problems 44 through 47, rewrite the given series of statements as a single statement that will yield the same final result. For example, this series of statements,

$$A = B + 1$$
$$A = A + 2$$

could be replaced by

$$A = B + 3$$

44
```
M = N + 1
M = M - 1
N = N + M
```

45
```
E = Y**2 + 1.0
X = E*X
X = E*X
```

46
```
Y = Y + 2
Z = X + Y
```

47
```
X = Y + 2.5
Z = (X + Y)/Y
```

48 Give an assignment statement to convert X from inches to feet.

49 Give an assignment statement to compute HOURS where HOURS is the number of hours in DAYS, a variable that represents a number of days.

50 The distance between points (X_a, Y_a) and (X_b, Y_b) is given by

$$DIST = \sqrt{(X_a - X_b)^2 + (Y_a - Y_b)^2}$$

You are given the coordinates of three points

point 1: (X1,Y1)
point 2: (X2,Y2)
point 3: (X3,Y3)

Give assignment statements to calculate the distance DIST12 between points 1 and 2, the distance DIST13 between points 1 and 3, and the distance DIST23 between points 2 and 3.

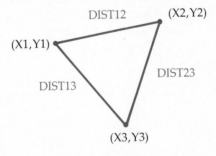

51 The approximate time for electrons to travel from the cathode to the anode of a rectifier tube is given by:

$$TIME = \left(\frac{2 \cdot M}{Q \cdot V}\right)^{1/2} \cdot R1 \cdot Z\left(1 + \frac{Z}{3} + \frac{Z^2}{10} + \frac{Z^3}{42} + \frac{Z^4}{216}\right)$$

where Q = charge of the electron = 1.60206×10^{-19} coulombs
M = mass of the electron = 9.1083×10^{-31} kilograms
V = accelerating voltage in volts
R1 = radius of the inner tube (cathode)
R2 = radius of the outer tube (anode)
Z = natural logarithm of $\left(\dfrac{R2}{R1}\right)$

Assume that the variables V, R1, and R2 have already been initialized. Give assignment statements to initialize Q and M. Then calculate Z and TIME.

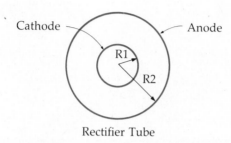

Rectifier Tube

52 Give a series of assignment statements that will take TOTMIN minutes and correctly determine the respective number of hours, HOURS, and the remaining minutes, REMAIN. For example, when TOTMIN = 65, then the computations should yield HOURS = 1 and REMAIN = 5. Assume TOTMIN, HOURS, and REMAIN have been typed in an INTEGER statement.

53 Give assignment statements to calculate the thickness of a hollow ball. Assume that VOLIN contains the volume inside the ball and that VOL-OUT contains the total volume occupied by the ball. The volume of a sphere is related to the radius r by:

$$V = (4/3)\pi \cdot r^3$$

54 Assume that AVE contains the mean value μ in a group of values that have a Gaussian distribution. Using the following equation, give assignment statements to compute the difference in the y values that correspond to the value x if the standard deviation σ changes from 0.5 to 1.5.

$$y = \frac{1}{\sqrt{2\pi\sigma^2}} \cdot e^{-\frac{(x-\mu)^2}{2\sigma^2}}$$

Courtesy of Barbara Johnston

SAMPLE PROBLEM – Nutrition Research

A research scientist performed nutrition tests using three animals. Data on each animal includes an identification number, the weight of the animal at the beginning of the experiment, and the weight of the animal at the end of the experiment. Write a complete program to read this information and print a report. The report is to include the original information plus the percentage increase or decrease in weight for each test animal. (For solution, see Example 3-21, page 73.)

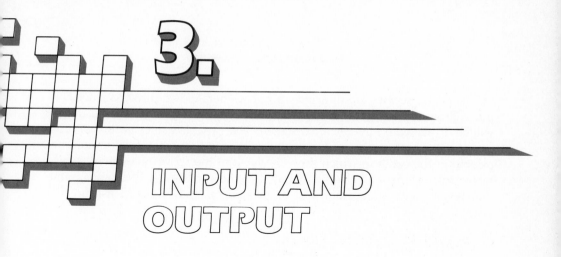

INPUT AND OUTPUT

INTRODUCTION

Nearly all programs compute values that need to be output in some form so that the results can be used. Many programs also read input data that will be needed by the program. For example, a program to compute test averages will need to read the individual test scores in order to compute the average, which then needs to be output. This chapter will examine input and output (I/O) statements in detail. We will also discuss the STOP and END statements in order to write complete FORTRAN programs.

3-1   LIST-DIRECTED OUTPUT

If we wish to print the value stored in a variable, it is necessary to tell the computer the variable's name. The computer can then access the storage location and print the contents, usually on computer paper or a terminal screen. Sometimes we are only interested in printing the value; other times we may also want to print the value on a new page of computer paper or center it on the output line. If we are interested in only the value of a variable, we use *list-directed* output; if we are interested in controlling where the value is printed, as we would for formal reports, we use *formatted* output. This section will discuss the list-directed statements PRINT and WRITE.

The general form of the PRINT statement is:

PRINT* , *variable list*

The asterisk specifies list-directed output. Generally, list-directed batch output will be printed by the line printer and list-directed time-sharing output will be displayed on the terminal screen. The variable names in the list must be separated by commas, and the values stored in those memory locations are printed in the order in which they are listed in the PRINT statement. Arithmetic expressions may also be included in the variable list. We will assume that seven digits of accuracy will be printed for real values in list-directed output.

EXAMPLE 3-1 VOLTS and LBS

Print the stored values of the variables VOLTS and LBS.

Solution

Computer Memory LBS | 13 |

VOLTS | 9 .05 |

FORTRAN Statement PRINT*, VOLTS, LBS

Computer Output   9.050000 13

The symbol that contains the computer output represents printed output. ◊

List-directed output enables us to select the variables whose values are printed and to determine the order in which they are printed. We cannot, however, control the spacing between the values. Also, if the value to be printed is very large or very small, many compilers will automatically print the value in exponential notation instead of decimal notation. Some compilers print all list-directed output in exponential form. We will assume that all values not between 1 and 100 will be printed in exponential form.

EXAMPLE 3-2 Density, DENS

Print the stored value of the variable DENS.

Solution

Computer Memory DENS | 0 .0000156 |

FORTRAN Statement PRINT*, DENS

Computer Output

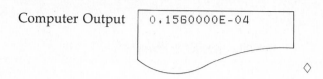

0.1560000E-04

◇

Descriptive information (sometimes called *literal information* or *literals*) may also be included in the variable list by enclosing the information in single quote marks or apostrophes. This descriptive information is then printed on the output line along with the values of any variables also on the PRINT statement.

EXAMPLE 3-3   Literal and Variable Information

Print the variable DENS with a literal that identifies the value as representing a density.

Solution

Computer Memory   DENS $\boxed{0.0000156}$

FORTRAN Statement

    PRINT*, 'THE DENSITY IS', DENS, 'KG/M**3'

Computer Output

THE DENSITY IS 0.1560000E-04 KG/M**3

◇

Another common list-directed output statement has the following general form:

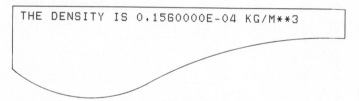

WRITE(*unit number,*)*variable list*

This WRITE statement is very similar to the PRINT statement. The only new element is the unit number. You will recall from Chapter 1 that different types of output devices exist. Some of the more common devices are the line printer, card punch, CRT terminal, hard-copy terminal, and plotter. Since many of these devices may be connected to a single computer, we must have some way of indicating which output device we want to use. Hence, we assign each device a unit number, and then put the unit number of the desired device in the WRITE statement. Many computers assign the unit number 6 to the line printer. If you are using a terminal, the unit number 6 will usually apply to the terminal output instead of the line printer. Hence, a typical list-directed WRITE statement with a specified unit number is:

```
WRITE(6,*)SIDE,   PERI,   AREA
```

An asterisk in the unit number specifies that the output is to be on the standard output unit, and can be used as shown in the following statement:

```
WRITE(*,*)SIDE,   PERI,   AREA
```

If we want values printed on different lines, we can use separate output statements. Thus,

```
WRITE(*,*)TIME,   TEMP
```

will print two values on the same line, while

```
WRITE(*,*)TIME
WRITE(*,*)TEMP
```

will print the two values on different lines. This example would also execute similarly with PRINT statements.

3-2 COMPLETE PROGRAMS

We have studied statements to assign values, compute values, and print values. Two short statements, STOP and END, are all that are needed now to enable s to write complete programs.

The END statement identifies the physical end of our FORTRAN program for the compiler. The compiler stops translating statements when it reaches the END statement. Every FORTRAN program must end with the END statement, whose general form is:

The STOP statement is a signal to the computer to terminate execution of our program. It can be anywhere in the program that makes sense, but usually it is physically just before the END statement. Its general form is:

Both the STOP and the END statements are executable statements. If an END statement is executed, it also terminates execution of the program.

Finally, before we begin to write some simple programs, we introduce the PROGRAM statement. The general form of the PROGRAM statement is:

```
PROGRAM   program name
```

The purpose of this statement is to clearly identify the beginning of a program and assign the program a name. Like a variable name, the program name can be 1 to 6 characters in length, begins with a letter, and contains only letters and digits. Some sample PROGRAM statements are:

```
PROGRAM   TEST
PROGRAM   COMPUT
PROGRAM   SORT2
```

3-3   APPLICATION – SLOPE OF LINE THROUGH TWO POINTS

In the following example, we develop a complete FORTRAN program to compute the slope of a line through two points. For clarity, it is helpful to begin programs with comment lines that describe the purpose of the program. Recall from Chapter 1 that comment statements are indicated with a C or an asterisk in column 1 and that they do not affect the execution of a program. We shall also use comment lines to separate portions of a program.

EXAMPLE 3-4   Slope of Line Through Two Points

Write a complete program to find the slope of a straight line through two points whose coordinates are (5.5,3.1) and (0.5,−1.6). Print the coordinates of the two points and the slope of the line.

Solution

The slope of a straight line is computed by dividing the change in Y by the change in X. Given two points on the line, (x_1,y_1) and (x_2,y_2), we can compute the slope with the following equation:

$$slope = \frac{y_2 - y_1}{x_2 - x_1}$$

FORTRAN Program

```
      PROGRAM  SLOPE1
C
C   THIS PROGRAM COMPUTES THE SLOPE
C   OF A STRAIGHT LINE THROUGH TWO POINTS
C
      X1 = 5.5
      Y1 = 3.1
      X2 = 0.5
      Y2 = -1.6
C
      SLOPE = (Y2 - Y1)/(X2 - X1)
C
      PRINT*, 'POINT 1 ', X1, Y1
      PRINT*, 'POINT 2 ', X2, Y2
      PRINT*, 'SLOPE ', SLOPE
C
      STOP
      END
```

Computer Output

```
POINT 1   5.500000 3.100000
POINT 2   0.5000000E+00  -0.1600000E+01
SLOPE   0.9400000E+00
```

The comment statements are intended to provide identification or information, and to improve overall "readability."   ◊

When running a program with computer cards there will also be additional information required by your particular computer and compiler. This *job control* information, as it is called, will be unique to your computer. It consists of information such as your name, the compiler you are using, and a computer user number. Your instructor or the computer center documentation will provide you with the job control requirements for the computer you will be using. The placement of the control cards, along with the program we have just written to calculate the slope of the line between two points, is given in Figure 3-1.

3-4   LIST-DIRECTED INPUT

We will frequently want to rerun a program to process a different set of data. For instance, the example in the previous section computes the slope of a line through two points. One way to run the program with new data points is to change the assignment statements at the beginning of the program to reflect the new values. However, this requires changing the program each time we want to use new data. A better solution is to incorporate a new statement,

```
                PROGRAM   SLOPE1
        C
        C  THIS PROGRAM COMPUTES THE
        C  SLOPE OF A STRAIGHT LINE
        C  THROUGH TWO POINTS
        C
           X1 = 5.5
           Y1 = 3.1
           X2 = 0.5
           Y2 = -1.6
        C

           SLOPE = (Y2 - Y1)/(X2 - X1)
        C

           PRINT*, 'POINT 1 ', X1, Y1
           PRINT*, 'POINT 2 ', X2, Y2
           PRINT*, 'SLOPE ', SLOPE
        C

           STOP
           END
```

FORTRAN Program {

Job Control Cards { (system dependent)

Figure 3-1   Job control information placement and FORTRAN program.

READ, that will read values from a data line on a terminal, from a data card, or from another input device. Thus, we can change the data to run the program with new values, without having to change the program itself.

Another reason that we use the READ statement is that large amounts of data, which would otherwise require individual assignment statements, can be read with a single READ statement. Returning to our slope calculation program, we saw that four assignments were necessary to initialize the coordinates of the points. In contrast, it takes only one READ statement to initialize the coordinates.

The general form of a list-directed READ statement is:

READ* , *variable list*

The asterisk specifies list-directed input. Generally, list-directed batch input will read the data from computer cards, and list-directed time-sharing input will read the data from the terminal. Again, the variable names in the list must be separated by commas. The variables receive new values in the order in which they are listed in the READ statement. These values must agree in type (integer or real) with the variables in the list. When the program is run on a terminal, a special character, such as a question mark, will be printed when the READ statement is being executed. At that time, you enter the new values for the variables, separated by commas or blanks. For card systems, the data card contains the new values, separated by commas or blanks. The location of the data card is very important. It does not go after the READ statement, but rather, after the complete program. As we mentioned in the previous section, there will be job control cards needed with all card programs. Typically, there are control cards before a program, between the program and its data, and following the data. Figure 3-2 contains the placement of job control cards, the program that calculates the slope (modified to use list-directed READ and PRINT statements), and the data card that contains the coordinates of the two points. Observe that a job control card follows the program and more job control cards follow the data.

A READ statement will read as many data lines or data cards as needed to find new values for the variables in its list. Also, each READ statement will begin with a new line or data card.

EXAMPLE 3-5   Coordinates of Two Points

Read the coordinates of point 1 from one data input line and the coordinates of point 2 from the next data input line.

Solution 1

FORTRAN Statement   `READ*, X1, Y1, X2, Y2`

Data Lines   5.5, 3.1
                 0.5, −1.6

Computer Memory   X1 | 5.5 |

Y1 | 3.1 |

X2 | 0.5 |

Y2 | −1.6 | ◊

Solution 2

FORTRAN Statements   `READ*, X1, Y1`
                         `READ*, X2, Y2`

Data Lines   5.5, 3.1
                 0.5, −1.6

Computer Memory   X1 | 5.5 |

Y1 | 3.1 |

X2 | 0.5 |

Y2 | −1.6 | ◊

```
JOB CONTROL CARDS  { (system dependent)

                       PROGRAM   SLOPE2
                  C
                  C   THIS PROGRAM COMPUTES THE
                  C   SLOPE OF A STRAIGHT LINE
                  C   THROUGH TWO POINTS
                  C
                      READ*, X1, Y1, X2, Y2
FORTRAN PROGRAM   C
                      SLOPE = (Y2 - Y1)/(X2 - X1)
                  C
                      PRINT*, 'POINT 1 ' ,X1, Y1
                      PRINT*, 'POINT 2 ' ,X2, Y2
                      PRINT*, 'SLOPE ' ,SLOPE
                  C
                      STOP
                      END

JOB CONTROL CARDS  { (system dependent)

DATA               { 5.5, 3.1, 0.5, -1.6

JOB CONTROL CARDS  { (system dependent)
```

FIGURE 3-2   Job control information placement and FORTRAN program with data.

Data lines or data cards may occasionally contain more information than is needed in a program. If the numbers that are not needed precede the data we desire, we have to read the unnecessary data to get to the desired data. The variables used to store the unnecessary data are called *dummy variables*. If the numbers that are not needed follow the data we desire, we do not need to read them.

EXAMPLE 3-6   First Test Score

A set of five integer test scores has been punched on a data card. Read the first test score into a variable TEST1.

Solution

FORTRAN Statements
```
INTEGER   TEST1
READ*, TEST1
```

Data Card   83, 52, 73, 81, 78

Computer Memory   TEST1   83

Since the other four test scores follow the one that we need, we do not need to read them. However, note that another READ statement would not read the value 52, but instead would begin with the next data card.   ◇

EXAMPLE 3-7   Third Test Score

A set of five integer test scores has been punched on a data card. Read the third test score into a variable TEST3.

Solution

FORTRAN Statements
```
INTEGER   TEST1, TEST2, TEST3
READ*, TEST1, TEST2, TEST3
```

Data Card   83, 52, 73, 81, 78

Computer Memory   TEST1 $\boxed{83}$

TEST2 $\boxed{52}$

TEST3 $\boxed{73}$

While we did not have to read all five test scores, we did have to read the first two scores to enable us to read the third one.   ◇

Since the input device and output device are the same in time-sharing systems, *conversational computing* can be used in our programs that are run on terminals. Before data is to be entered, we can print a message that describes the data and the order of data values to be entered. After reading the data, we can print it for a validity check. This interaction between the program and the user who is entering the data resembles a conversation, and thus the technique is called conversational computing. In the next example, the slope-computation program has been modified to include more of a conversation between the program and the user.

EXAMPLE 3-8   Slope of Line with Data

Write a complete program to find the slope of a straight line through two points whose coordinates are entered using a terminal. Print the coordinates of the two points and the slope of the line.

Solution

This modification of the solution in Figure 3-2 will illustrate the interaction that can take place between the user and a program. Recall that the system will prompt you to enter data with a question mark when it executes a READ statement.

FORTRAN Program

```
      PROGRAM  SLOPE3
C
C  THIS PROGRAM COMPUTES THE SLOPE
C  OF A STRAIGHT LINE THROUGH TWO POINTS
C
      PRINT*, 'ENTER X AND Y COORDINATES OF POINT 1'
      READ*, X1, Y1
      PRINT*, 'POINT 1 ', X1, Y1
C
      PRINT*, 'ENTER X AND Y COORDINATES OF POINT 2'
      READ*, X2, Y2
      PRINT*, 'POINT 2 ', X2, Y2
C
      SLOPE = (Y2 - Y1)/(X2 - X1)
C
      PRINT*, 'SLOPE ', SLOPE
C
      STOP
      END
```

Computer Output

```
ENTER X AND Y COORDINATES OF POINT 1
?5.5, 3.1
POINT 1   5.500000 3.100000
ENTER X AND Y COORDINATES OF POINT 2
?0.5, -1.6
POINT 2   0.50000000E+00 -0.1600000E+01
SLOPE    0.9400000E+00
```

◊

Another list-directed input statement has the general form:

READ(*unit number,*)variable list*

As in the WRITE statement, the unit number designates the specific device. Many computers assign the unit number 5 to their primary input device, which may be the terminal or the card reader. Again, an asterisk specifies this standard input unit. Hence, typical list-directed READ statements are:

```
      READ(5,*)TEST1
      READ(*,*)TEST1
```

These statements execute just like the previously discussed forms without the unit number designation.

If you will not be using formatted READ and WRITE statements, you should skip Sections 3-5 and 3-6. In succeeding examples and problem solutions that use formatted statements, you will be able to follow the FORTRAN code by ignoring the FORMAT statement and simply using the variable lists for the READ or WRITE statements to tell you which variables are being used. For instance, if a program included

```
READ(5,2)AREA, VOL
2 FORMAT(F4.1,2X,F4.1)
```

then you should mentally read it as

```
READ(*,*)AREA, VOL
```

and skip the FORMAT statement. If a program included

```
WRITE(6,1)AREA, VOL
1 FORMAT(1X,F5.1,2X,F8.3)
```

then you should mentally read it as

```
WRITE(*,*)AREA, VOL
```

or

```
PRINT*, AREA, VOL
```

and skip the FORMAT statement.

3-5 WRITE/FORMAT COMBINATIONS

If we want to specify the form in which data values are printed, and where on the output line they are printed, formatted WRITE statements are necessary. The general form of a formatted WRITE statement is

> WRITE(*unit number,format reference number*)*variable list*

where the variable list is optional. Recall that the unit number selects the specific output device, and the list of variables designates the storage locations whose contents will be printed or arithmetic expressions whose values will be printed. The list of variables also determines the order in which the data values will be printed. The other information still needed is the spacing desired between variables, what part of the page (top, bottom, next line, etc.) is to be used when printing the line, and how many digits are to be printed for the variable values. This information is all given in the FORMAT statement.

Each FORMAT statement has a statement number that is used in the WRITE statement to tie the two together. A sample WRITE/FORMAT combination would thus be:

```
WRITE(6,5)TIME, DIST
5 FORMAT(1X,F5.1,2X,F7.2)
```

Note that the WRITE statement identifies the statement with statement number 5 as the FORMAT statement to be used with it. The same formatted WRITE statement that uses the standard output device is:

```
WRITE(*,5)TIME, DIST
5 FORMAT(1X,F5.1,2X,F7.2)
```

The general form of the FORMAT statement is:

k FORMAT(specification list)

where k is a statement number. The specification list tells the computer the vertical spacing and horizontal spacing to be used when printing the variables. The vertical spacing options include printing on the top of a new page, the next line (single-spacing), double spacing, and no spacing. Horizontal spacing includes indicating how many digits will be used for each value, how many blanks will be between numbers, and how many values are to be printed per line.

In order to understand the specifications that are used to describe the vertical and horizontal spacing, we must first examine the output from a line printer or terminal. These are the most common output devices, but other forms of output have similar characteristics.

The line printer prints on computer paper that is a series of connected pages, each separated by perforations so that it is easy to separate the pages. A common size for a computer page is 11 inches by 14 7/8 inches. Typically 55 to 75 lines of information can be printed per page, and each line can contain up to 132 characters. In our discussion of printed output, we will assume that an output line contains 132 characters. Most line printers print either 6 lines per inch or 8 lines per inch. The WRITE/FORMAT combination describes specifically how each line is to be printed on the page (vertical spacing) and which characters, in the 132 possible characters, will contain data (horizontal spacing).

The computer uses the specification list to construct each output line internally in the memory before actually printing the line. This internal memory region, which contains 133 characters, is called a *buffer*. The buffer is automatically filled with blanks before it is used to construct a line of output. The first character of the buffer is called the *carriage control* character. It determines the vertical spacing for the line. The remaining 132 characters represent the line to be printed.

Output buffer

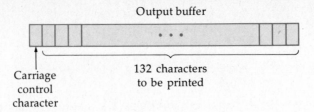

Carriage
control
character

132 characters
to be printed

The following table shows some of the valid carriage control characters and the vertical spacing that they generate. When needed for clarity in either FORMAT statements or Buffer Contents, a blank will be indicated by the character b placed one-half space below the regular line.

CARRIAGE CONTROL	VERTICAL SPACING
1	new page
blank, ♭	single-spacing
0	double-spacing
+	no vertical spacing

When a plus sign is in carriage control, no spacing will occur and the next line of information will print over the last line printed. Some of the examples to follow will contain applications for this *overprinting*. On most computers, an invalid carriage control character will cause single spacing.

When a terminal is used as the output device, the width of the line may be less than 132 positions. Although terminal systems do not always use carriage control, the internal buffer will contain one character more than the line width if carriage control applies. Since a terminal does not have the same capability as a line printer for spacing to a new page, a 1 in carriage control usually becomes an invalid control character and causes single spacing.

We will now examine five FORMAT specifications that will describe how to fill the output buffer. Commas are used to separate specifications in the FORMAT statement.

LITERAL SPECIFICATION

The literal specification allows you to put characters directly into the buffer. The characters must be enclosed in single quote marks or apostrophes. These characters can represent the carriage control character or the characters in a literal. The following examples will illustrate the use of the literal specification in FORMAT statements.

EXAMPLE 3-9 Title Heading

Print a title heading, TEST RESULTS, on the top of a new page, *left-justified* (i.e., no blanks to the left of the heading).

Solution

FORTRAN Statements

```
WRITE(6,4)
4 FORMAT('1','TEST RESULTS')
```

Buffer Contents | 1TEST_bRESULTS |

Computer Output

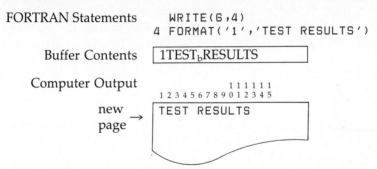

```
                    1 1 1 1 1 1
          1 2 3 4 5 6 7 8 9 0 1 2 3 4 5
new   →   TEST RESULTS
page
```

The buffer is filled according to the FORMAT. No variable names were listed on the WRITE statement; hence, no values are printed. The literal specifications cause the characters 1TEST RESULTS to be put in the buffer, beginning with the first position in the buffer. After filling the buffer as instructed by the FORMAT, the carriage control is examined to determine vertical spacing. The character 1 in the carriage control position tells the computer to space the computer paper to the beginning of a new page. The rest of the buffer, 132 positions, is then printed. Notice that the carriage control character is not printed. The row of small numbers above the computer output shows the specific column of the output line. That is, the first T is in column 1, the second T is in column 4, and the third T is in column 11.   ◊

EXAMPLE 3-10   Column Headings

Double-space from the last line printed, and then print column headings 1979 SALES and 1980 SALES, with no blanks on the left side of the paper and five blanks between the two column headings.

Correct Solution

FORTRAN Statements

```
WRITE(6,3)
3 FORMAT('0','1979b SALESbbbbb1980b SALES')
```

Buffer Contents

| 01979_bSALES_{bbbbb}1980_bSALES |

Computer Output

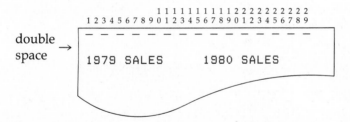

```
                    1 1 1 1 1 1 1 1 1 1 2 2 2 2 2 2 2 2 2 2
          1 2 3 4 5 6 7 8 9 0 1 2 3 4 5 6 7 8 9 0 1 2 3 4 5 6 7 8 9
double →  - - - - - - - - - - - - - - - - -
space
          1979 SALES       1980 SALES
```

The line of dashes in the computer output represents the previous line of output. The first character inserted in the buffer is a zero, to indicate double-spacing from the previous line of output. Then the column headings are specified with five blanks between them. ◇

Incorrect Solution

FORTRAN Statements

```
        WRITE(6,3)
      3 FORMAT('1979ₐSALESₐₐₐₐₐ1980ₐSALES')
```

Buffer Contents

1979bSALESbbbbb1980bSALES

Computer Output

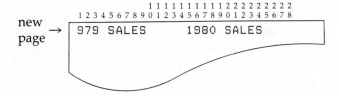

In this example we forgot to specify the carriage control; however, the computer does not forget. The first position of the buffer contains a 1, which indicates spacing to a new page. The rest of the buffer, 979bSALESbbbbb1980bSALES, is then printed. ◇

X SPECIFICATION

The X specification will insert blanks into the buffer. Its general form is nX, where n represents the number of blanks to be inserted in the buffer. An example using both the X specification and the literal specification follows:

EXAMPLE 3-11   Centered Heading

Print the heading EXPERIMENT NO. 1, centered at the top of a new page.

Solution

FORTRAN Statements

```
       WRITE(6,35)
    35 FORMAT('1',58X,'EXPERIMENT NO. 1')
```

Buffer Contents

1	EXPERIMENT NO. 1

$$\underbrace{}$$

58 blanks

Computer Output

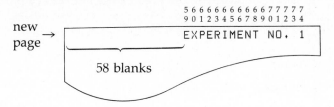

This heading could have been done without the 58X specification, but would require a literal specification of a 1, followed by 58 blanks, followed by EXPERIMENT NO. 1. ◇

I SPECIFICATION

The literal specification and the X specification already discussed allow us to specify carriage control and to print headings. They cannot, however, be used to print variable values. We will now look at a specification that is used for printing the contents of integer variables. The form of the specification is Iw, where w represents the number of positions (width) to be assigned in the buffer for printing the value of an integer variable. The value is always *right-justified* (no blanks to the right of the value) in those positions in the buffer. Extra positions on the left are filled with blanks. Thus, if the value 16 is printed with an I4 specification, the four positions contain two blanks followed by 16. If there are not enough positions to print the value, including a minus sign if the value is negative, the positions are filled with asterisks. Hence, if we print the value 132 or −12 with an I2 specification, the two positions are filled with asterisks. It is important to recognize that the asterisks do not necessarily indicate that there is an error in the value; instead, the asterisks may indicate that you need to assign a larger width in the corresponding I specification.

Often, more than one variable name will be listed on the WRITE statement. When interpreting a WRITE/FORMAT combination, the compiler will match the first variable name to the first specification for printing values, the second variable name to the second specification for printing values, and so on. Thus, there should generally be the same number of specifications for printing values as there are variables on the WRITE statement list.

EXAMPLE 3-12   Integer Values

Print the values of the integer variables SUM, MEAN, and N on the same line, single-spaced from the previous line.

Solution

Computer Memory	SUM	12
	MEAN	−14
	N	−146

FORTRAN Statements   `WRITE(6,30)SUM, MEAN, N`
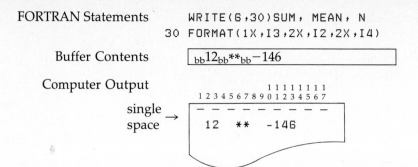
                 `30 FORMAT(1X,I3,2X,I2,2X,I4)`

Buffer Contents   bb12bb**bb−146

Computer Output

single → / space →

    11111111
1 2 3 4 5 6 7 8 9 0 1 2 3 4 5 6 7

   12   **   -146

The computer will print SUM with an I3 specification, MEAN with an I2 specification, and N with an I4 specification. The value of SUM is 12, so the three corresponding positions are $_b12$. The value of MEAN, −14, requires at least three positions, so the two specified positions are filled with asterisks. The value of N fills all four allotted positions. The carriage control character is a blank and thus the line of output is single-spaced from the previous line. ◇

EXAMPLE 3-13   Literal and Variable Information

On separate lines, print the values of MEAN and SUM, along with an indicator of the name of each of the integer variables.

Solution

Computer Memory   SUM | 12 |

                     MEAN | −14 |

FORTRAN Statements   `WRITE(6,2)MEAN`
                 `2 FORMAT(1X,'MEAN = ',I4)`
                 `WRITE(6,3)SUM`
                 `3 FORMAT(1X,'SUM = ',I4)`

Buffer Contents   bMEANb=bb−14

                     bSUMb=bbb12

Computer Output

single → / space →

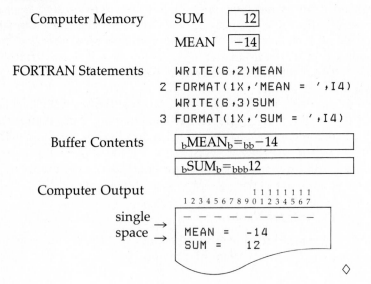

    11111111
1 2 3 4 5 6 7 8 9 0 1 2 3 4 5 6 7

MEAN =   -14
SUM =   12

◇

F SPECIFICATION

The F specification is used to print real numbers in a decimal form (e.g., 36.21), as opposed to an exponential form (0.3621E+02). The general form for an F specification is Fw.d, where w represents the total width or number of positions to be used in printing the real value, and d represents the number of those positions that will represent decimal positions on the right of the decimal point. For example, the minimum size F specification that can be used to print 34.186 is F6.3, a total of six positions counting the decimal point with three decimal positions. Before the value is inserted in the buffer, the decimal point is located in the specified position. The form for F6.3 is then

X X . X X X

DECIMAL

WIDTH

If the value to be printed has fewer than d decimal positions, zeros are inserted on the right side. Thus, if the value 21.6 is printed with an F6.3 specification, the output is 21.600. If the value to be printed has more than d decimal positions, only d decimal positions are printed, dropping the rest. Thus, if the value 21.86342 is printed with an F6.3 specification, the output is 21.863. Many compilers will round to the last decimal position printed. Thus, if the value 18.98662 is printed with an F6.3 specification, the output is 18.987.

If the integer portion of a real value requires fewer positions than allotted in the F specification, the extra positions on the left are filled with blanks. Thus, if the value 3.123 is printed with an F6.3 specification, the output is ₆3.123. If the integer portion of a real value, including the minus sign if the value is negative, requires more positions than allotted in the F specification, the entire field is filled with asterisks. Thus, if the value 312.6 is printed with an F6.3 specification, the output is ******.

If a value is between −1 and +1, positions must usually be allowed for both a leading zero to the left of the decimal point and a minus sign if the value can be negative. Thus, the smallest F specification that could be used to print −.127 is F6.3, which would be output as −0.127. If a smaller specification width were used, all the positions would be filled with asterisks.

EXAMPLE 3-14   Angle THETA

Print the value of an angle called THETA. Construct the Greek symbol for theta (θ) and print in this form:

$$\theta \;=\; XX.XX$$

Solution

Computer Memory   THETA $\boxed{3\,.184}$

FORTRAN Statements
```
  WRITE(6,1)
1 FORMAT(' ','-')
  WRITE(6,2)THETA
2 FORMAT('+','0 = ',F5.2)
```

Buffer Contents

$\boxed{\text{b}-}$

$\boxed{+0_b=_{bb}3.18}$

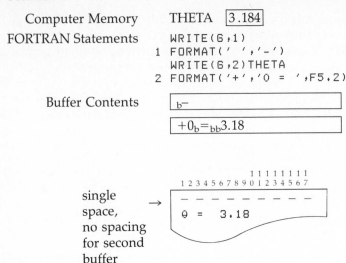

single
space,   →
no spacing
for second
buffer

The first WRITE printed a dash in the first position of the output line after single-spacing. The second WRITE had a plus sign in the carriage control which caused no vertical spacing. Thus, the character zero is printed on top of the character dash, thus giving the Greek symbol θ. The value of THETA is printed on the same line.   ◇

EXAMPLE 3-15   Sine and Cosine Computation

Print the values of the sine of the angle THETA and the cosine of the angle THETA. Assume that THETA is in radians. Use descriptive literals.

Solution

Computer Memory   THETA $\boxed{1\,.26}$

FORTRAN Statements
```
  WRITE(6,1)
1 FORMAT('1',3X,'0',3X,'SINE_b0',
+            3X,'COSINE 0')
  WRITE(6,2)
2 FORMAT('+',3X,'-',8X,'-',10X,'-')
  WRITE(6,3)THETA, SIN(THETA), COS(THETA)
3 FORMAT(2X,F4.2,3X,F4.2,5X,F4.2)
```

Buffer Contents

$\boxed{1_{bbb}0_{bbb}\text{SINE}_b0_{bbb}\text{COSINE}_b0}$

$\boxed{+_{bbb}-_{bbbbbbbb}-_{bbbbbbbbbb}-}$

$\boxed{_{bb}1.26_{bbb}0.95_{bbbbb}0.31}$

Computer Output

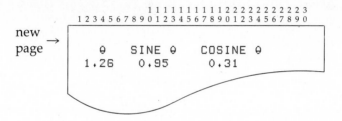

new
page →

The first line was printed on a new page, the second line was over-printed on the same line as the first to build the symbol θ, and the third line was printed after single-spacing. Note that, if either the sine or cosine of THETA had been negative, the corresponding output field would have been filled with asterisks because there is not room for a minus sign. ◇

E SPECIFICATION

Real numbers may be printed in an exponential form with the E specification. This specification is primarily used for very small values, or very large values, or when you are uncertain of the magnitude of a number. If you use an F format or an I format that is too small for a value, the output field will be filled with asterisks. In contrast, a real number will always fit in an E specification field.

The general format for an E specification is Ew.d. The w again represents the total width or number of positions to be used in printing the value. The d represents the number of positions to the right of the decimal point, assuming that the value is in exponential form. The framework for printing a real value in an exponential specification with three decimal places is:

S0.XXXESXX

DECIMAL

WIDTH

The symbol S indicates that positions must be reserved for the sign of the value and the sign of the exponent in case they are negative. Note that with all the extra positions, the total width becomes 10 positions. Three of the 10 positions are the decimal positions and the other 7 are positions that are always needed for an E format. Thus, the total width of an E specification must be at least d + 7. The above specification is then E10.3.

If there are more decimal positions in the specification than are in the exponential form of the value, the extra decimal positions are filled on the right with zeros.

If the total width of the E specification is more than 7 plus the decimal positions, the extra positions appear as blanks on the left side of the value.

EXAMPLE 3-16   Exponential Value

Print the value of TIME in an exponential form with four decimal positions.

Solution 1

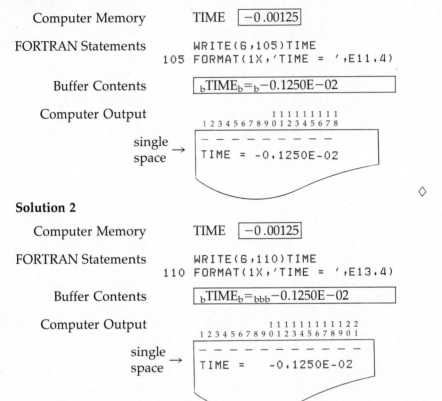

Computer Memory   TIME $\boxed{-0.00125}$

FORTRAN Statements
```
      WRITE(6,105)TIME
  105 FORMAT(1X,'TIME = ',E11.4)
```

Buffer Contents $\boxed{\text{ьTIME}_{ь}=_{ь}-0.1250\text{E}-02}$

Computer Output

```
                        1 1 1 1 1 1 1 1 1
            1 2 3 4 5 6 7 8 9 0 1 2 3 4 5 6 7 8
single      _ _ _ _ _ _ _ _ _ _ _ _ _ _ _ _ _ _
space  →    TIME = -0.1250E-02
```

◇

Solution 2

Computer Memory   TIME $\boxed{-0.00125}$

FORTRAN Statements
```
      WRITE(6,110)TIME
  110 FORMAT(1X,'TIME = ',E13.4)
```

Buffer Contents $\boxed{\text{ьTIME}_{ь}=_{ьbb}-0.1250\text{E}-02}$

Computer Output

```
                        1 1 1 1 1 1 1 1 1 1 2 2
            1 2 3 4 5 6 7 8 9 0 1 2 3 4 5 6 7 8 9 0 1
single      _ _ _ _ _ _ _ _ _ _ _ _ _ _ _ _ _ _ _ _
space  →    TIME =      -0.1250E-02
```

◇

EXAMPLE 3-17   Polynomial Computation

Calculate and print the value of the polynomial $X^6 + 2X^4 - 6X$ for the number stored in the variable X. Since X may be a small number, use an E format to print both the value of X and the value of the polynomial.

Correct Solution

Computer Memory
(Before Execution)   X $\boxed{0.00143}$

FORTRAN Statements

```
   POLY = X**6 + 2.0*X**4 - 6.0*X
   WRITE(6,5)X, POLY
 5 FORMAT('0','X = ',E11.3,' POLYNOMIAL = ',E11.3)
```

Computer Memory
(After Execution)   X   [0.00143]

      POLY   [−0.00858]

Buffer Contents

| 0X$_b$=$_{bbb}$0.143E−02$_b$POLYNOMIAL$_b$=$_{bb}$−0.858E−02 |

Computer Output

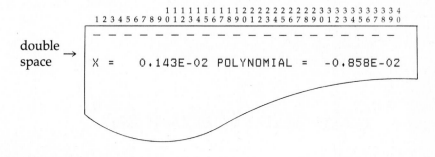

Incorrect Solution

Computer Memory
(Before Execution)   X   [0.00143]

FORTRAN Statements

```
POLY = X**6 + 2.0*X**4 - 6.0*X
WRITE(6,6)POLY, X
6 FORMAT('0','X = ',E11.3,' POLYNOMIAL = ',E11.3)
```

Computer Memory   X
(After Execution)   [0.00143]

      POLY   [−0.00858]

Buffer Contents

| 0X$_b$ = $_{bb}$−0.858E−02$_b$POLYNOMIAL$_b$=$_{bbb}$0.143E−02 |

Computer Output

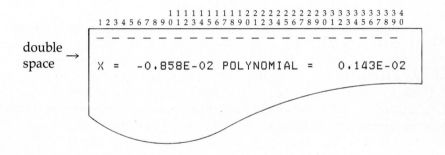

Note that the only difference between the correct solution and the incorrect solution is the order of the variables in the WRITE statement. Thus, in the incorrect solution, the output has the values interchanged. This is obviously a serious error but, unfortunately, one that the computer cannot detect.   ◇

The PRINT statement can also be used with formats, as shown in these statements:

```
        PRINT 10, X
    10 FORMAT(1X,'X = ',F4.2)
```

It is not possible, however, to specify an output device other than the standard output device with a PRINT statement.

3-6   READ/FORMAT COMBINATIONS

If we want to specify the columns to be used in reading data from a data line or a data card, we use a formatted READ statement. The general form of a formatted READ statement is:

READ(*unit number, format reference number*)*variable list*

The unit number designates the input device to be used. The list of variable names determines the order in which new values are stored, and the format reference number refers to a FORMAT statement that will describe the positions to be read. A typical READ/FORMAT combination is:

```
    READ(5,2)DIST, VEL
    2 FORMAT(F4.1,3X,F4.2)
```

The same formatted READ statement, which specifies the standard input device, is:

```
    READ(*,2)DIST, VEL
    2 FORMAT(F4.1,3X,F4.2)
```

The form of the FORMAT appears to be the same as that used with WRITE statements. Even the specifications in the FORMAT look familiar. There are, however, differences between the specifications used for reading data values and those used to write data values. Also, no carriage control is needed with READ statements. Each READ statement begins reading at column one of a new terminal input line or a new card. We will assume that the input unit is a terminal or a card reader, but the examples will illustrate fundamental rules that apply to other forms of input also.

We now look at each specification individually, as we did for the WRITE statement specifications. We will start with the X specification instead of the literal specification because it is invalid to use a literal specification when reading data.

X SPECIFICATION

The X specification will skip positions on the data line. Its general form is nX, where n represents the number of positions to skip. Thus, we do not have to use dummy variables with formatted READ statements to get to the data we want to use. We just skip over unnecessary values.

I SPECIFICATION

The I specification is required when reading a value into an integer variable. The form of this specification is Iw where w represents the number of positions to use on the data line. Any blanks in the w positions will be interpreted as zeros. Any character besides numbers, plus or minus signs, and blanks will cause an execution error to occur. Thus, 5.0 cannot be read with an I3 specification, but $_{bb}5$ will be read correctly with an I3 specification.

EXAMPLE 3-18   MEAN and NORM

Read the values of the variables MEAN and NORM from a data line. MEAN is in columns 1–4 and NORM is in columns 10–11.

Correct Solution

FORTRAN Statements	`READ(5,1)MEAN, NORM` `1 FORMAT(I4,5X,I2)`
Data Line	$_b123_{bbbbb}10$
Computer Memory	MEAN $\boxed{123}$
	NORM $\boxed{10}$

The first four columns, $_b123$, are used to assign a value to MEAN. The first blank is interpreted as a zero, and thus 0123 is stored in MEAN. We then skip the next five columns. From columns 10–11 we pick up the value 10 for NORM.   ◇

Incorrect Solution

FORTRAN Statements	`READ(5,2)MEAN, NORM` `2 FORMAT(1X,I4,5X,I2)`
Data Line	$_b123_{bbbbb}10$
Computer Memory	MEAN $\boxed{1230}$
	NORM $\boxed{0}$

If carriage control is used with READ statements, incorrect values may be stored in memory. Using the above format, we skip the first column and use the next four columns for determining the value of MEAN. These columns contain 123_b, which is interpreted as 1230. We then skip five columns, and use the next two columns for determining the value of NORM. The contents 0_b will be interpreted as 0.

$\diamond$

F SPECIFICATION

The F specification can be used to read a value for a real variable. The form of this specification is Fw.d, where w represents the total number of positions to use on the data line and d represents the number of decimal positions. As with the I specification, any blanks in the w positions will be interpreted as zeros. If there is a decimal point punched in the w positions, the value will be stored as it is punched, regardless of what value has been given to d. Thus, if a real value DIST is read with a F4.1 specification, and the four characters are 1.26, then the value of DIST is 1.26. If there is no decimal point punched in the specified positions, then the value of d is used to position a decimal place before storing the value. Thus, if the characters 1246 are read with an F4.1 specification, the value stored is 124.6, a value with one decimal position. Note that printing this value would require an F5.1 specification. Thus, the same specification will not always work for both input and output.

EXAMPLE 3-19   TIME and TEMP

Read two variables, TIME and TEMP. TIME will be in columns 10–13, with two decimal positions, and TEMP will be in columns 16–18, with one decimal position.

Solution

FORTRAN Statements
```
        READ(5,200)TIME, TEMP
    200 FORMAT(9X,F4.2,2X,F3.1)
```

Data Line   bbbbbbbbb4.66bb125

Computer Memory   TIME $\boxed{4.66}$

                     TEMP $\boxed{12.5}$

Since there was no decimal point in the TEMP field, which was read with F3.1, one was positioned in the three numbers such that one position was a decimal position. $\diamond$

In Figure 3-2 we gave an example of a program for a card system used to calculate and print the slope of the line through two data points using list-directed statements. Figure 3-3 contains the same program, now using formatted statements.

```
JOB CONTROL
CARDS              { (system dependent)

                            PROGRAM   SLOPE4
                   C
                   C   THIS PROGRAM COMPUTES THE SLOPE
                   C   OF A STRAIGHT LINE THROUGH TWO POINTS
                   C
                            READ(5,10)X1, Y1, X2, Y2
                   10 FORMAT(F4.1,F4.1,F4.1,F4.1)
                   C
FORTRAN                     SLOPE = (Y2 - Y1)/(X2 - X1)
PROGRAM            C
                            WRITE(6,20)X1, Y1, X2, Y2, SLOPE
                   20 FORMAT('1','THE SLOPE OF THE '
                          +        'LINE THROUGH (',F4.1,',',
                          +        F4.1,') AND (',F4.1,',',
                          +        F4.1,') IS',F4.1)
                   C
                            STOP
                            END

JOB CONTROL
CARDS              { (system dependent)

DATA               { b5.5b3.1b0.5-1.6

JOB CONTROL
CARDS              { (system dependent)
```

FIGURE 3-3   Job control information placement
and FORTRAN program with formatted data.

The output from the program of Figure 3-3 is:

```
          1 1 1 1 1 1 1 1 1 1 2 2 2 2 2 2 2 2 2 2 3 3 3 3 3 3 3 3 3 3 4 4 4 4 4 4 4 4 4 4 5 5 5 5 5 5 5 5 5 5 6 6 6 6 6
1 2 3 4 5 6 7 8 9 0 1 2 3 4 5 6 7 8 9 0 1 2 3 4 5 6 7 8 9 0 1 2 3 4 5 6 7 8 9 0 1 2 3 4 5 6 7 8 9 0 1 2 3 4 5 6 7 8 9 0 1 2 3 4
THE SLOPE OF THE LINE THROUGH ( 5.5, 3.1) AND ( 0.5,-1.6) IS 0.9
```

new page

E SPECIFICATION

The E specification is used in a READ/FORMAT combination when a variable is entered in an E format, or exponential form. The general form is Ew.d, where w represents the total number of positions that are being considered, and d represents the number of decimal positions when the value is expressed in exponential form. If a decimal point is included, then its placement will override the value of d. If no decimal point is included, then one is located, according to d, before storing the value. It is not necessary that the width be at least seven positions greater than the number of decimal positions as was necessary for output with an E format. In fact, for READ statements, the E format will accept many forms of input. The following list shows some of the different ways in which the value 1.26 can be entered in a field read with E9.2. Note that the data can even be in an F specification form.

Data Card	Value Stored
0.126E$_b$01	1.26
1.26$_b$E$_b$00	1.26
1.26$_{bbbbb}$	1.26
12.60E-01	1.26
bbb.126E1	1.26
bbbbbb126	1.26

Remember that the system will use two positions for the exponent if they are available. Thus $_{bbb}$.126E1 will be interpreted as 1.26, but $_{bb}$.126E1$_b$ will be interpreted as $_{bb}$.126E10, or 0.126×10^{10}.

EXAMPLE 3-20   Job Number and Computer Time

Read two values. The first value, in columns 2–6, represents an integer job number assigned to a computer run, and the second value, in columns 10–16, represents the number of computer seconds used to run the program. This computer time will be entered in an exponential form, with two decimal places.

Solution

FORTRAN Statements
```
      READ(5,10)NUM,  CTIME
   10 FORMAT(1X,I5,3X,E7.2)
```

Data Line $_b$13034$_{bbb}$.36E−02

Computer Memory   NUM   [13034]

CTIME   [0.0036] ◇

3-7 APPLICATION – NUTRITION RESEARCH RESULTS

In the application presented in this section, we give a solution to the problem stated at the beginning of the chapter. In the solution, we use list-directed input and formatted output. This is a very common way of performing I/O on terminals.

EXAMPLE 3-21 Nutrition Research Results

A research scientist performed nutrition tests using three animals. Data on each animal includes an identification number, the weight of the animal at the beginning of the experiment, and the weight of the animal at the end of the experiment. The data for one animal are on one line, with each data value separated from other values by commas. Write a complete program to read this information and print a report. The report is to include the original information plus the percentage increase in weight for each test animal.

Solution

We must first determine the steps that are necessary to prepare the desired report. We could read the data, compute the percentage increase in weight, and print the test results for the first animal; then read, compute, and print the results for the second animal; and finally, read, compute, and print the results for the last animal. As an alternative solution, we could read the information for all three animals first, then compute the weight increases for all three, and then print the results for all three. This last technique is the one used in the following solution.

FORTRAN PROGRAM

```
      PROGRAM   RESRCH
C
C  THIS PROGRAM PRINTS A REPORT ON THE RESULTS OF
C  AN EXPERIMENT INVOLVING THREE TEST ANIMALS
C
      READ*, N1, BWT1, FWT1
      READ*, N2, BWT2, FWT2
      READ*, N3, BWT3, FWT3
C
      PERC1 = (FWT1 - BWT1)/BWT1*100.0
      PERC2 = (FWT2 - BWT2)/BWT2*100.0
      PERC3 = (FWT3 - BWT3)/BWT3*100.0
C
      WRITE(6,5)
    5 FORMAT('1','TEST RESULTS')
      WRITE(6,10)
   10 FORMAT('0','NUMBER   INITIAL WT  FINAL
     +        'WT   PERCENTAGE INCREASE')
C
      WRITE(6,20)N1, BWT1, FWT1, PERC1
      WRITE(6,20)N2, BWT2, FWT2, PERC2
      WRITE(6,20)N3, BWT3, FWT3, PERC3
   20 FORMAT(1X,I4,6X,F4.1,7X,F4.1,6X,F10.5)
C
      STOP
      END
```

Data Input

10, 5.3, 6.2
11, 5.2, 5.2
12, 5.3, 5.1

Computer Output

```
                1 1 1 1 1 1 1 1 1 1 2 2 2 2 2 2 2 2 2 2 3 3 3 3 3 3 3 3 3 3 4 4 4 4 4 4 4 4 4 4 5
1 2 3 4 5 6 7 8 9 0 1 2 3 4 5 6 7 8 9 0 1 2 3 4 5 6 7 8 9 0 1 2 3 4 5 6 7 8 9 0 1 2 3 4 5 6 7 8 9 0
TEST RESULTS

NUMBER    INITIAL WT    FINAL WT    PERCENTAGE INCREASE
  10         5.3          6.2            16.98112
  11         5.2          5.2             0.00000
  12         5.3          5.1            -3.77359
```

3-8 DATA FILES

The construction of *data files* is a feature that allows you to build a data file and store it separately from your program. Another program can then access the data file to obtain the information, if needed. Thus, the data does not have to be entered by hand every time that it is needed. You only have to build the data file once, and use the editing capabilities of the computer system to correct and update the file. To use this feature, a statement that assigns the file to a device number or unit number is required. READ/WRITE statements that use this device number can then access the data file directly. The general form of the statement that assigns a device number to the data file is:

OPEN(UNIT=*integer expression*, FILE=*file name*, STATUS=*literal*)

The integer expression designates the unit number to be used in READ/WRITE statements. Do not use the device numbers assigned to the standard input and output devices on your system. Thus, in our examples, we will not assign data files to units 5 and 6. The file name refers to the name given to the file. The STATUS literal tells the computer whether we are opening an input file to be used with READ statements or an output file to be used with PRINT or WRITE statements. If the file is an input file, then it already has data in it and is specified with STATUS = 'OLD'. If the file is an output file, then it does not contain data yet, and is specified with STATUS = 'NEW'. Some systems require a REWIND statement after opening an input file. This statement and additional information on building and accessing data files are presented in Chapter 9.

EXAMPLE 3-22 Parallel Resistance

A data file RES3 contains three data lines, each containing a resistance value from a resistor in an instrumentation circuit. Write a complete program to read the three resistances and compute their combined resistance R_c for a parallel arrangement, as shown below:

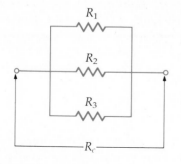

$$R_c = \frac{1}{\dfrac{1}{R_1} + \dfrac{1}{R_2} + \dfrac{1}{R_3}}$$

Print the value of R_c.

Solution

Data File RES3

1000.0
1100.0
2000.0

FORTRAN Program

```
      PROGRAM  RESIS1
C
C   THIS PROGRAM READS A DATA FILE WITH THREE
C   RESISTANCE VALUES AND COMPUTES THEIR EQUIVALENT
C   PARALLEL VALUE
C
      OPEN(UNIT=10, FILE='RES3', STATUS='OLD')
C
      READ(10,*)R1, R2, R3
C
      RC = 1.0/(1.0/R1 + 1.0/R2 + 1.0/R3)
C
      WRITE(*,*)RC, 'OHMS'
C
      STOP
      END
```

Computer Output

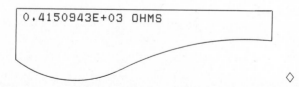

0.4150943E+03 OHMS

Example 3-22 used a small data file, but the advantages of using a data file become more obvious with large data files. Once the data file is built, no matter how many times you run a program that uses the file, you do not have to reenter the data. Also, it is very easy to make changes and updates to a data file with the editing capabilities available on terminal systems.

Data files can also be built by a FORTRAN program with WRITE statements. Thus, instead of using a printer as our output device, we can write the values in a data file. This is often used when plotting data. The data to be plotted is first entered into a data file, and the plotter then accesses the data file. Carriage control is not used with a formatted WRITE to a data file because the output is not actually being printed, but instead is being stored internally in the computer.

EXAMPLE 3-23   Parallel Resistance with Files

Modify the program in the solution of Example 3-22 such that the combined resistance R_c is printed and also stored in a file called RESC.

Solution

Data File RES3

1000.0
1100.0
2000.0

FORTRAN Program

```
      PROGRAM  RESIS2
C
C   THIS PROGRAM READS A DATA FILE WITH THREE
C   RESISTANCE VALUES AND COMPUTES THEIR EQUIVALENT
C   PARALLEL VALUE
C
      OPEN(UNIT=10, FILE='RES3', STATUS='OLD')
      OPEN(UNIT=11, FILE='RESC', STATUS='NEW')
C
      READ(10,*)R1, R2, R3
C
      RC = 1.0/(1.0/R1 + 1.0/R2 + 1.0/R3)
C
      WRITE(*,*)RC, 'OHMS'
      WRITE(11,*)RC
C
      STOP
      END
```

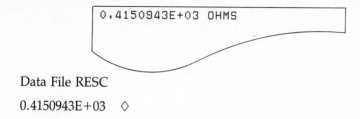

Data File RESC

0.4150943E+03   ◇

3-9   ADDITIONAL FORMAT FEATURES

REPETITION

If we have two specifications in a row that are the same, we can use a constant in front of the specification to indicate repetition. For instance, I2, I2, I2 can be replaced by 3I2. Often our FORMAT statements can be made shorter with repetition constants. The following pairs of FORMAT statements represent equivalent specifications.

```
10 FORMAT(3X,I2,3X,I2)
10 FORMAT(2(3X,I2))

20 FORMAT(1X,F4.1,F4.1,1X,I3,1X,I3)
20 FORMAT(1X,2F4.1,2(1X,I3))
```

SLASH

The FORMAT statement may also contain the character slash, /. Commas around the slash in a FORMAT are optional. If the slash is in a READ statement, a new data line or a new data card will be read when the slash is encountered.

EXAMPLE 3-24   Real Values

Read the values of HT1 and HT2 from one data line, TIME from a second line, and VEL from a third data line. Each number is entered in four columns, with one decimal position. There are no extra columns between HT1 and HT2.

Solution 1

FORTRAN Statements
```
   READ(5,15)HT1, HT2, TIME, VEL
15 FORMAT(2F4.1/F4.1/F4.1)
```

Data Lines
16.518.2
00.5
−4.6

Computer Memory	HT1	16.5
	HT2	18.2
	TIME	0.5
	VEL	−4.6 ◇

Solution 2

In this solution, we do not use the slash. Notice the extra READ statements that are required.

FORTRAN Statements

```
      READ(5,15)HT1, HT2
   15 FORMAT(2F4.1)
      READ(5,16)TIME
      READ(5,16)VEL
   16 FORMAT(F4.1)
```

Data Lines

```
16.518.2
00.5
−4.6
```

Computer Memory	HT1	16.5
	HT2	18.2
	TIME	0.5
	VEL	−4.6 ◇

The slash can be used with WRITE statements also. It is very important, however, to interpret the slash as a signal that says "print the current buffer and start a new one." If you interpret it this way, you see that the carriage control character following the slash will determine whether the spacing between lines is single-spacing, double-spacing, or some other spacing.

EXAMPLE 3-25 Title and Headings

Print the heading TEST RESULTS followed by column headings TIME and HEIGHT. Start on a new page.

Solution 1

FORTRAN Statements

```
      WRITE(6,5)
    5 FORMAT('1','bb TEST RESULTS'/
    +       1X,'TIMEbbbbbHEIGHT')
```

Buffer Contents

| 1bb TEST RESULTS |
| bTIMEbbbbbHEIGHT |

Computer Output

When the slash is encountered, we "print the current buffer." The carriage control character is a 1, and thus the first line is printed on a new page. We then "start a new buffer." The 1X specification puts a blank first in the buffer. Thus, when we reach the end of the FORMAT, this line will be single-spaced from the first line. If the 1X had been omitted, the character T would have been used for carriage control. This is an undefined carriage control character and thus also causes single-spacing. However, the computer output would be:

◇

Solution 2

FORTRAN Statements

```
      WRITE(6,20)
   20 FORMAT('1','bbTEST RESULTS'/
      +       '0','TIMEbbbbbHEIGHT')
```

Buffer Contents

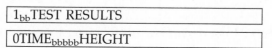

Computer Output

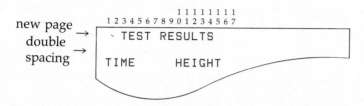

The only difference between the statements in this solution and the first solution is that the carriage control character for the second buffer is a 0. Thus, we have double-spacing between the lines instead of single-spacing. ◇

TAB SPECIFICATION

The tab specification, Tn, allows you to shift directly to a specified position, n, in the input or output buffer. The following pairs of FORMAT statements function exactly the same.

```
500 FORMAT(58X,'EXPERIMENT NO. 1')
500 FORMAT(T59,'EXPERIMENT NO. 1')

550 FORMAT('1','SALES',10X,'PROFIT',10X,'LOSS')
550 FORMAT('1','SALES',T17,'PROFIT',T33,'LOSS')

600 FORMAT(F6.1,15X,I7)
600 FORMAT(F6.1,T22,I7)
```

NUMBER OF SPECIFICATIONS

Suppose there are more FORMAT specifications than variables on a READ or WRITE list, as shown below:

```
READ(5,1)SPEED, DIST
1 FORMAT(4F5.2)
```

In these cases, the computer uses as much of the specification list as is needed, and ignores the rest. Thus, in our example, SPEED and DIST would be matched to the first two specifications, and the last two specifications would be ignored. This rule allows us to occasionally use the same FORMAT with several statements.

Suppose there are fewer FORMAT specifications than variables on a READ or WRITE list, as shown below:

```
WRITE(5,20)TEMP, VOL
20 FORMAT(1X,F6.2)
```

In these cases, we match variables and specifications until we reach the end of the FORMAT. Then, two events occur:

1 With a READ instruction, we go to the next data line or data card; with a WRITE instruction, we print the current buffer and start a new one.

2 We back up in the FORMAT specification list with both READ and WRITE statements until we reach a left parenthesis, and we again begin matching the remaining variables to the specifications at that point.

Thus, in the previous statements, TEMP would be matched to the F6.2 specification. Since there is not a specification for VOL, we do the following:

1 Print the value of TEMP after single spacing.

2 Back up to the beginning of the FORMAT specification list (first left parenthesis) and match the F6.2 to the value of VOL. We then reach the end of the list and single space to print the value of VOL. Thus TEMP and VOL are printed on separate lines.

SUMMARY

We have studied statements that allow us to READ data and also to PRINT or WRITE data. These statements are usually needed to write meaningful programs. List-directed statements are easy to use, but to be able to control the form of input and output, we must use FORMAT statements with our READ and WRITE statements. With these I/O statements, we can now write complete programs that read data values, perform calculations using the data values, and then print the new values calculated.

KEY WORDS

buffer
carriage control
conversational computing
data file
dummy variable
END statement
FORMAT specification
FORMAT statement
formatted I/O
job control information

left-justified
list-directed
literal
OPEN statement
overprinting
PRINT statement
READ statement
right-justified
STOP statement
WRITE statement

DEBUGGING AIDS

The following steps will help you correct input and output statements that are not working properly.

LIST-DIRECTED AND FORMATTED I/O

1   Check to be sure you have given values to all variables on a WRITE list.

2   *Echo* values that you read. That is, immediately after reading values, print them for a comparison check.

FORMATTED I/O

3   If any of your output contains asterisks, enlarge the width w of the corresponding specifications or use an E format.

4   Be sure that the order of variables on the input or output list match the order you used when writing the FORMAT.

5   Check *every* line of output to be sure that you have correctly specified carriage control. Look for incorrect spacing between lines or missing first letters or numbers.

6　Be sure that you have as many FORMAT specifications as variable names in the READ/WRITE list. In general, do not try to share FORMAT statements.

7　Always print integer values with I specifications, and real values with F or E specifications.

8　Be sure you do not have the characters I and 1 interchanged, or the characters O (letter) and 0 (number) interchanged.

9　Be sure that you have not gone past column 72 on long statements.

10　Do not try to combine too many lines of output in a single WRITE statement.

11　Use unformatted statements to print values first. After you have determined that the values are correct, then change to formatted statements, if needed.

12　Check input FORMATS to be sure that you have not included carriage control.

13　Do not split a literal specification when continuing a long FORMAT to the next line. For example, consider the following FORMAT statement:

```
10 FORMAT('1',20X,'EXPERIMENTAL RESULTS
+   FROM PROJECT #1')
```

Any blanks between the word RESULTS and column 72 of the first line, and the blanks between the continuation character + and the word FROM, will be inserted in the literal. Thus, the heading would appear something like this:

```
EXPERIMENTAL RESULTS            FROM PROJECT #1
```

STYLE/TECHNIQUE GUIDES

Except for the first three guidelines, the following refer mainly to formatted input and output statements.

1　Develop the habit of echo printing values that you have read.

2　Print the physical units that correspond to numerical values that are being printed. This information is vital for proper interpretation of results.

3　Use a PROGRAM statement with an appropriate name at the beginning of each program. Follow the PROGRAM statement with comment statements that briefly describe the function of the program.

4 Be consistent about your placement of FORMAT statements. Either put the FORMAT immediately after the READ or WRITE that uses it, or place them all just before the END statement in your program.

5 Label FORMAT numbers so that they are in ascending order, and fit into the order of other statements in your program. Do not, however, number statements sequentially. Leave a difference of at least 10 between statement numbers in case you need to insert additional statements later.

6 Make your carriage control evident. For instance, use (1X,F4.1) instead of (F5.1).

7 Label values printed. Use (1X,'X=',F3.1) instead of (1X,F3.1).

8 Use an E format to print values for which you cannot approximate the size. Then, if desired, after seeing the answer, you can change the E specification to an F specification that will accommodate the value.

9 Do not print more significant digits than you have. For instance, if you computed sums with values that had one decimal position, do not print the result with three decimal positions.

10 Generally, it is best to use the same number of specifications in the FORMAT as there are variable names on the READ/WRITE variable list.

11 Do not use extremely long FORMAT statements. Instead, use additional READ or WRITE statements with separate FORMAT statements.

12 Remember that the slash character must always be followed by carriage control in WRITE statements.

PROBLEMS

In problems 1 through 5, express the following values with the specified FORMAT. Be sure to indicate blanks when needed. The first is done as an example.

	VALUE	FORMAT	OUTPUT
	1000.3	F8.2	$_b$1000.30
1	.0004	E9.2	
2	136	I4	
3	−16	I2	
4	163.21	F8.1	
5	−7.6	F4.2	

In problems 6 through 8, show the output from the following WRITE statements. Be sure to indicate the vertical spacing as well as the horizontal spacing. Use the following variables and corresponding values:

TIME	4.55
RESP1	0.00074
RESP2	56.83

6
```
    WRITE(6,5)TIME, RESP1, RESP2
  5 FORMAT('0',F6.2,5X,2F7.4)
```

7
```
    WRITE(6,4)TIME, RESP1, TIME, RESP2
  4 FORMAT(' ','TIME = ',F5.2,2X,'RESPONSE 1 = ',F8.5/
  +        ' ','TIME = ',F5.2,2X,'RESPONSE 2 = ',F8.5)
```

8
```
    WRITE(6,1)TIME, RESP1, RESP2
  1 FORMAT('1','EXPERIMENT RESULTS'/1X,'TIME',2X,
  +        'RESPONSE 1',2X,'RESPONSE 2'/
  +        1X,F4.2,2E12.3)
```

In problems 9 and 10, show the values that will be stored in the variables after execution of the following READ statements.

9
```
            READ(5,15)ID, HT, WIDTH
         15 FORMAT(I4,2X,2F4.1)
```

Data Line $1456_{bb}14.6_{bb}.7$

ID	
HT	
WIDTH	

10
```
            READ(5,7)ID, HT, WIDTH
          7 FORMAT(I2,F4.1,2X,F4.2)
```

Data Line $_{bb}13.7_{bb}.865$

ID	
HT	
WIDTH	

In problems 11 through 14, tell how many data lines or data cards are required for the following READ/WRITE combinations to work correctly. Indicate which variables are on each line or card and the columns that must be used.

11
```
    READ(5,4)TIME, DIST, VEL, ACCEL
  4 FORMAT(4F6.3)
```

12
```
    READ(5,14)TIME, DIST, VEL, ACCEL
 14 FORMAT(F6.2)
```

```
13    READ(5,2)TIME, DIST, VEL, ACCEL
   2 FORMAT(F3.2/F4.1)

14    READ(5,3)TIME, DIST
      READ(5,3)VEL, ACCEL
   3 FORMAT(4F6.3)
```

15 Write a complete program to read the diameter of a circle from columns 1–5 of a data card, in the form XX.XX. Compute the radius, circumference, and area of the circle. Print these new values in the following form:

$\begin{matrix}\text{new} \\ \text{page}\end{matrix} \rightarrow$ PROPERTIES OF A CIRCLE WITH DIAMETER XX.XX

             (1) RADIUS = XX.XX
             (2) CIRCUMFERENCE = XXX.XX
             (3) AREA = XXXX.XXXX

16 Write a complete program to read the coordinates of three points (X_1, Y_1), (X_2, Y_2), (X_3, Y_3) from one data line with:

columns		
1–4	X_1	XX.X
6–9	Y_1	XX.X
11–14	X_2	XX.X
16–19	Y_2	XX.X
21–24	X_3	XX.X
26–29	Y_3	XX.X

Assume that the name of the file is POINTS. Compute the area of the triangle formed from these points using

$$AREA = 1/2\,|X_1Y_2 - X_2Y_1 + X_2Y_3 - X_3Y_2 + X_3Y_1 - X_1Y_3|$$

Print the coordinates and the area in the following form:

double space $\rightarrow$ Triangle vertices:
         (1) XX.X, XX.X
         (2) XX.X, XX.X
         (3) XX.X, XX.X
       Triangle area:
         XXXX.XX

17 Write a complete program to read an integer value from columns 10–13 on a data card. This value represents a measurement in meters. Print the value read followed by the units, 'METERS'. Convert the measurement to kilometers, and print on the next line, again with the correct units. Convert the measurement to miles, and print on the third line, with correct units. Give some careful thought to both the type of variables that you should use and the size of output field that you will need.

18 Write a complete program to read the following integer information from one line in a data file called LABOR:

columns 1–4   year
          10–17   number of people in civilian labor force
          20–27   number of people in military labor force

Compute the percentage of the labor force that is civilian and the percentage that is military. Print the following information:

LABOR FORCE – YEAR XXXX

	NUMBER OF WORKERS (IN THOUSANDS)	PERCENTAGE OF WORKERS
CIVILIAN	XXXXX.X	XX.X
MILITARY	XXXXX.X	XX.X
TOTAL	XXXXXX.X	XXX.X

19 When N is an integer greater than or equal to zero, the expression N! (read N factorial) represents the product of all integers from 1 through N. We define 0! to be equal to 1. A few factorials and their corresponding values are shown below:

$$0! = 1$$
$$1! = 1$$
$$2! = 1 \cdot 2 = 2$$
$$3! = 1 \cdot 2 \cdot 3 = 6$$

An approximation to N! can be computed using Stirling's formula,

$$N! = \sqrt{2\pi N}\left(\frac{N}{e}\right)^N$$

where e = 2.718282. Write a complete program that reads a value of N and then computes an approximation of N! using Stirling's formula. Print the following message before you read the value of N from a terminal:

ENTER N WHERE N IS BETWEEN 1 AND 10

The output of the program should be:

XX! IS APPROXIMATELY XXXXXXX

Courtesy of Sandia Peak Tramway

SAMPLE PROBLEM – Cable Car Velocity

A 1000-foot cable is stretched between two towers, with a supporting tower midway between the two end towers. The velocity of the cable car depends on its position on the cable. When the cable car is within 30 feet of a tower, its velocity is given by:

$$\text{vel} = 2.425 + 0.00175d^2 \text{ ft/sec}$$

where d is the distance in feet from the cable car to the nearest tower. If the cable car is not within 30 feet of a tower, its velocity is given by:

$$\text{vel} = 0.625 + 0.12d - 0.00025d^2 \text{ ft/sec}$$

Print a table starting with the cable car at the first tower and moving to the last tower in increments of 10 feet. At each increment of 10 feet, print the number of the nearest tower (1 = first, 2 = middle, 3 = end), the distance from the first tower, and the velocity of the cable car. (For solution, see Example 4-5, page 109.)

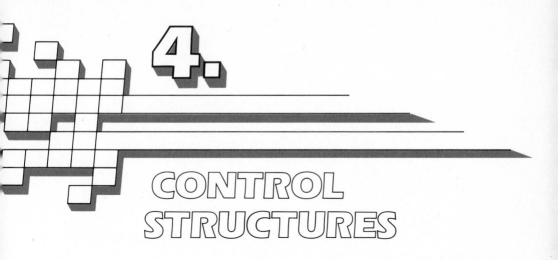

4.

CONTROL STRUCTURES

INTRODUCTION

As we read the cable car velocity problem we recognize the need to be able to ask the computer the question: "Which tower is closest?" We also need an IF-THEN-ELSE combination: "IF the cable car is within 30 feet of a tower, THEN use formula 1 to compute velocity, ELSE use formula 2 to compute velocity." These requirements relate to program control. In most programs, we will control the flow of the program, or the order in which certain statements are executed, with the IF-THEN-ELSE statement. This statement allows us to compare values stored in variables; then, based on the comparison, we can determine the closest tower and compute the velocity with the correct equation. Another very important control structure is the *WHILE loop*, a group of statements that will be executed while a specified condition is true. We certainly do not want to write separate instructions for the situation where the cable car is 10 feet from Tower 1, 20 feet from Tower 1, and so on until it is 1000 feet from Tower 1. Instead, we want a group of statements that are repeated while the distance from Tower 1 is not greater than 1000 feet.

4-1 LOGICAL IF STATEMENT

We compare variables with *logical expressions.* While an arithmetic expression represents a numerical value, a logical expression represents either a "true" or "false" situation. A logical expression is formed using one of the following *relational operators:*

RELATIONAL OPERATOR	ALGEBRAIC INTERPRETATION
.EQ.	is equal to
.NE.	is not equal to
.LT.	is less than
.LE.	is less than or equal to
.GT.	is greater than
.GE.	is greater than or equal to

Arithmetic expressions are used on both sides of the relational operator to complete the logical expression, but the logical expression always has the value "true" or "false."

The general form of the logical IF statement is:

> I F*(logical expression)executable statement*

A typical IF statement is:

```
IF(A.LT.B)SUM = SUM + A
```

When this statement is executed, the logical expression in parentheses is evaluated. If it is "true," then the statement following the parentheses is executed. If the logical expression is "false," then control passes to the next statement. Thus, if the value of A is less than the value of B, then the value of A is added to SUM. If the value of A is greater than or equal to B, then control passes to whatever statement follows the IF statement in the program.

Some example IF statements are:

```
IF(TIME.GT.1.5)STOP
IF(DEN.LE.0.0)WRITE(6,5)DEN
IF(-4.NE.NUM)NUM = NUM + 1
```

Any executable statement except another IF statement can be used after the logical expression. We can also combine two logical expressions into a *compound* logical expression with the connectors .OR. and .AND.. When two logical expressions are joined by .OR., the entire expression is "true" if either, or both, expressions are "true." It is "false" only when both expressions are "false." When two logical expressions are joined by .AND., the entire expression is "true" only if both expressions are "true." These connectors can be used only with complete logic expressions on both sides of the connector. For example, A.LT.B.OR.A.LT.C is a valid compound logical expression because .OR. joins A.LT.B and A.LT.C. However, A.LT.B.OR.C is an invalid compound expression because C is a variable, not a complete logical expression.

Logical expressions can also be preceded by the connector .NOT.. This connector changes the value of the expression to the opposite value. Hence, if A.GT.B is "true," then .NOT.A.GT.B is "false." The following statement

$$IF(.NOT.A.LT.B)X = 1.5$$

is also equivalent to

$$IF(A.GE.B)X = 1.5$$

A logical expression may contain several connectors, as in

$$IF(.NOT.(A.LT.15.0).OR.KT.EQ.ISUM)WRITE(6,5)A$$

The hierarchy of execution of connectors, from highest to lowest, is .NOT., .AND., .OR.. Thus, in the above statement, the logical expression A.LT.15.0 would be evaluated, and its value, "true" or "false," would be reversed by the .NOT. connector. Then this value would be used, along with the value of KT.EQ.ISUM, with the connector .OR..

4-2 IF-THEN-ENDIF STRUCTURE

We can perform only one statement in a logical IF statement assuming the logical expression is "true." Yet there are many instances where we would like to perform more than one statement if a logical expression is "true." The IF-THEN-ENDIF structure allows us to perform any number of statements if a logical expression is "true," using the following general form:

```
IF(logical expression)THEN
    statement 1
    statement 2
        .
        .
        .
    statement n
ENDIF
```

Execution consists of the following steps:

1   If the logical expression is "true," we execute statement 1 through statement n, and then go to the statement following ENDIF.

2   If the logical expression is "false," we jump immediately to the statement following ENDIF.

Although not required, the statements to be performed when the logical expression is "true" should be indented to indicate that they are a group of statements within the IF-THEN-ENDIF structure.

EXAMPLE 4-1   Zero Divide

Assume that you have calculated the numerator NUM (explicitly typed REAL) and the denominator DEN of a fraction. Before dividing the two values, you want to see if DEN is zero. If DEN is zero, you want to print an error message and stop the program. If DEN is not zero, you want to compute the decimal value and print it. Write the statements to perform these steps.

Solution

```
          ┊
      IF(DEN.EQ.0.0)THEN
          WRITE(6,50)
   50     FORMAT('0','DENOMINATOR IS ZERO')
          STOP
      ENDIF
   C
      FRACT = NUM/DEN
      WRITE(6,60)FRACT
   60 FORMAT('0','FRACTION =  ',F7.2)
          ┊   ◇
```

The IF-THEN-ENDIF structures can also be nested. The following form includes an IF-THEN-ENDIF within an IF-THEN-ENDIF.

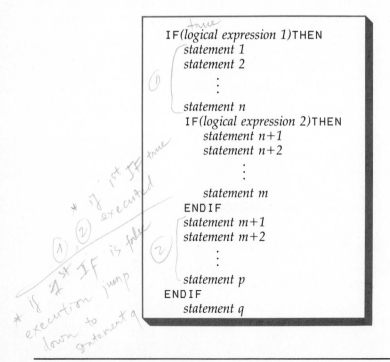

Again, the indenting of statements within an IF-ENDIF construction is not required but makes the construction much easier to follow. If logical expression 1 is "true," we then always execute statements 1 through n, and statements $m+1$ through p. If logical expression 2 is "true," then we also execute statements $n+1$ through m. If logical expression 1 is "false," we immediately go to the statement after the second ENDIF, statement q.

4-3   FLOWCHARTS AND PSEUDOCODE

Flowcharts and pseudocode are tools used in organizing our thoughts into a stepwise solution to a problem. We do not concern ourselves with the details of FORTRAN statements until we are ready to convert the flowchart or the pseudocode into a program. In the remainder of the text, we will alternate between flowcharts and pseudocode as we develop algorithms so that you can become familiar with both techniques.

FLOWCHARTS

As we begin to use the logical IF, the IF-THEN-ENDIF, and other similar structures in the following sections, it can be very helpful to use symbols instead of FORTRAN statements, thus emphasizing the structure of our programs. These symbols are called *flowchart symbols,* and the process of outlining the flow of an algorithm using the symbols is called *flowcharting.*

The types of processes or steps in algorithms that we have covered and their corresponding flowchart symbols are listed below:

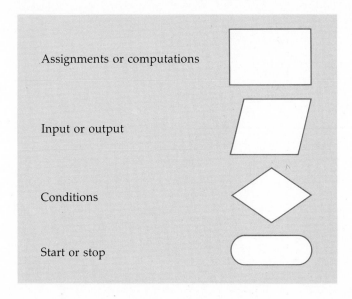

Assignments or computations

Input or output

Conditions

Start or stop

In the logical IF and the IF-THEN-ENDIF structures flowcharted below, the term *condition* is used to represent the logical expression whose value determines the path or branch to take.

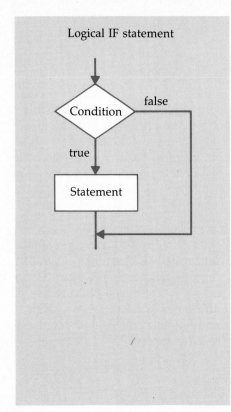

Logical IF statement

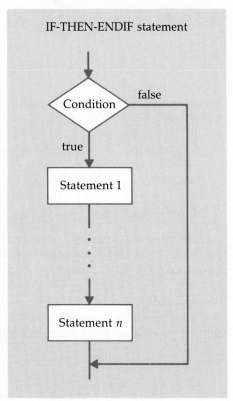

IF-THEN-ENDIF statement

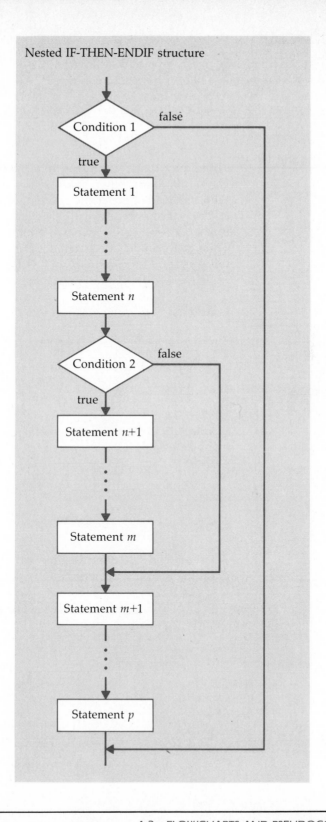

Nested IF-THEN-ENDIF structure

PSEUDOCODE

Another tool frequently used in place of a flowchart is *pseudocode*. With pseudocode, we list the steps of an algorithm in an English-like form instead of a graphical form. While pseudocode is English-like, there are standard entries for the types of processes and steps that we have covered.

Assignment or computation

$$A \leftarrow 0$$

To indicate that a variable is to be initialized or computed from other values, use an arrow with the head of the arrow pointed to the name of the variable receiving the new value. The arrow can be read "is assigned the value." Thus, the pseudocode statement above is read, "*A* is assigned the value zero," while

$$B \leftarrow C + 4.0$$

is read as "*B* is assigned the value *C* plus 4.0."

Input or output

READ TEMP
PRINT heading
PRINT DIST, VEL

Condition

$A = B$
$TIME = 0.0$

Conditions in pseudocode statements use the symbols: $>, \geq, <, \leq, =, \neq$.

Start or stop

PROGRAM ROCKET

.

.

.

STOP

A pseudocode solution begins with the program name and ends with STOP.

In the pseudocode for the logical IF and the IF-THEN-ENDIF structures on page 97, note the importance of indenting properly.

Logical IF statement	IF condition THEN statement

```
IF-THEN-ENDIF          IF condition THEN
structure                  statement 1
                               .
                               .
                               .
                           statement n
                       ENDIF
```

```
Nested                 IF condition 1 THEN
IF-THEN-ENDIF              statement 1
structure                     .
                              .
                              .
                          statement n
                          IF condition 2 THEN
                              statement n+1
                                  .
                                  .
                                  .
                              statement m
                          ENDIF
                          statement m+1
                              .
                              .
                              .
                          statement p
                       ENDIF
```

4-4   THE WHILE LOOP STRUCTURE

There are a large number of definitions of *structured programming,* all of which are somewhat different and some of which are very abstract. The common thread in most of these definitions is summarized by the phrase "techniques for making coding, debugging, and modification easier, faster, and less expensive through simpler programs." There are many techniques proposed to accomplish this and thereby structure your programs. One of the most important techniques for simplifying your program logic is to use *top-down* code—a code that flows from the beginning of the program to the end of the program. The IF-THEN-ENDIF structure splits into two paths that ultimately merge together again and thus fits the requirement of flowing from top to bottom. Another type of structure necessary is a WHILE loop (a group of statements that are executed as long as a specified condition is true). In the development of the WHILE loop structure that follows, observe the top-down structure—one way into the loop and one way out of the loop.

The WHILE loop structure can be flowcharted as:

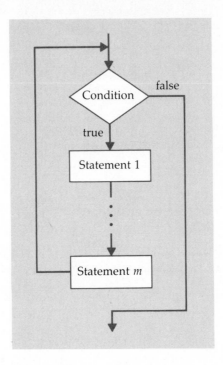

While the condition is "true," statements 1 through m are executed. After executing the group of statements, the condition is again tested. If the condition is still "true," the group of statements is executed again. When the condition is "false," execution continues with the statement following the WHILE loop. The variables modified in the group of statements in the WHILE loop must involve the variables tested in the condition of the WHILE loop, or the value of the condition will never change.

In pseudocode, the WHILE loop structure is:

WHILE condition DO
statement 1
.
.
.
statement m
ENDWHILE

Unfortunately, standard FORTRAN 77 does not include a WHILE statement. However, we can implement the WHILE loop with the IF-THEN-ENDIF structure:

```
n  IF(condition)THEN
      statement 1
          .
          .
          .
      statement m
      GO TO n
   ENDIF
```

In this implementation, we have used an unconditional transfer statement, whose general form is:

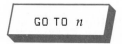

```
GO TO n
```

where n is the statement number of an executable statement in the program. The execution of the GO TO statement causes the flow of program control to transfer to statement n.

When developing an algorithm, all loop structures should be constructed from WHILE loops. As you refine the algorithm or parts of the algorithm to more detailed processes, the WHILE loop structures should remain. When translating the refined pseudocode or flowchart to FORTRAN, implement the WHILE loop with the IF-THEN-ENDIF structure and the GO TO statement.

4-5 APPLICATION – Degree to Radian Conversion Table

One of the simplest types of programs that uses a loop is a program to compute and print a table of data. This table could be a conversion table that converts a given value in one set of units to the corresponding value in another set of units. Another type of table that is useful computes the interest on an initial amount deposited and prints the simple interest, compound interest, and new principle after each year. In the examples mentioned, the loop exit might be made when the value to be converted exceeded a specified value or when the interest had been computed for a specified number of years.

EXAMPLE 4-2   Degree Conversion

Write a complete program that will print a table converting degrees to radians. Begin with 0°, and increment by 10°, through the final value of 360°. Use the form shown below for output.

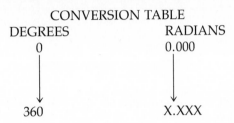

CONVERSION TABLE

DEGREES	RADIANS
0	0.000
360	X.XXX

Solution

As we develop an algorithm, we want to consider two tasks at the beginning: printing headings and initializing variables. Since these functions will be involved in most programs, you should develop the habit of considering them at the beginning of every program. After printing the headings for this conversion table, we need to initialize a variable DEGREE to zero. Then with the use of the WHILE loop structure, DEGREE is converted to RADIAN, and the two values are printed. DEGREE is incremented by 10, and we repeat the loop as long as DEGREE is less than or equal to 360. Now, refer to the flowchart for this algorithm.

First, we print headings and initialize an integer variable DE-GREE to zero. While DEGREE is less than or equal to 360°, we convert DEGREE to a real variable RADIAN, print both values, increment DEGREE by 10°, and repeat the process. It is important to carefully check our "exit" from the WHILE loop to avoid building a loop that never terminates. Actually, the computer will not stay in a loop indefinitely—after a large number of times through a loop, execution will be halted and an execution error will be printed that indicates that the time limit has been exceeded. By placing the flowchart next to the code, you can see that the flowchart provides an excellent guide or outline for writing the program. It is an invaluable tool for organizing and constructing programs of any size.   ◇

Flowchart

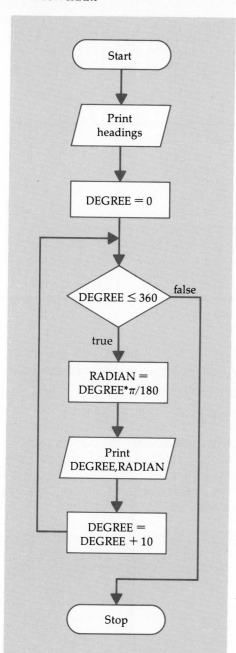

FORTRAN Program

```
      PROGRAM  CONVRT
C
C   THIS PROGRAM PRINTS A
C   CONVERSION TABLE
C   CONVERTING DEGREES TO
C   RADIANS FOR 0 TO 360
C   DEGREES IN INCREMENTS OF
C   10 DEGREES
C
      INTEGER  DEGREE
C
      WRITE(6,1)
    1 FORMAT(1X,5X,
     +        'CONVERSION ',
     +        'TABLE'/' ',
     +        'DEGREES',12X,
     +        'RADIANS')
C
      DEGREE = 0
C
   10 IF(DEGREE.LE.360)THEN
         RADIAN = DEGREE*
     +        (3.141593/
     +        180.0)
         WRITE(6,20)DEGREE,
     +        RADIAN
   20    FORMAT(1X,I4,15X,
     +        F5.3)
         DEGREE =
     +        DEGREE + 10
      GO TO 10
      ENDIF
C
      STOP
      END
```

```
          CONVERSION TABLE
      DEGREES              RADIANS
        0                  0.000
       10                  0.175
       20                  0.349
         .                   .
         .                   .
         .                   .
      340                  5.934
      350                  6.109
      360                  6.283
```

Observe that the flowchart of Example 4-2 does not contain FOR-TRAN statements. A flowchart or pseudocode should be language independent; that is, programmers in any high-level language should be able to work from the same flowchart or pseudocode. ◇

4-6 ELSE STRUCTURES

Two structures can be added to the IF-THEN-ENDIF structure to give us the ability to execute one set of statements if a condition is true, and to execute another set of statements if the condition is not true.

IF-THEN-ELSE-ENDIF STRUCTURE

The general form for the IF-THEN-ELSE-ENDIF structure is shown below:

```
IF(logical expression)THEN
    statement 1
    statement 2
        .
        .
        .
    statement n
ELSE
    statement n+1
    statement n+2
        .
        .
        .
    statement m
ENDIF
```

If the logical expression is "true," then statements 1 through n are executed. If the logical expression is "false," then statements $n+1$ through m are executed. Any of the statements can also be other IF-THEN-ENDIF or IF-THEN-ELSE-ENDIF structures to provide a nested structure to the statements.

The IF-THEN-ELSE-ENDIF structure can be flowcharted as:

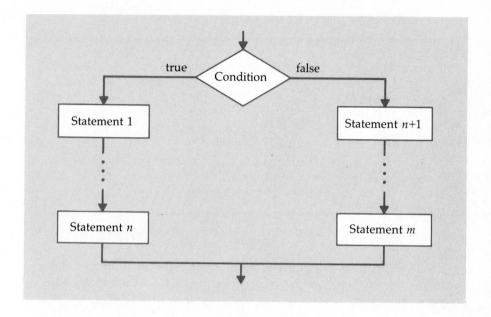

In pseudocode, the IF-THEN-ELSE-ENDIF becomes:

```
IF condition THEN
    statement 1
        .
        .
        .
    statement n
ELSE
    statement n+1
        .
        .
        .
    statement m
ENDIF
```

EXAMPLE 4-3   Velocity Computation

Give the statements for calculating the velocity VEL of a cable car. The variable DIST contains the distance of the cable car from the nearest tower. Use

$$vel = 2.425 + 0.00175d^2 \text{ ft/sec}$$

if the cable car is within 30 feet of the tower. Use

$$vel = 0.625 + 0.12d - 0.00025d^2 \text{ ft/sec}$$

if the cable car is more than 30 feet from the tower.

Correct Solution

```
IF(DIST.LE.30.0)THEN
    VEL = 2.425 + 0.00175*DIST*DIST
ELSE
    VEL = 0.625 + 0.12*DIST - 0.00025*DIST*DIST
ENDIF
```

Incorrect Solution

```
IF(DIST.LE.30.0)VEL = 2.425 + 0.00175*DIST*DIST
VEL = 0.625 + 0.12*DIST - 0.00025*DIST*DIST
```

This incorrect solution points out a very common error. Let us follow the execution of these two statements to find the error. Suppose DIST is greater than 30. Then the first logical expression is "false," and we thus proceed to the next statement to calculate VEL. This part works fine. But now suppose the logical expression is "true"; that is, DIST is less than or equal to 30. We then execute the assignment statement on the IF statement, thus correctly calculating VEL when DIST is less than or equal to 30. But the next statement that is executed is the other assignment statement that replaces the correct value in VEL with an incorrect value.   ◇

IF-THEN-ELSEIF-ENDIF STRUCTURE

When we nest several levels of IF-THEN-ELSE-ENDIF structures, it can become difficult to determine what conditions must be true (or false) in order to execute a particular set of statements in the structure. In these cases, the ELSEIF structure can often be used to clarify the program logic. The general form of the ELSEIF structure is illustrated by:

```
IF(condition 1)THEN
    statement 1
        .
        .
        .
    statement m
ELSEIF(condition 2)THEN
    statement m+1
        .
        .
        .
    statement n
ELSEIF(condition 3)THEN
    statement n+1
        .
        .
        .
    statement p
ENDIF
```

We have shown three ELSEIF statements, but there may be more or less in an actual structure. With the ELSEIF structure, if condition 1 is true, then only statements 1 through m will be executed. If condition 1 is false and condition 2 is true, then only statements m+1 through n will be executed. If conditions 1 and 2 are false and condition 3 is true, then only statements n+1 through p are executed. If more than one condition is true, then the first one encountered will be the only one executed. The flowchart and pseudocode presentations of the ELSEIF structure are given on pages 106–107.

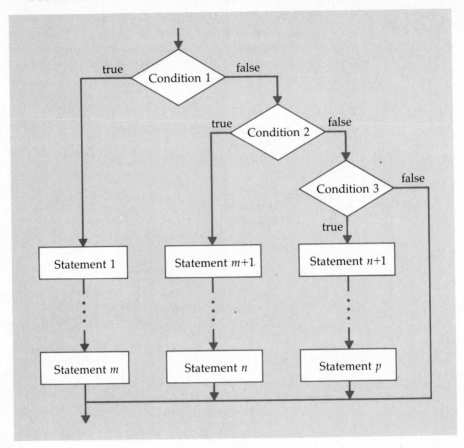

IF condition 1 THEN
    statement 1
        .

        .

        .

    statement m
ELSEIF condition 2 THEN
    statement m+1
        .

        .

        .

    statement n
ELSEIF condition 3 THEN
    statement n+1
        .

        .

        .

    statement p
ENDIF

An ELSE statement may also follow the last ELSEIF.

EXAMPLE 4-4   Weight Category

An analysis of a group of weight measurements involves converting a weight value into an integer category number that is determined as follows:

CATEGORY	WEIGHT (POUNDS)
1	$weight \le 50.0$
2	$50.0 < weight \le 125.0$
3	$125.0 < weight \le 200.0$
4	$200.0 < weight$

Write FORTRAN statements that will put the correct value (1, 2, 3, or 4) into CATEGR based on the value of WEIGHT.

Solution 1

```
        .
        .
        .
IF(WEIGHT.LE.50.0)THEN
    CATEGR = 1
ELSE
    IF(WEIGHT.LE.125.0)THEN
        CATEGR = 2
    ELSE
        IF(WEIGHT.LE.200.0)THEN
            CATEGR = 3
        ELSE
            CATEGR = 4
        ENDIF
    ENDIF
ENDIF
        .
        .
        .
```

Solution 2

```
        .
        .
        .
IF(WEIGHT.LE.50.0)THEN
    CATEGR = 1
ELSEIF(WEIGHT.LE.125.0)THEN
    CATEGR = 2
ELSEIF(WEIGHT.LE.200.0)THEN
    CATEGR = 3
ELSEIF(WEIGHT.GT.200.0)THEN
    CATEGR = 4
ENDIF
```

Solution 2, as you can see, is more compact than Solution 1. It combines the ELSE and IF statements into the single statement ELSEIF and eliminates two of the ENDIF statements. Both solutions use the same logic pattern and follow the recommended top-down program flow. The one you choose to use is a matter of personal preference and the specific application.   ◇

4-7 APPLICATION – Cable Car Velocity

In this section we present a solution to the cable car problem described at the beginning of this chapter. A flowchart is developed first; then, pseudocode is given; and finally two different FORTRAN programs are shown. The first program solution uses IF-THEN-ELSE-ENDIF constructions. The second program solution uses only the simple IF statement. Comparison of these two programs illustrates the power of the IF-THEN-ELSE-ENDIF construction. Note also the difference in readability. A top-down program, one with few or no GO TO statements, is much easier to follow and thus requires less documentation.

EXAMPLE 4-5 Cable Car Velocity

A 1000-foot cable is stretched between two towers, with a supporting tower midway between the two end towers. The velocity of the cable car depends on its position on the cable. When the cable car is within 30 feet of a tower, its velocity is given by:

$$vel = 2.425 + 0.00175d^2 \text{ ft/sec}$$

where d is the distance in feet from the cable car to the nearest tower. If the cable car is not within 30 feet of a tower, its velocity is given by:

$$vel = 0.625 + 0.12d - 0.00025d^2 \text{ ft/sec}$$

Print a table starting with the cable car at the first tower and moving to the last tower in increments of 10 feet. At each increment of 10 feet, print the number of the nearest tower (1 = first, 2 = middle, 3 = end), the distance from the first tower, and the velocity of the cable car.

Solution

Let us first look at a flowchart for a general solution to this problem using the WHILE loop structure.

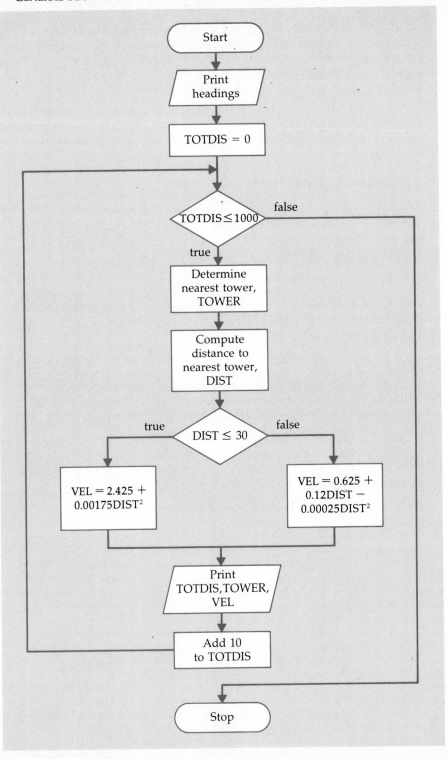

This general flowchart has been useful in determining the order of the steps that need to be performed. However, it is not detailed enough to begin coding the solution in FORTRAN statements. For instance, how will we compute the nearest tower number? Or, how will we compute the distance to the nearest tower? To answer these questions, we will look at a simplified sketch.

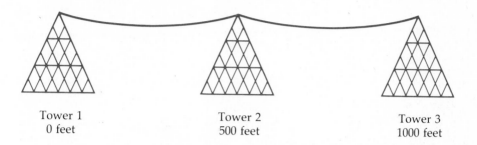

Tower 1
0 feet

Tower 2
500 feet

Tower 3
1000 feet

The cable car will be closest to Tower 1 if the total distance TOTDIS of the cable car from Tower 1 is 0 to 250 feet. When TOTDIS is greater than 250 but less than 750, the cable car is closest to Tower 2. When TOTDIS is greater than or equal to 750, the cable car is closest to Tower 3. (Note that when TOTDIS = 250 we really could have chosen Tower 1 or 2. A similar situation occurs when TOTDIS = 750.) Furthermore, the distance to the nearest tower is TOTDIS if TOTDIS is less than or equal to 250. When TOTDIS is between 250 and 750, the distance to the nearest tower is |TOTDIS − 500|. We used the absolute value here so that the distance is always positive. Finally, the distance to the nearest tower when TOTDIS is greater than 750 is 1000 − TOTDIS. Pick a few values of TOTDIS and use these formulas to convince yourself that they are correct. Now, we add these details to the flowchart to get a refined flowchart. These details are also included in refined pseudocode so that you can compare the two techniques for describing the algorithm.

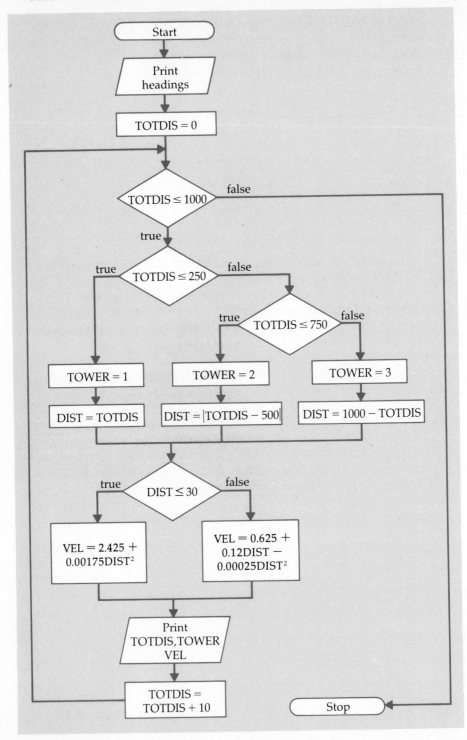

```
PROGRAM   CABLE1
    PRINT headings
    TOTDIS ← 0
    WHILE TOTDIS ≤ 1000 DO
        IF TOTDIS ≤ 250 THEN
            TOWER ← 1
            DIST ← TOTDIS
        ELSE
            IF TOTDIS ≤ 750 THEN
                TOWER ← 2
                DIST ← |TOTDIS − 500|
            ELSE
                TOWER ← 3
                DIST ← 1000 − TOTDIS
            ENDIF
        ENDIF
        IF DIST ≤ 30 THEN
            VEL ← 2.425 + 0.00175DIST²
        ELSE
            VEL ← 0.625 + 0.12DIST − 0.00025DIST²
        ENDIF
        PRINT TOTDIS, TOWER, VEL
        TOTDIS ← TOTDIS + 10
    ENDWHILE
STOP
```

```
      PROGRAM   CABLE1
C
C  THIS PROGRAM COMPUTES THE VELOCITY OF A CABLE CAR ON
C  A THOUSAND-FOOT CABLE WITH THREE TOWERS
C
      INTEGER   TOTDIS, DIST, TOWER
C
      WRITE(6,1)
    1 FORMAT('1',9X,'CABLE CAR REPORT'//' ','DISTANCE',
     +        2X,'NEAREST TOWER',2X,'VELOCITY'/1X,2X,
     +        '(FT)',19X,'(FT/SEC)')
C
      TOTDIS = 0
C
    5 IF(TOTDIS.LE.1000)THEN
C
          IF(TOTDIS.LE.250)THEN
            TOWER = 1
            DIST = TOTDIS
          ELSE
            IF(TOTDIS.LE.750)THEN
               TOWER = 2
               DIST = IABS(TOTDIS - 500)
            ELSE
               TOWER = 3
               DIST = 1000 - TOTDIS
            ENDIF
          ENDIF
C
          IF(DIST.LE.30)THEN
             VEL = 2.425 + 0.00175*DIST*DIST
          ELSE
             VEL = 0.625 + 0.12*DIST - 0.00025*DIST*DIST
          ENDIF
C
          WRITE(6,40)TOTDIS, TOWER, VEL
   40     FORMAT(' ',I4,11X,I1,9X,F7.2)
C
          TOTDIS = TOTDIS + 10

C
          GO TO 5
C
      ENDIF
C
      STOP
      END
```

```
      PROGRAM  CABLE2
C
C THIS PROGRAM COMPUTES THE VELOCITY OF A CABLE CAR ON
C A THOUSAND-FOOT CABLE WITH THREE TOWERS
C
      INTEGER  TOTDIS, DIST, TOWER
C
      WRITE(6,1)
    1 FORMAT('1',9X,'CABLE CAR REPORT'/' ','DISTANCE',
     +        2X,'NEAREST TOWER',2X,'VELOCITY'/1X,2X,
     +        '(FT)',19X,'(FT/SEC)')
C
      TOTDIS = 0
C
    5 IF(TOTDIS.GT.250)GO TO 10
         TOWER = 1
         DIST = TOTDIS
         GO TO 20
C
   10 IF(TOTDIS.GT.750)GO TO 15
         TOWER = 2
         DIST = IABS(TOTDIS - 500)
         GO TO 20
C
   15 TOWER = 3
      DIST = 1000 - TOTDIS
C
   20 IF(DIST.LE.30)VEL = 2.425 + 0.00175*DIST*DIST
      IF(DIST.GT.30)VEL = 0.625 + 0.12*DIST -
     +                    0.00025*DIST*DIST
C
      WRITE(6,40)TOTDIS, TOWER, VEL
   40 FORMAT(' ',I4,11X,I1,9X,F7.2)
C
      TOTDIS = TOTDIS + 10
C
      IF(TOTDIS.LE.1000)GO TO 5
C
      STOP
      END
```

```
                 CABLE CAR REPORT
    DISTANCE    NEAREST TOWER    VELOCITY
     (FT)                        (FT/SEC)
       0             1             2.42
      10             1             2.60
      20             1             3.13
       ·             ·              ·
       ·             ·              ·
       ·             ·              ·
     980             3             3.13
     990             3             2.60
    1000             3             2.42
```

◇

4-8   END-OF-DATA SIGNALS

Many programs require the computer to read a number of data values, such as test scores or experimental results. The WHILE loop is a handy tool for the programmer to use to accomplish this task. For instance, if 50 data values are to be read, we could use a WHILE loop of this form:

$$
\begin{aligned}
&\text{COUNT} \leftarrow 0 \\
&\text{WHILE} \quad \text{COUNT} < 50 \quad \text{DO} \\
&\quad \text{READ data} \\
&\qquad \cdot \\
&\qquad \cdot \\
&\quad \text{COUNT} \leftarrow \text{COUNT} + 1 \\
&\text{ENDWHILE}
\end{aligned}
$$

If the number of data values to be read is available in another variable, we can use a WHILE loop of this form:

$$
\begin{aligned}
&\text{COUNT} \leftarrow 0 \\
&\text{WHILE} \quad \text{COUNT} < \text{NUM} \quad \text{DO} \\
&\quad \text{READ data} \\
&\qquad \cdot \\
&\qquad \cdot \\
&\quad \text{COUNT} \leftarrow \text{COUNT} + 1 \\
&\text{ENDWHILE}
\end{aligned}
$$

There are also situations where you do not know prior to executing your program exactly how many data values need to be read. These situations must be handled carefully because, if we execute a READ statement for which there is no data card or data line, an execution error occurs and the execution of our program will be stopped. Two techniques for handling this situation of an unspecified number of input data values are now presented.

The first technique involves the use of a *trailer card* or a *trailer line*. These trailer signals are data values that signal the end of data. For example, a valid identification number for a student record may be three digits, ranging from 000 to 500. If we were reading student records, we could use an identification number of 999 as a trailer signal. Thus, as we read each data card, we test the identification number for the value 999. When we find the value 999, we then exit the loop. This process can be structured in a WHILE loop, but since the condition will use a value from a data card, we must read one student record before entering the WHILE loop.

.
.
.

```
READ ID, student data
WHILE   ID ≠ 999   DO
    process student data
    READ ID, student data
ENDWHILE
```

.
.
.

If we need to know the number of data values read, a counter can be used in the WHILE loop. Be sure not to count the trailer value as a valid data value.

If a data file does not have a trailer signal at the end, and if we do not know the number of data lines in the file, a different technique must be used with the WHILE loop. In pseudocode, we want to perform these steps:

```
WHILE   more data   DO
    READ ID, student data
    process data
ENDWHILE
```

To implement this in FORTRAN, we use an option available with the READ statement that tests for the end of the data. A READ statement that uses this option has the following form:

```
READ(5,10,END=20)A, B
```

As long as there are data lines or data cards, this statement executes exactly like the statement:

$$READ(5,10)A, B$$

However, if the last data line or data card has already been read and we execute the READ statement again, instead of getting an execution error, control will be passed to the statement referenced in the END option. In the above example, once the end of the data has been reached, the next execution of the READ statement will cause control to pass to the statement with statement number 20. However, if the READ statement were executed a second time after the end of the data, then an execution error would occur. Using this END option, we can now implement the WHILE loop as:

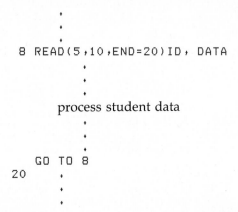

```
        .
        .
        .
8  READ(5,10,END=20)ID, DATA
        .
        .
        .
        process student data
        .
        .
        .
        GO TO 8
   20   .
        .
        .
```

This is a special implementation of the WHILE loop that is used only when you do not know the number of data lines or data cards to be read before executing the loop. We have still preserved the top-down structure with this implementation because there is only one way to enter the loop and only one way to exit the loop.

Observe that these two techniques should not be used together. If you have a trailer value, test for that value to exit the loop. If you do not use a trailer card, use the END option to branch out of the loop at the end of the data. Both these techniques will now be used in examples.

EXAMPLE 4-6   Test Scores with Trailer Signal

A group of test scores are punched on data cards, one score per card in columns 1–3. The last card contains a negative value to signal the end of the test scores. Write a complete program to read the data, compute the test average, and print the number of tests and the test average.

Solution

FLOWCHART

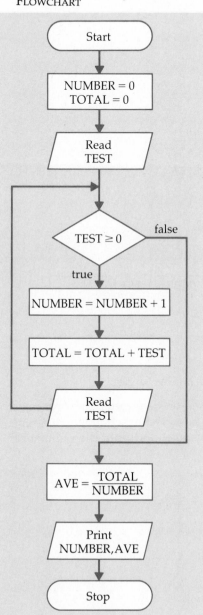

PSEUDOCODE

```
PROGRAM   AVERG1
    NUMBER ← 0
    TOTAL ← 0
    READ TEST
    WHILE   TEST ≥ 0   DO
        NUMBER ← NUMBER + 1
        TOTAL ← TOTAL + TEST
        READ TEST
    ENDWHILE
    AVE ← TOTAL/NUMBER
    PRINT NUMBER,AVE
STOP
```

```
C     PROGRAM   AVERG1
C
C     THIS PROGRAM COMPUTES THE AVERAGE OF A GROUP OF TEST
C     SCORES WHICH ARE FOLLOWED BY A TRAILER CARD
C
      INTEGER   TEST, TOTAL
C
      NUMBER = 0
      TOTAL = 0
C
      READ(5,15)TEST
   15 FORMAT(I3)
C
   20 IF(TEST.GE.0)THEN
         NUMBER = NUMBER + 1
         TOTAL = TOTAL + TEST
         READ(5,15)TEST
         GO TO 20
      ENDIF
C
      AVE = TOTAL/FLOAT(NUMBER)
C
      WRITE(6,30)NUMBER, AVE
   30 FORMAT('1','THE AVERAGE OF',I3,'TEST SCORES IS',
     +        F6.1)
C
      STOP
      END
```

SAMPLE OUTPUT

```
THE AVERAGE OF 10 TEST SCORES IS   89.4
```

◇

EXAMPLE 4-7   Test Scores without Trailer Signal

A group of test scores are punched on data cards, one score per card in columns 1–3, with no trailer card. Write a complete program to read the data, compute the test average, and print the number of tests and the test average.

Solution

FLOWCHART

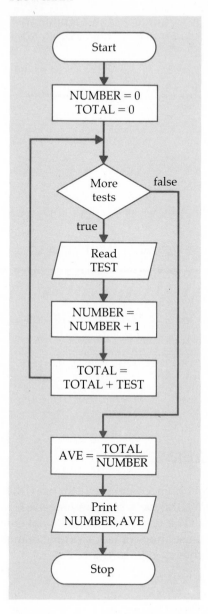

PSEUDOCODE

```
PROGRAM   AVERG2
   NUMBER ← 0
   TOTAL ← 0
   WHILE more tests DO
      READ TEST
      NUMBER ← NUMBER + 1
      TOTAL ← TOTAL + TEST
   ENDWHILE
   AVE ← TOTAL/NUMBER
   PRINT NUMBER, AVE
STOP
```

FORTRAN Program

```
      PROGRAM  AVERG2
C
C  THIS PROGRAM COMPUTES THE AVERAGE OF A GROUP'OF TEST
C  SCORES WHICH ARE NOT FOLLOWED BY A TRAILER CARD
C
      INTEGER  TEST, TOTAL
C
      NUMBER = 0
      TOTAL = 0
C
   10 READ(5,15,END=25)TEST
   15 FORMAT(I3)
         NUMBER = NUMBER + 1
         TOTAL = TOTAL + TEST
      GO TO 10
C
   25 AVE = TOTAL/FLOAT(NUMBER)
C
      WRITE(6,30)NUMBER, AVE
   30 FORMAT('1','THE AVERAGE OF',I3,'TEST SCORES IS',
     +       F6.1)
C
      STOP
      END
```

Computer Output

```
THE AVERAGE OF 37 TEST SCORES IS   79.4
```

◇

4-9   OTHER CONTROL STATEMENTS

Although this text will emphasize top-down coding, which uses the IF-THEN-ELSE-ENDIF statement and the WHILE loop, programmers need to be aware of other valid control statements. The use of these additional control statements is generally discouraged because they contain multiple branches. Debugging a program with many branches is a difficult job.

ARITHMETIC IF

The general form of the arithmetic IF statement is:

IF(*arithmetic expression*)*label 1, label 2, label 3*

Label 1, label 2, and label 3 must be numbers of executable statements in the program. The arithmetic expression is evaluated, and if it represents a negative value, control passes to the statement referenced by label 1. If the expression represents zero, then control passes to the statement referenced by label 2. Finally, if the expression represents a positive value, control passes to the statement referenced by label 3. In the following arithmetic IF statement, control will pass to statement 10 if A is greater than B, to statement 15 if A is equal to B, and to statement 20 if A is less than B.

```
IF(B - A)10, 15, 20
```

Thus, the arithmetic IF statement is a three-way branch, equivalent to the following statements:

```
IF(arithmetic expression.LT.0.0)GO TO label 1
IF(arithmetic expression.EQ.0.0)GO TO label 2
GO TO label 3
```

The early versions of FORTRAN did not include the logical IF statement. Hence, all IF statements were in the form of arithmetic IF statements at that time.

COMPUTED GO TO STATEMENT

The general form of the computed GO TO statement is:

GO TO(*label 1,label 2, . . ., label n),integer expression*

Label 1, label 2, . . ., and label n must be numbers of executable statements in your program. The computed GO TO statement is used for a multi-way branch of control. For example, if we wish to execute a different set of statements dependent on the rank (RANK) of a student, we could use the following computed GO TO statement, where RANK = 1 for freshman, 2 for sophomore, 3 for junior, 4 for senior, and 5 for graduate. Assume RANK is an integer variable.

```
INTEGER   RANK
   +
   +
   +
GO TO(11, 15, 20, 17, 17), RANK
WRITE(6,5)
5 FORMAT(1X,'RANK VALUE IN ERROR')
   +
   +
   +
```

If RANK = 1 (representing a freshman), then the computed GO TO will be executed as if it were:

GO TO 11

Similar branches would occur for RANK = 2 and RANK = 3. For seniors and graduate students (RANK = 4 and RANK = 5), control will transfer to statement 17, thus illustrating the fact that the statement labels do not have to be unique. If the value of RANK is such that it does not cause a branch (in this case, less than 1 or greater than 5), control passes to the next statement, which we have used to print an error message.

ASSIGN STATEMENT AND
ASSIGNED GO TO STATEMENT

The ASSIGN statement and the assigned GO TO statement work together to yield a multi-branch structure. The general forms of these two statements are given below:

ASSIGN *integer constant* TO *integer variable*

GO TO *integer variable,(label 1,label 2, . . .,label n)*

The assigned GO TO statement looks very similar to the computed GO TO statement but there are some significant differences.

1 The integer variable referenced in the assigned GO TO must have been initialized with the ASSIGN statement.

2 The integer variable can be used only to store statement references.

3 If the value of the integer variable is less than 1 or greater than n, an error occurs.

In the example below, the value 3 has been initially assigned to K. The IF statements may change the value stored in K to either 1 or 2. When the assigned GO TO statement is executed, control will transfer to statement 10 if K = 1, statement 5 if K = 2, or statement 15 if K = 3. Otherwise, an execution error occurs.

```
                    .
                    .
                    .
          ASSIGN 3 TO K
                    .
                    .
                    .
          IF(A.LT.B)ASSIGN 2 TO K
          IF(A.GE.C)ASSIGN 1 TO K
                    .
                    .
                    .
          GO TO K,(10, 5, 15)
                    .
                    .
                    .
```

SUMMARY

The inclusion of the IF-THEN-ELSE-ENDIF statement in our FORTRAN vocabulary has greatly expanded the type of problems that we can solve. This is due primarily to the ability to build WHILE loops. Also, as we solve longer and more complex problems, we will find flowcharts and pseudocodes very helpful in determining the order of the steps needed within the WHILE loops.

While the IF-THEN-ELSE-ENDIF statement is the primary statement used for control, there are other control statements in the FORTRAN language. In general, the use of these statements, such as the computed GO TO and the arithmetic IF, is strongly discouraged because they tend to cause multiple branches. It is more desirable to have a program that follows a top-down or sequential path rather than one that branches in many directions. The difficulties in following and debugging multi-branch statements are eliminated with the use of structured programming techniques.

KEY WORDS

arithmetic IF statement
ASSIGN statement
assigned GO TO statement
branch
compound logical expression
computed GO TO statement
connector
control structure
flowchart
GO TO statement
IF-THEN-ELSE-ENDIF
    structure

IF-THEN-ELSEIF-ENDIF
    structure
IF-THEN-ENDIF structure
logical expression
logical IF statement
logical value
loop
pseudocode
relational operator
structured programming
top-down
trailer signal
WHILE loop

DEBUGGING AIDS

The most helpful tool in debugging is the temporary WRITE or PRINT statement. Just knowing that your program is working incorrectly does not really tell you where to begin looking for errors. If you write the values of key variables at different points in your program, however, then it becomes easier to isolate the parts of the program that are not working correctly. The location of these *checkpoints*, or places to write the values of key variables, depends upon the program. Some of the obvious places are after initializing variables, after completing loops, and after branching. It is also a good idea to number the checkpoints and then print the checkpoint number along with the other values. For instance, if you print the values of X and Y at several checkpoints, it may not be obvious which set of X and Y values have been printed. However, the following output is very clear:

```
CHECKPOINT 3: X = 14.76   Y = -3.821
```

If you believe that a programming error is within a WHILE loop, then at the beginning of the loop, print the values of key variables. Since this information will be printed each time the loop is executed, you will be able to locate the trouble spot.

If you have narrowed the problem to an IF structure, then first check the logical expression. Did you use .LT. when you needed .LE.? Be careful when using .NOT. in an expression. It is less confusing to use A.NE.B rather than .NOT.A.EQ.B. Also, note that .NOT.(A.EQ.1.0.OR.B.EQ.2.0) is also equal to A.NE.1.0.AND.B.NE.2.0.

Another possible error with IF structures can be traced to values being very close to a desired value, but not exactly the desired value. For instance, suppose that the result of a mathematical computation should have a real value 5.0. Since computers do have limitations on the number of digits of accuracy, the result might be 4.9999 or 5.0001. Yet, if you check only for 5.0, you may not realize that you really have the correct value. One way to address this problem is to use the IF statement to look for values close to 5.0. For instance, if

$$|5.0 - X| < .001$$

then X is between 4.999 and 5.001. If this is close enough for the particular problem being solved, then replace the statement

```
IF(X.EQ.5.0)WRITE(6,5)TOTAL
```

with the statement

```
IF(ABS(5.0 - X).LT.0.001)WRITE(6,5)TOTAL
```

In summary, the longer a problem becomes, the more difficult it will be to locate errors. Use your flowchart or pseudocode to look for logic errors. When you think you have found a section of code with errors, use the WRITE or PRINT statement to print variables at strategic points to isolate the error.

STYLE/TECHNIQUE GUIDES

As a program grows in size, the more apparent the programmer's style becomes. Not only does bad style/technique become more obvious, it also becomes harder to correct. Therefore, practicing good style/technique in your small programs builds habits that will carry over into all your programming.

One of the best guides to good style when building loops is to consistently use the WHILE structure. With a little practice, you will find that all loops fit easily into this structure. The main advantage of the WHILE loop is the inherent top-down flow. Each WHILE loop has one entrance and one exit, and thus enhances readability and adds simplicity to your program.

Another characteristic of good style is the utilization of indenting to emphasize the statements in IF-ENDIF constructions. You can convince yourself of the importance of indenting if you try to follow a program written by someone else who has not indented statements within IF-THEN-ELSE-ENDIF structures.

Comment cards are yet another sign of style. The use of comment cards, however, can become excessive. Use only as many cards as are needed to show the program's organization and enhance its readability. There should always be initial comments to describe the purpose of the program. If needed, comments may be used throughout the program to identify processes, values, variables, etc. You will also notice that blank comment cards can be very effective in separating different steps within a program. This technique is often used in our example programs.

A final program exhibiting good style will save time in the long run since it is easier to debug. The programmers who may need to follow your program in future projects will also appreciate good style. Changing a few lines of FORTRAN code to achieve this will be time well spent.

PROBLEMS

In problems 1 through 10, use the values given below to determine whether the following logical expressions are "true" or "false."

$$A = 5.5 \qquad B = 1.5 \qquad I = -3 \qquad K = 12$$

1   A.LT.10.0

2   A + B.GE.6.5

3   I.NE.0

4   B−I.GT.A

5   .NOT.A.EQ.3*B

6   −I.LE.I+6

7   A.LT.10.0.AND.A.GT.5.0

8   IABS(I).GT.3.OR.K/5.GT.2

9   EXP(A).GT.1.0.OR.SQRT(A).LT.2.0

10   .NOT.(I.GE.K).AND.MOD(500,K).NE.0

In problems 11 through 16, give FORTRAN statements that perform the steps indicated.

11 If TIME is greater than 15.0, increment TIME by 1.0.

12 When the square root of POLY is less than 0.5, go to statement 50.

13 If the difference between VOLT1 and VOLT2 is larger than 10.0, stop the program.

14 If the value of DEN is less than 0.005, write the message 'DEN IS TOO SMALL'.

15 If the logarithm (base 10) of A is greater than or equal to the logarithm (base e) of Q, set TIME to zero.

16 If DIST is less than 50.0 and TIME is greater than 10.0, increment TIME by 0.05. Otherwise increment TIME by 2.0.

17 Complete the following IF-THEN-ENDIF structure so that the statements will read and print 200 cards.

```
 1    INTEGER   CTR
 2    CTR = 1
 3    IF(          )THEN
 4         READ(5,5)I, J
 5         FORMAT(2I2)
 6         WRITE(6,7)I, J
 7         FORMAT(1X,2I3)
 8         CTR = CTR + 1
 9         GO TO 3
10    ENDIF
11       .
         .
         .
```

18 How many values of TEMP will be read and printed by the following group of statements?

```
            .
            .
            .
      NUM = 0
 2    IF(NUM.LT.50)THEN
 3         READ(5,4)TEMP
 4         FORMAT(F4.2)
           WRITE(6,5)TEMP
 5         FORMAT(1X,F5.2)
           NUM = NUM + 1
           GO TO 2
      ENDIF
         .
         .
         .
```

19 What does the following set of statements do?

```
            .
            .
            .
      READ(5,1)I, J, K
  1   FORMAT(3I2)
      M = I
      IF(J.LT.M)M = J
      IF(K.LT.M)M = K
      WRITE(6,2)M
  2   FORMAT(1X,I2)
            .
            .
            .
```

20 Give statements to read three real values from a data card using a 3F4.1 format beginning in column 1. Determine the largest absolute value of the three values and print this largest absolute value.

21 Convert the following pair of logical IF statements to a single IF statement.

```
      IF(I.GT.M - N)K = L + 1
      IF(I.EQ.6)K = L + 1
```

22 Convert the following IF statement to the IF-THEN-ENDIF structure without a compound logical expression.

```
      IF(ABS(A).LT.5.0.AND.B.GE.C)WRITE(6,10)X
```

23 Give the statements necessary to compute the salary of a student who works in the Engineering College Computer Center. Assume that the hourly rate is RATE and the total number of hours worked is HRS. Pay the student according to the following schedule.

HOURS WORKED	HOURLY RATE
hours ≤ 40	regular rate
$40 <$ hours ≤ 50	regular rate for 40 hours
	1.5 times regular rate for hours above 40
hours > 50	regular rate for 40 hours
	1.5 times regular rate for 10 hours
	2.0 times regular rate for hours above 50

24 As a practicing engineer, you have been collecting data on the performance of a new solar device. You have been measuring the sun's intensity and the voltage produced by a photovoltaic cell exposed to the sun. These measurements have been taken every half hour of the day for 2 months. Since the sun sets at a different time each day, the number of measurements may vary from day to day. To indicate the end of data, a card that contains 9999 in the first four columns is placed after the last valid data card. The valid data cards are of the form:

columns 1–4   Sun's Intensity (Integer)
        8–11   Time (Military form where 1430 represents 2:30 pm)
    20–30   Voltage (Exponential with two decimal places)

Write a complete program to read this data and compute and print the total number of measurements, the average intensity of the sun, and the average voltage value. Develop a flowchart or pseudocode before beginning to code the problem.

25 Develop an algorithm and use it to write a complete program that will read the value of N from columns 1–3 of a data card. If N is zero or negative, stop the program. Otherwise, use N to specify how many cards of the following form to read.

columns 1–3   ID Number   XXX
        8–11   Initial Weight   XX.X
    20–23   Final Weight   XX.X

Print a table containing the ID number of an animal subject in an experiment, the initial weight, the final weight, and the percentage increase in weight. Number the lines. (*Hint:* Use an integer variable for the line number and increment it each time a line is printed.)

NUTRITION STUDY

	ID	INITIAL WT	FINAL WT	PERCENT INCREASE
1.	XXX	XX.X	XX.X	XXX.X
2.	XXX	XX.X	XX.X	XXX.X
.	.	.	.	.
.	.	.	.	.
.	.	.	.	.
N.	XXX	XX.X	XX.X	XXX.X

26 A small test rocket is being designed for use in testing a retrorocket that is intended to permit "soft" landings. The designers have derived the following equations that they believe will predict the performance of the test rocket.

(t = elapsed time in seconds)

$$\text{Acceleration in ft/sec}^2 = 4.25 - .015t^2 + \frac{6.07t^{2.751}}{9995}$$

$$\text{Velocity in ft/sec} = 4.25t - \frac{.015t^3}{3} + \frac{6.07t^{3.751}}{3.751(9995)}$$

$$\text{Distance in ft} = 90 + \frac{4.25t^2}{2} - \frac{.015t^4}{12} + \frac{6.07t^{4.751}}{4.751(37,491)}$$

(*Note:* The distance equation gives the height above ground level at time t and the first term (90) is the height in feet above ground level of the launch platform that will be used.) In order to check the predicted performance, the rocket will be "flown" on a computer, using the derived equations. Develop an algorithm and use it to write a complete program to cover a maximum flight of 100 seconds. The data print-out is to be in the following form:

TIME (SEC)	ACCELERATION (FT/SEC**2)	VELOCITY (FT/SEC)	DISTANCE (FT)
XXX.XX	XX.XX	XXXX.XX	XXXX.XX
(Starting with 0.0 sec)			
.	.	.	.
.	.	.	.
.	.	.	.

Increments of time are to be 2.0 seconds, from launch through the ascending and descending portions of the trajectory until the rocket descends to within 50 feet of ground level. Below 50 feet the time increments are to be 0.05 second. If the rocket impacts prior to 100 seconds, the program is to be stopped immediately after impact.

27 Write a complete program that reads a data file called EXAMS that has 40 lines of data with three numbers per line in a 3I3 format. Each line represents exam scores on EXAM1, EXAM2, and EXAM3 for a student. There are 40 students. Exam grades can be any integer between 0 and 100. Find the maximum score on each exam and print the following:

MAXIMUM SCORE ON EXAM 1 = XXX
MAXIMUM SCORE ON EXAM 2 = XXX
MAXIMUM SCORE ON EXAM 3 = XXX

28 Write a complete program that will read a student registration file, called STUDNT, containing a student number in columns 1–4 and the hours completed in columns 8–10, for each student that attends the university. The last line of the data is indicated with student number 9999, which does not represent a student. A student's classification is based on the following table:

CLASSIFICATION	HOURS COMPLETED
FRESHMAN	hours < 30
SOPHOMORE	30 ≤ hours < 60
JUNIOR	60 ≤ hours < 90
SENIOR	90 ≤ hours

Print the following report:

REGISTRATION REPORT

STUDENT ID	HOURS COMPLETED	CLASSIFICATION
XXXX	XXX	XXXXXXXXX
.	.	.
.	.	.
.	.	.
XXXX	XXX	XXXXXXXXX

29 Modify the program of problem 28 so that a final summary report follows
the registration report and has the following form:

REGISTRATION SUMMARY

FRESHMEN	XXXX
SOPHOMORES	XXXX
JUNIORS	XXXX
SENIORS	XXXX
TOTAL STUDENTS	XXXXX

SAMPLE PROBLEM – Population Study

The population of Shakespeare, New Mexico, has had large increases and decreases as it grew to a large mining community and then eventually became a ghost town. The population of Shakespeare, for the years 1880 through 1980, has been entered in a data file. Determine the 2 consecutive years in which the percentage increase was the greatest. (For solution, see Example 5-6, page 148.)

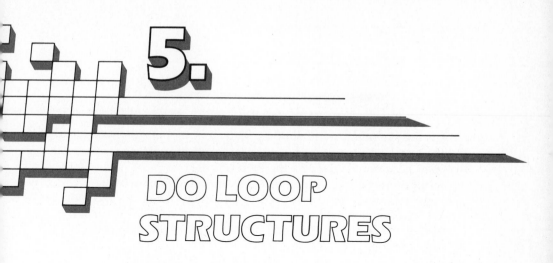

5.

DO LOOP STRUCTURES

INTRODUCTION

In the previous chapter we used the IF-THEN-ENDIF structure to build WHILE loops. A special case of the WHILE loop is the counting loop or *iteration* loop. An iteration loop generally involves initializing a counter before entering the loop, modifying the counter within the loop, and exiting the loop when the counter reaches a specified value. These three steps can certainly be incorporated in a WHILE loop, but the three steps still require three statements. A special statement, the DO statement, combines all three steps into one statement. Using the DO statement to construct a loop results in a construction called a *DO loop*. The sample problem on population increases requires a loop to read the population data and compute the population increase each year. Instead of building a WHILE loop that is executed "while YEAR is less than 1981," we will use a DO loop that is executed 101 times, since there are 101 years from 1880 through 1980.

5-1 GENERAL FORM OF A DO LOOP

The general form of the DO statement is

$$\boxed{\text{DO}\quad k,\ index = initial, limit, increment}$$

where *k* is the statement number of the statement that represents the end of the loop,

index is a variable used as the loop counter,

initial represents the initial value given to the loop counter,

limit represents the value used to determine when the DO loop has been completed, and

increment represents the value to be added to the loop counter each time that the loop is executed.

The comma after *k* is optional.

The values of initial, limit, and increment are called the *parameters* of the DO loop. If the increment is omitted, an increment of 1 is assumed. When the value of the index is greater than the limit, control is passed to the statement following the end of the loop. The end of the loop is usually indicated with the CONTINUE statement, whose general form is:

$$\boxed{k\quad \text{CONTINUE}}$$

where k is the statement number referenced on the corresponding DO statement. Before we list all the rules that must be followed when using a DO loop, we look at a simple example.

EXAMPLE 5-1 Integer Sum

The sum of the integers 1 through 50 is represented mathematically as

$$\sum_{i=1}^{50} i = 1 + 2 + \cdots + 49 + 50$$

Obviously we do not want to write one long assignment statement of the form:

$$\text{SUM} = 1 + 2 + 3 + 4 + 5 + 6 + \cdots + 50$$

A better solution is to build a loop that we execute 50 times, and add a number to the sum each time through the loop.

WHILE Loop Solution

```
        INTEGER   SUM
           .
           .
           .
        SUM = 0
        NUMBER = 1
   10   IF(NUMBER.LE.50)THEN
           SUM = SUM + NUMBER
           NUMBER = NUMBER + 1
           GO TO 10
        ENDIF
           .
           .
           .
```

DO Loop Solution

```
        INTEGER   SUM
           .
           .
           .
        SUM = 0
        DO 10 NUMBER=1,50
           SUM = SUM + NUMBER
   10   CONTINUE
           .
           .
           .
```

The DO statement identifies statement 10 as the end of the loop. The index NUMBER is initialized to 1. The loop will be repeated until the value of NUMBER is greater than 50. Since the third parameter is omitted, the index NUMBER will be automatically incremented by 1 at the end of each loop. Comparing the DO loop solution with the WHILE loop solution, we see that the DO loop solution is shorter than the WHILE loop solution, but both would compute the same value for SUM. ◇

Now that you have seen a DO loop in a simple example, we will summarize the general rules to be followed when building a DO loop. The rules will be divided into two groups, rules relating to the structure of the DO loop and rules relating to the execution of the DO loop. Following these rules are the flowchart and pseudocode descriptions of a DO loop.

STRUCTURE OF A DO LOOP

1 The index of the DO loop must be a variable, but it may be either real or integer type.

2 The parameters of the DO loop may be variables or expressions and can also be real or integer type.

3 The increment must be nonzero.

4 A DO loop may end on any executable statement that is not a transfer, an IF-ENDIF, or another DO. The CONTINUE statement is an executable statement that was designed expressly for the purpose of closing a DO loop. Although other statements may also be used, we strongly encourage the consistent use of CONTINUE to clearly indicate the end of all loops.

EXECUTION OF A DO LOOP

1 The test for completion is done at the beginning of the loop, as in a WHILE loop. Thus, if the initial value of the index is greater than the limit, the loop will not be executed. For instance, the statement

```
DO 10 I=5,2
```

sets up a loop that ends at statement 10. The initial value of the index I is 5, which is greater than the limit 2. Therefore, the statements within the loop will be skipped, and control passes to the statement following statement 10.

2 The value of the index should not be modified by other statements during the execution of the loop.

3 After the loop begins execution, changing the values of the parameters will have no effect on the loop.

4 If the increment is negative, the exit from the loop will occur when the value of the index is less than the limit.

5 You may branch out of a DO loop before it is completed. The value of the index will be the value just before the branch.

6 Upon completion of the DO loop, the index contains the last value that exceeded the limit.

7 Always enter a DO loop through the DO statement so that it will be initiated properly.

8 The number of times that a DO loop will be executed, assuming that the limit is greater than or equal to the initial value, can be computed as follows

$$\left[\frac{\text{limit} - \text{initial}}{\text{increment}}\right] + 1$$

The brackets around the first term represent the greatest integer function. That is, we drop any fractional portion (truncate) in the fraction. Hence, if we had a DO statement

$$\text{DO } 35 \text{ } K = 5, 83, 4$$

the corresponding DO loop would be executed the following number of times.

$$\left[\frac{83 - 5}{4}\right] + 1 = \left[\frac{78}{4}\right] + 1 = 20$$

The value of the index K would be 5, then 9, then 13, and so on until the final value of 81. The loop would not be executed with the value 85 because that value is greater than the limit, 83.

FLOWCHART SYMBOL FOR A DO LOOP

The flowchart symbol that we will use for a DO statement is shown below:

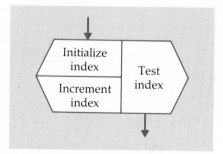

Note that it is separated into three parts to correspond to the three steps in generating a loop—initialize index, test index, and increment index.

For the DO statement

$$DO \ 10 \ I = 1,50$$

the corresponding flowchart symbol is

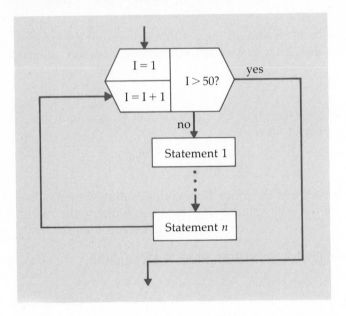

We enter the DO symbol at the initialization step, $I = 1$. The statements in the loop follow the NO response from the test. After executing the statements in the loop, we reenter the DO symbol at the increment, $I = I + 1$. When the index is greater than 50, we exit the DO symbol at YES and pass control to whatever statement follows the loop.

PSEUDOCODE FOR A DO LOOP

In pseudocode, a DO loop is indicated with a DO-ENDDO structure, similar to the WHILE-ENDWHILE construction. Instead of the condition used in the WHILE-ENDWHILE, we need to give the initial value of the index, the limit, and its increment. An example of the pseudocode for a DO loop is:

$$DO \ NUMBER = 2,60,2$$

.
.
.

ENDDO

Now that we have summarized the rules for building DO loops, a number of examples are needed to illustrate these rules. The statements in a DO loop should always be indented to clearly identify it.

EXAMPLE 5-2   Polynomial Model with Integer Time

Polynomials are often used to model data and experimental results. Assume that the polynomial

$$3t^2 + 4.5$$

models the results of an experiment where t represents time in seconds. Write a complete program to evaluate this polynomial for the period of time from 1 second to 10 seconds in increments of 1 second (i.e., let t = 1, 2, 3, 4, 5, 6, 7, 8, 9, 10). For each value of time, print the time and the polynomial value.

Solution

FLOWCHART

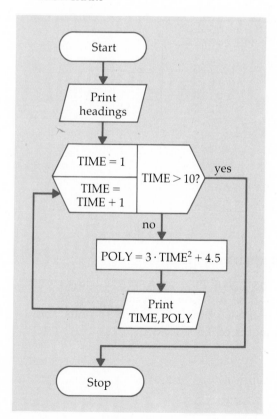

PSEUDOCODE

```
PROGRAM   POLY1
    PRINT headings
    DO TIME=1,10
        POLY ← 3*TIME² + 4.5
        PRINT TIME, POLY
    ENDDO
STOP
```

FORTRAN Program

```
      PROGRAM   POLY1
C
C  THIS PROGRAM PRINTS A TABLE OF VALUES FOR A POLYNOMIAL
C
      INTEGER   TIME
C
      WRITE(6,5)
    5 FORMAT('1','POLYNOMIAL MODEL'/1X,'TIME',3X,
     +         'POLYNOMIAL'/1X,'(SEC)')
C
      DO 15 TIME=1,10
         POLY = 3.0*TIME**2 + 4.5
         WRITE(6,10)TIME, POLY
   10    FORMAT(1X,I3,6X,F6.1)
   15 CONTINUE
C
      STOP
      END
```

Computer Output

```
POLYNOMIAL MODEL
TIME    POLYNOMIAL
(SEC)
  1         7.5
  2        16.5
  3        31.5
  4        52.5
  5        79.5
  6       112.5
  7       151.5
  8       196.5
  9       247.5
 10       304.5
```

◇

EXAMPLE 5-3   Polynomial Model with Real Time

We again assume that the polynomial $3t^2 + 4.5$ models an experiment where t represents time in seconds. Write a program to evaluate this polynomial for time beginning at zero seconds and ending at 5 seconds in increments of 0.5 second.

FORTRAN Program

```
      PROGRAM   POLY2
C
C  THIS PROGRAM PRINTS A TABLE OF VALUES FOR A POLYNOMIAL
C
      WRITE(6,5)
   5 FORMAT('1','POLYNOMIAL MODEL'/1X,'TIME',3X,
     +        'POLYNOMIAL'/1X,'(SEC)')
C
      DO 15 TIME=0.0,5.0,0.5
         POLY = 3.0*TIME**2 + 4.5
         WRITE(6,10)TIME, POLY
  10     FORMAT(1X,F3.1,6X,F6.1)
  15 CONTINUE
C
      STOP
      END
```

Computer Output

```
POLYNOMIAL MODEL
TIME    POLYNOMIAL
(SEC)
0.0         4.5
0.5         5.3
1.0         7.5
1.5        11.3
2.0        16.5
2.5        23.3
3.0        31.5
3.5        41.3
4.0        52.5
4.5        65.3
5.0        79.5
```

◇

EXAMPLE 5-4   Polynomial Model with Variable Time

Assume that we want to evaluate the polynomial $3t^2 + 4.5$, beginning at t equal to zero, in increments of 0.25, for a variable number of seconds. Write a complete program to read an integer NSEC that represents the number of seconds to be used for evaluating the polynomial. Then, print the corresponding table.

FLOWCHART

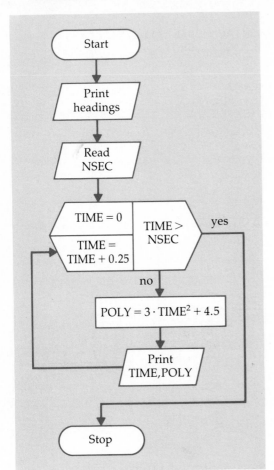

PSEUDOCODE

```
PROGRAM   POLY3
   PRINT headings
   READ   NSEC
   DO TIME=0.0, NSEC, 0.25
      POLY ← 3*TIME² + 4.5
      PRINT  TIME, POLY
   ENDDO
STOP
```

FORTRAN Program

```
      PROGRAM   POLY3
C
C   THIS PROGRAM PRINTS A TABLE OF VALUES FOR A POLYNOMIAL
C
      WRITE(6,5)
    5 FORMAT('1','POLYNOMIAL MODEL'/1X,'TIME',3X,
     +        'POLYNOMIAL'/1X,'(SEC)')
C
      READ(5,8)NSEC
    8 FORMAT(I3)
C
      DO 15 TIME=0.0,NSEC,0.25
         POLY = 3.0*TIME**2 + 4.5
         WRITE(6,10)TIME, POLY
   10    FORMAT(1X,F4.2,5X,F6.1)
   15 CONTINUE
C
      STOP
      END
```

Data Input

004

Computer Output

```
POLYNOMIAL MODEL
TIME    POLYNOMIAL
(SEC)
0.00        4.5
0.25        4.7
0.50        5.3
0.75        6.2
1.00        7.5
1.25        9.2
1.50       11.3
1.75       13.7
2.00       16.5
2.25       19.7
2.50       23.3
2.75       27.2
3.00       31.5
3.25       36.2
3.50       41.3
3.75       46.7
4.00       52.5
```

◇

5-2 APPLICATION – Timber Management Economics

In this section we will present an application that uses a DO loop to compute the amount of timber present at the end of each year over a period of 20 years for an area in which not all the trees have been harvested.

EXAMPLE 5-5   Timber Management

A problem in timber management is to determine how much of an area to leave uncut so that the harvested area is reforested in a certain period of time. It is assumed that reforestation takes place at a known rate per year, depending on climate and soil conditions. The reforestation rate expresses this growth as a function of the amount of timber standing. For example, if 100 acres are left standing and the reforestation rate is 0.05, then there are $100 + 0.05 \times 100$ or 105 acres forested at the end of the first year. At the end of the second year, the number of acres forested is $105 + 0.05 \times 105$ or 110.25 acres.

Assume that the total area to be forested, the uncut area, and the reforestation rate are read from a card. Write a complete program to determine the total area that is forested after 20 years. The output should be on a new page in the form indicated by the following sample output:

REFORESTATION DATA

AREA NUMBER	TOTAL ACRES	UNCUT ACRES	REFORESTATION RATE
45	10000.00	100.00	0.05

YEAR	ACRES REFORESTED	ACRES FORESTED
1	5.00	105.00
2	5.25	110.25
.	.	.
.	.	.
.	.	.
20	XX.XX	XXXX.XX

Use the following data values:

area number	192
total acres	14,000
uncut acres	2,500
reforestation rate	0.02

Solution

We must read the area number, total acres, uncut area, and the reforestation rate before we can print the headings, since the headings include this data. Then, we perform a loop 20 times, computing and printing the number of acres reforested and the cumulative acres forested.

PSEUDOCODE

```
PROGRAM   TIMBER
    READ NUMBER, TOTACR, TREES, RATE
    PRINT headings
    DO YEAR=1,20
        NEWFOR ← RATE*TREES
        TREES ← TREES + NEWFOR
        PRINT YEAR, NEWFOR, TREES
    ENDDO
STOP
```

FORTRAN PROGRAM

```
      PROGRAM   TIMBER
C
C  THIS PROGRAM COMPUTES A REFORESTATION SUMMARY FOR
C  AN AREA WHICH HAS NOT BEEN COMPLETELY HARVESTED
C
      INTEGER   YEAR
      REAL   NEWFOR
C
      READ(5,*)NUMBER, TOTACR, TREES, RATE
C
      WRITE(6,10)NUMBER, TOTACR, TREES, RATE
   10 FORMAT('1',23X,'REFORESTATION DATA'/1X,
     +        'AREA NUMBER', 5X,'TOTAL ACRES',4X,
     +        'UNCUT ACRES',4X,'REFORESTATION RATE'/
     +        1X,2X,I5,10X,F8.2,7X,F8.2,12X,F4.2/1X,8X,
     +        'YEAR',10X,'ACRES REFORESTED',5X,
     +        'ACRES FORESTED')
C
      DO 24 YEAR=1,20
         NEWFOR = TREES*RATE
         TREES = TREES + NEWFOR
         WRITE(6,20)YEAR, NEWFOR, TREES
   20    FORMAT(1X,9X,I2,15X,F8.2,13X,F8.2)
   24 CONTINUE
C
      STOP
      END
```

```
                    REFORESTATION DATA
AREA NUMBER      TOTAL ACRES     UNCUT ACRES     REFORESTATION RATE
    192          14000.00         2500.00              0.02
         YEAR            ACRES REFORESTED     ACRES FORESTED
          1                  50.00               2550.00
          2                  51.00               2601.00
          3                  52.02               2653.02
          4                  53.06               2706.08
          5                  54.12               2760.20
          6                  55.20               2815.41
          7                  56.31               2871.71
          8                  57.43               2929.15
          9                  58.58               2987.73
         10                  59.75               3047.49
         11                  60.95               3108.44
         12                  62.17               3170.60
         13                  63.41               3234.02
         14                  64.68               3298.70
         15                  65.97               3364.67
         16                  67.29               3431.96
         17                  68.64               3500.60
         18                  70.01               3570.62
         19                  71.41               3642.03
         20                  72.84               3714.87
```

◇

5-3   APPLICATION – Population Study

In this section we solve the problem described at the beginning of this chapter.

EXAMPLE 5-6   Population Analysis

The population of Shakespeare, New Mexico, for the years 1880 through 1980, has been entered in a data file POPNM. Each line of the data file contains the year and the corresponding population in the format I4, 1X, I5. The data lines are in ascending order by year. Write a complete program to read the data and determine the 2 consecutive years in which the percentage increase in population was the greatest.

Solution

Before we begin a flowchart, let us look at some typical data and compute the percentage increase in the data each year to be sure that we understand the computations involved.

YEAR	POPULATION	PERCENTAGE INCREASE
1950	82	
		−32% [(56 − 82)/82∗100]
1951	56	
		27% [(71 − 56)/56∗100]
1952	71	
		21% [(86 − 71)/71∗100]
1953	86	
		19% [(102 − 86)/86∗100]
1954	102	

In the years above, the largest percentage increase was from 1951 to 1952. Note that this was not the largest increase in actual population. The largest increase in actual population occurred from 1953 to 1954.

When we read a data line, we will need not only the information on that line but also the information on the previous data line in order to compute the population increase. Thus, we will need to use the following variables:

YRNEW: the year just read from a data line

YROLD: the year from the previous data line

POPNEW: the population just read from a data line

POPOLD: the population from the previous data line

GPIYR: the year in which there was the greatest percentage increase

GPI: the percentage that represents the greatest percentage increase

In the flowchart (see page 150), we read the first line of data outside the loop. The loop is then executed 100 times to read the rest of the data and compute population increases.

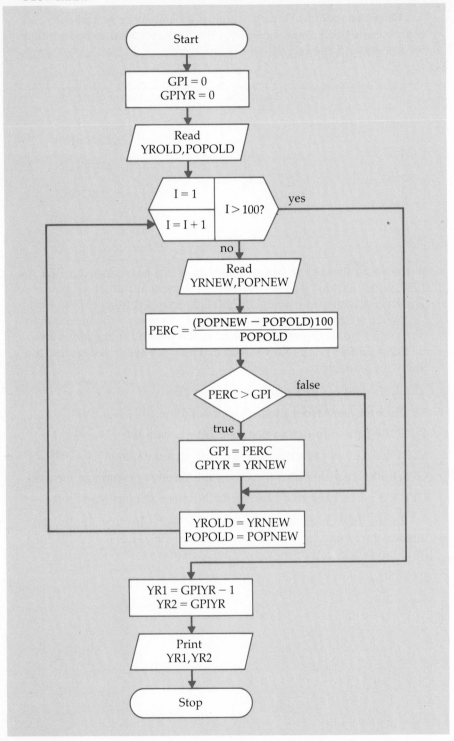

FORTRAN Program

```
      PROGRAM   GROWTH
C
C THIS PROGRAM READS 101 POPULATION VALUES AND
C DETERMINES THE YEARS OF GREATEST PERCENTAGE INCREASE
C
      INTEGER  YR1, YR2, YRNEW, YROLD, POPNEW, POPOLD,
     +         GPIYR
C
      GPI = 0.0
      GPIYR = 0
C
      OPEN(UNIT=15, FILE='POPNM', STATUS='OLD')
C
      READ(15,10)YROLD, POPOLD
   10 FORMAT(I4,1X,I5)
C
      DO 50 I=1,100
         READ(15,10)YRNEW, POPNEW
         PERC = (POPNEW - POPOLD)*100.0/POPOLD
         IF(PERC.GT.GPI)THEN
            GPI = PERC
            GPIYR = YRNEW
         ENDIF
         YROLD = YRNEW
         POPOLD = POPNEW
   50 CONTINUE
C
      YR1 = GPIYR - 1
      YR2 = GPIYR
C
      WRITE(6,70)YR1, YR2
   70 FORMAT(1X,'GREATEST PERCENT INCREASE OCCURRED ',
     +        'BETWEEN',I5,' AND',I5)
C
      STOP
      END
```

Computer Output

```
GREATEST PERCENT INCREASE OCCURRED BETWEEN 1890 AND 1891
```

◇

5-4 NESTED DO LOOPS

DO loops may be independent of each other, or they may be nested within other DO loops. Overlapping loops, however, are not allowed. Note that we have drawn brackets on the left side of the statements below to connect the beginning and ending of DO loops. These brackets prove to be very helpful in spotting invalid nesting of DO loops. The structures below compare valid and invalid loop structures.

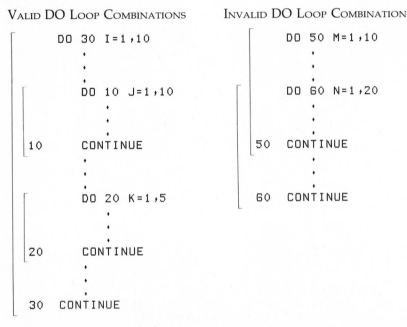

VALID DO LOOP COMBINATIONS   INVALID DO LOOP COMBINATION

```
        DO 30 I=1,10                    DO 50 M=1,10
            .                               .
            .                               .
            .                               .
           DO 10 J=1,10                     DO 60 N=1,20
               .                               .
               .                               .
               .                               .
  10       CONTINUE              50       CONTINUE
            .                               .
            .                               .
            .                               .
           DO 20 K=1,5           60       CONTINUE
               .
               .
               .
  20       CONTINUE
            .
            .
            .
  30    CONTINUE
```

In the valid DO loop construction, the two inside loops, DO 10 and DO 20, are independent of each other. However they are both within the loop, DO 30. Independent loops may use the same index. Thus, the DO 10 loop and the DO 20 loop could have used the same index J. However, the DO 30 loop index could not be used on either of the inside loops because the inside loops are not independent of the outside loop.

It is valid for two nested DO loops to end on the same statement, but is not encouraged because of the lack of clarity. With separate CONTINUE statements, each DO statement and its CONTINUE can be indented the same number of positions to emphasize the structure, with the statements inside the loop indented further.

When one loop is nested within another loop, the inside loop is completely executed each pass through the outer loop. To illustrate this, consider the following program.

```
       PROGRAM   NEST
C
C   THIS PROGRAM PRINTS THE INDEXES IN NESTED DO LOOPS
C
       WRITE(6,1)
     1 FORMAT(1X,2X,'I   J'/)
C
       DO 10 I=1,5
          DO 5 J=1,3
             WRITE(6,2)I, J
     2       FORMAT(1X,2I3)
     5    CONTINUE
    10 CONTINUE
C
       STOP
       END
```

The output from this program is shown below:

```
I   J

1   1
1   2
1   3
2   1
2   2
2   3
3   1
3   2
3   3
4   1
4   2
4   3
5   1
5   2
5   3
```

The first time through the outer loop, I is initialized to the value 1. Then we begin executing the inner loop. The variable J is initialized to the value 1. After executing the WRITE statement, we reach statement 5. Since this is the end of the inner loop, control returns to the DO 5 statement, and J is incremented to the value 2. We again write values and return to the DO 5 statement and increment J to the value 3. After writing values, we return to the DO 5 and increment J to the value 4. This value of J is now greater than the test value 3. We have completed the inner loop; so I is incremented to 2, and we begin the DO 5 loop with J equal to the value 1. The process is repeated until I is greater than 5.

EXAMPLE 5-7   Experimental Sums

Write a complete program to read 100 data values. Each data value has been punched in columns 10–15 of a card, with one decimal position. Compute the sum of the first 20 numbers, the next 20 numbers, and so on. Print the five sums.

Solution

While we need to read 100 values, we will need only 20 at a time, and thus an outer loop is needed to read 5 sets of data. Each set of data is 20 values; so the inner loop reads the 20 values. It is very important to set the variable being used to store the sum to zero before the inner loop is begun. Thus, we add 20 values, print the sum, and then set the sum back to zero before we read the next 20 values.

FLOWCHART

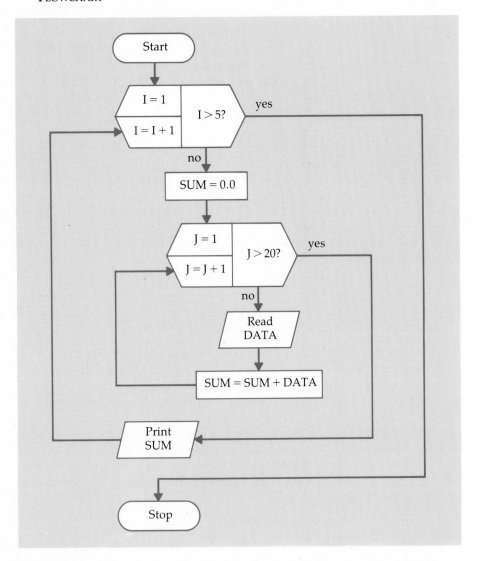

Pseudocode

PROGRAM SUMS
   DO I=1,5 ·
     SUM ← 0
     DO J=1,20
       READ DATA
       SUM ← SUM + DATA
     ENDDO
     PRINT SUM
   ENDDO
STOP

FORTRAN Program

```
      PROGRAM  SUMS
C
C  THIS PROGRAM READS 100 NUMBERS AND PRINTS
C  THE SUM OF EACH GROUP OF 20 VALUES
C
      DO 200 I=1,5
C
         SUM = 0.0
C
         DO 50 J=1,20
            READ(5,10)DATA
  10        FORMAT(9X,F6.1)
            SUM = SUM + DATA
  50     CONTINUE
C
         WRITE(6,60)I, SUM
  60     FORMAT(1X,'SUM ',I1,' = ',F6.1)
C
  200 CONTINUE
C
            STOP
            END
```

Computer Output

```
SUM 1 =     36.8
SUM 2 =    125.2
SUM 3 =     68.0
SUM 4 =     10.5
SUM 5 =     83.7
```

◇

EXAMPLE 5-8 Factorial Computation

Write a complete program to compute the factorial of an integer read from columns 3–4 of a data card. A few factorials and their corresponding values are shown below (an exclamation point after a number symbolizes a factorial):

$$0! = 1$$
$$1! = 1$$
$$2! = 2 \cdot 1$$
$$3! = 3 \cdot 2 \cdot 1$$
$$4! = 4 \cdot 3 \cdot 2 \cdot 1$$
$$5! = 5 \cdot 4 \cdot 3 \cdot 2 \cdot 1$$

Compute and print the factorial for four different values that are read from cards.

Solution

Since the factorial of a negative number is not defined, we should include in our algorithm an error check for this condition with an appropriate error message. In computing a factorial, we use a DO loop to perform the successive multiplications.

PSEUDOCODE

```
PROGRAM    FACT
   DO I=1,4
      READ N
      IF N < 0  THEN
         PRINT error message
      ELSE
         NFACT ←1
         IF N > 1 THEN
            DO K=1,N
               NFACT ←NFACT*K
            ENDDO
         ENDIF
         PRINT N, NFACT
      ENDIF
   ENDDO
STOP
```

FORTRAN Program

```
      PROGRAM  FACT
C
C  THIS PROGRAM COMPUTES THE FACTORIAL
C  OF FOUR VALUES READ FROM DATA CARDS
C
      DO 200 I=1,4
C
         READ(5,10)N
   10    FORMAT(2X,I2)
C
         IF(N.LT.0)THEN
            WRITE(6,15)N
   15       FORMAT(1X,'INVALID N = ',I2)
         ELSE
            NFACT = 1
            IF(N.GT.1)THEN
               DO 50 K=1,N
                  NFACT = NFACT*K
   50          CONTINUE
            ENDIF
            WRITE(6,110)N, NFACT
  110       FORMAT(' ',I2,'! = ',I8)
         ENDIF
C
  200 CONTINUE
C
      STOP
      END
```

Data Input

Card 1	03
Card 2	−2
Card 3	11
Card 4	00

Computer Output

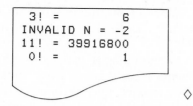

```
 3! =         6
INVALID N = -2
11! = 39916800
 0! =         1
```

SUMMARY

The DO statement has provided a simple and convenient way to build iteration or counting loops by combining the three steps of initializing a counter, incrementing the counter, and testing the counter into one statement. It is important to recognize that loops built with the DO statement are still just special cases of the WHILE loop.

KEY WORDS

CONTINUE statement
DO loop
DO statement
increment value
index

initial value
iteration loop
limit value
nested DO loop
parameter

DEBUGGING AIDS

Since a DO loop is a special type of loop, an iteration loop, most errors involve the parameters that specify the iterations. Therefore, when a program error seems to involve a DO loop, print the value of the index immediately after the DO statement. After executing the loop with this output statement, you can answer the following questions:

1 Did the index start with the correct value?

2 Did the index increment by the proper amount?

3 Did the index have the correct value during the last execution of the loop?

If the answer to any of these questions is no, check the DO statement itself. You probably have an error in the parameters that you specified.

If the error is not in your original specification of parameters in the DO statement, print the values of the index, both immediately after the DO statement and immediately before the CONTINUE statement. After executing the loop with these two output statements, you will be able to determine if the value of the index is changed by the statements inside the loop. If the index is being modified, you have either used the index inadvertently, which can be corrected, or you do not have an iteration loop and, hence, you should replace the DO loop with a WHILE loop.

Another common error associated with DO loops occurs when a similar variable name is used instead of the index. For instance, if the index of the DO loop is INDEX, use INDEX and not I inside the loop when you intend to use the index value.

STYLE/TECHNIQUE GUIDES

Since DO loops are contained in many programs, good style and technique with DO loops become important. The following guides will help you develop a smooth style when constructing DO loops.

1 Use comment cards to separate DO loops from the surrounding statements.

```
                         .
                         .
                         .
              READ(5,10)N
         10  FORMAT(I2)
      C
              DO  15  I=1,N
                         .
                         .
                         .
         15  CONTINUE
      C
              WRITE(6,20)SUM
                         .
                         .
                         .
```

2 Indent nested loops.

```
                    .
                    .
                    .
         DO  5  I=1,10
            DO  3  J=1,10
               DO  1  K=1,10
                         .
                         .
                         .
         1          CONTINUE
         3       CONTINUE
         5  CONTINUE
                    .
                    .
                    .
```

3 Indent the statements within a DO loop.

```
                 .
                 .
                 .
         DO  5  NUM=5,100,5
            POLY = NUM**2 - 5.0*NUM + 6.0
            WRITE(*,*)NUM, POLY
         5  CONTINUE
                 .
                 .
                 .
```

4 Use CONTINUE to close DO loops. While other statements are valid, the CONTINUE clearly identifies the end of a loop. Do not close more than one loop with the same CONTINUE statement.

5 Use DO loops instead of building loops with IF statements when possible. The only time you should use IF statements to build loops is when you do not have an iteration loop—then use the WHILE loop structure.

PROBLEMS

In problems 1 through 8, compute the number of times that statements will be executed that are within the loop associated with each of the following DO statements:

1 `DO 10 J=0,20`   2 `DO 30 KTR=2,20,2`

3 `DO 26 T=5,200,0.5`   4 `DO 37 LL=5,203,5`

5 `DO 40 N=10,10`   6 `DO 94 I=10,5,4`

7 `DO 150 JI=40,0,-1`   8 `DO 200 RQ=0,-5,-0.75`

In problems 9 through 14, give the value in COUNTR after each of the following loops is executed. Assume COUNTR represents an integer variable.

9
```
          ,
          ,
          ,
     COUNTR = 0
     DO 5 I=1,10
         COUNTR = COUNTR + 1
   5 CONTINUE
          ,
          ,
          ,
```

10
```
          ,
          ,
          ,
     COUNTR = 0
     DO 5 I=1,10,2
         COUNTR = COUNTR + 1
   5 CONTINUE
          ,
          ,
          ,
```

11
```
         .
         .
         .
      COUNTR = 1
      DO 5 I=2,10,2
         COUNTR = COUNTR + 1
    5 CONTINUE
      COUNTR = COUNTR + 1
         .
         .
         .
```

12
```
         .
         .
         .
      COUNTR = 1
      DO 5 B=5,10,0.5
         COUNTR = COUNTR + 1
    5 CONTINUE
      DO 10 K=2,6
         COUNTR = COUNTR + 2
   10 CONTINUE
         .
         .
         .
```

13
```
         .
         .
         .
      COUNTR = 1
      DO 5 I=1,10
         DO 4 K=2,10,2
            COUNTR = COUNTR + 1
    4    CONTINUE
    5 CONTINUE
         .
         .
         .
```

14
```
         .
         .
         .
      COUNTR = 0
      DO 5 MM=15,5,-2
         COUNTR = COUNTR + 1
         DO 2 LL=10,20,4
            COUNTR = COUNTR + 1
    2    CONTINUE
    5 CONTINUE
         .
         .
         .
```

In problems 15 through 18, convert the following WHILE loops to DO loops. Assume that SUM and COUNTR represent integer variables.

15
```
              .
              .
              .
     COUNTR = 0
     SUM = 0
  4  IF(COUNTR.LT.50)THEN
         SUM = SUM + COUNTR
         COUNTR = COUNTR + 1
         GO TO 4
     ENDIF
              .
              .
              .
```

16
```
              .
              .
              .
     COUNTR = 0
     SUM = 0
  5  IF(COUNTR.LE.50)THEN
         SUM = SUM + COUNTR
         COUNTR = COUNTR + 1
         GO TO 5
     ENDIF
              .
              .
              .
```

17
```
              .
              .
              .
     COUNTR = 1
     SUM = 0
     READ(5,1)NUM
  1  FORMAT(I2)
  3  IF(COUNTR.LE.NUM)THEN
         SUM = SUM + COUNTR
         COUNTR = COUNTR + 1
         GO TO 3
     ENDIF
              .
              .
              .
```

18
```
            ·
            ·
            ·
      COUNTR = 0
  20  IF(COUNTR.LT.M)THEN
         READ(5,21)X
  21     FORMAT(F4.1)
         WRITE(6,22)X
  22     FORMAT(1X,F4.1)
         COUNTR = COUNTR + 1
         GO TO 20
      ENDIF
            ·
            ·
            ·
```

19 What are the values of I, SUM, and CALC after completing this segment of a FORTRAN program?

```
      INTEGER   SUM, CALC
            ·
            ·
            ·
      SUM = 0
      DO 100 I=1,50,10
         SUM = SUM + 1
         CALC = I*2
  100 CONTINUE
            ·
            ·
            ·
```

20 What is the value of L1 after the following statements are executed?

```
            ·
            ·
            ·
      L1 = 0
      DO 100 I=1,15
         IF(I.LT.13)L1 = L1 + I
  100 CONTINUE
            ·
            ·
            ·
```

21 What is the value of KT after the following is executed?

```
            ·
            ·
            ·
      KT = 0
      DO 6 I=4,20
         IF(I.LT.11)KT = KT + 1
    6 CONTINUE
            ·
            ·
            ·
```

In problems 22 through 24, write FORTRAN statements to print tables showing the values of the variables and the function using DO loops to control the loops.

Example: $K = 3M$ for $M = 1, 2, 3, 4$
Solution:
```
          DO 6 M=1,4
             K = 3*M
             WRITE(6,1)M, K
1            FORMAT(1X,2I5)
6         CONTINUE
                  .
                  .
                  .
```

22 $K = I^2 + 2I + 2$ for $I = 0, 1, 2, \ldots, 20$

23 $Y = \dfrac{X^2 - 9}{X^2 + 2}$ for $X = 1.5, 2.0, 2.5, \ldots, 9$

24 $F = \dfrac{X^2 - Y^2}{2XY}$ for $X = 1, 2, \ldots, 9$
and $Y = 0.5, 0.75, 1.0, \ldots, 2.5$

25 Write a complete program to print a table giving consecutive even integers beginning with 2 and squaring each value, until the value of I is greater than 200.

I	I*I
2	4
4	16
.	.
.	.
.	.

26 Write a complete program to read a value FINAL from columns 1 through 4 of a data card in an F4.1 format. Print a table that prints values of X and X^2, starting with $X = 0.0$, in increments of 0.5, until X is greater than FINAL.

X	X*X
0.0	0.0
0.5	0.25
.	.
.	.
.	.

27 A biologist, after discovering the omega germ, had spent 5 years determining the characteristics of the new virus. She has found that the germ has a constant growth rate. If there are 10 cells present with a growth factor of 0.1, the next generation will have $10 + 10(0.1) = 11$ cells. Write a complete program that will compute and print a report with the following form:

OMEGA GERM GROWTH

CULTURE NUMBER	NUMBER OF CELLS INITIALLY	PETRI DISH DIAMETER (CM)	GROWTH RATE
XXXX	XXXX	XXX	XX.XX

GENERATION	NUMBER OF CELLS	% AREA OF PETRI DISH COVERED
1	XXXXX	XXX.XX
.	.	.
.	.	.
.	.	.
14	XXXXX	XXX.XX

The output for each set of data is to be on a new page. Ten cells occupy 1 mm². If the covered area of the dish is ever greater than or equal to 100 percent, stop calculations, print out an appropriate message, and then continue with next set of data. Use the following data.

CULTURE NUMBER	NUMBER OF CELLS INITIALLY	PETRI DISH DIAMETER	GROWTH RATE
1984	100	10 cm	0.50
1776	1300	5 cm	0.16
1812	600	15 cm	0.55
1056	700	8 cm	0.80

28 The current-voltage relationship in an ideal *p-n* junction diode is described by the equation:

$$I = I_s(\exp{(QV/kT)} - 1)$$

where I = current through diode, amps
V = voltage across diode, volts
I_s = saturation current, amps
Q = electron charge, 1.6E−19 coulomb
k = Boltzmann's constant, 1.38E−23 joule/°K
T = junction temperature, °K

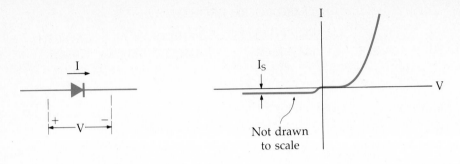

Write a complete program that calculates I as V varies from $-0.250\,V$ to $0.500\,V$ in increments of $0.125\,V$, for junction temperatures of 32, 100, 212°F. (*Note:* °K = (°F -32)*5/9 + 273.16.) Saturation current, I_s, which is also a function of temperature, will be 1 μA in all three cases. Your output should be in the following format:

JUNCTION TEMPERATURE = XXX.XX F = XXX.XX K

VOLTAGE ACROSS DIODE	CURRENT THROUGH DIODE
$-0.250\,V$	$\pm 0.XXXXE \pm XX\,A$
$-0.125\,V$	$\pm 0.XXXXE \pm XX\,A$
.	.
.	.
.	.
$0.500\,V$	$\pm 0.XXXXE \pm XX\,A$

29 Forty-eight temperature measurements for two compounds have been taken at 10-minute intervals over a period of time. The measurements have been put in a data file TEMP, with each pair of temperatures on a new line in a 2F6.2 format in the order that the measurements were made. Write a complete program to read the data and print it in the following manner:

TEMPERATURE MEASUREMENTS

TIME ELAPSED		COMPOUND	COMPOUND
HOURS	MINUTES	1	2
0	0	XXX.XX	XXX.XX
0	10		
0	20	.	.
0	30		
0	40	.	.
0	50		
1	0	.	.
.	.		
.	.	.	.
.	.		
7	50	XXX.XX	XXX.XX

*30 Modify the program of problem 29 so that the following output lines are printed after the temperature measurements:

	MINIMUM TEMPERATURE	TIME ELAPSED	
		HOURS	MINUTES
COMPOUND 1	XXX.XX	X	XX
COMPOUND 2	XXX.XX	X	XX

*31 The function $\sin^2 X$ can be represented by the following series:

$$\sin^2 X = X^2 - \frac{2^3 X^4}{4!} + \frac{2^5 X^6}{6!} - \cdots = \sum_{n=1}^{\infty} \frac{(-1)^{n+1} 2^{2n-1} X^{2n}}{(2n)!}$$

Write a complete program to evaluate this series for $X = 2.0$, printing the results after 2, 4, 6, 8, . . . , 14 terms and comparing to the true solution. The program should read the value of X. Note that the term for $n = 1$ is X^2, and that all consecutive terms can be obtained by multiplying the previous term by

$$\frac{-(2X)^2}{2n(2n-1)}$$

The computer print-out is to have the following form:

COMPARISON OF VALUES OF SINE SQUARED

NUMBER OF TERMS	SERIES SUMMATION	INTRINSIC FUNCTION	ABSOLUTE DIFFERENCE
2	---	---	---
4	---	---	---
6	---	---	---
.	.	.	.
.	.	.	.
.	.	.	.
14	---	---	---

Courtesy of New Mexico Tourism and Travel Division

SAMPLE PROBLEM – National Park Data

The National Park Service conducts annual surveys comparing snowfall statistics for each of the National Parks. Assume data is available that includes the snowfall recorded each day in January for Yellowstone National Park. Determine the daily snowfall average for January and the number of days with snowfall above this daily average. (For solution, see Example 6-5, page 179.)

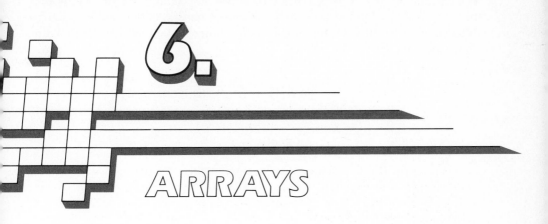

INTRODUCTION

The objective of this chapter is to develop a method for storing groups of values without explicitly giving each value a different name. The group of values have a common name but individual values have a unique subscript. This technique allows us to analyze the data using loops, where the common name remains the same, but the subscript becomes a variable that changes with each pass through the loop. Since the data values are stored in separate memory locations, we can also access the data as often as needed without rereading it. The use of an array to store the snowfall data in the sample problem is necessary because we need to have all the snowfall data available after we have computed the average. Each snowfall value is then compared to the average, and a counter is incremented if the value is greater than the average snowfall value.

6-1   STORAGE AND INITIALIZATION OF ONE-DIMENSIONAL ARRAYS

An *array* is a group of storage locations that have the same name. Individual members of an array are called *elements* and are distinguished by using the common name followed by a subscript in parentheses. Subscript numbers are consecutive integers, usually beginning with the integer 1. A one-dimensional array can be visualized as either one column of data or one row of data. The storage locations and associated names for a one-dimensional integer array J of five elements and a one-dimensional real array DIST with four elements are shown below:

J(1)	2
J(2)	−5
J(3)	14
J(4)	80
J(5)	−12

1.2	−0.8	36.9	−0.07
DIST(1)	DIST(2)	DIST(3)	DIST(4)

The DIMENSION statement, a nonexecutable statement, is used to reserve memory space or storage for an array. In the general form of the DIMENSION statement, a list of array names and their corresponding sizes follow the word DIMENSION.

> DIMENSION   *array1(size), array2(size), . . .*

A DIMENSION statement that will reserve storage for the two arrays previously mentioned is:

DIMENSION   J(5), DIST(4)

The number in parentheses after the array name gives the total number of values to be stored in that array. Two separate DIMENSION statements, with one array listed in each statement, would also be valid, but not preferable because it requires an extra statement. All DIMENSION statements must be placed before any executable statements in your program because they are specification statements.

The type of values stored in an array can be specified implicitly through the choice of array name, or explicitly with a REAL or INTEGER statement. For example, the following statement specifies that AREA is an array of 15 elements that contains integer values:

INTEGER   AREA(15)

The typing of an array, whether implicit or explicit, applies to all elements of the array; hence, an array cannot contain some real values and some integer values. Explicitly typed array names do not appear on DIMENSION statements because the array size has also been specified in the type statement.

The range of subscripts associated with an array can be specified with a beginning subscript number and an ending subscript number, both of which must be integers separated by a colon and following the array name in the

DIMENSION statement. The following statement reserves storage for a REAL array ZX whose elements are ZX(0), ZX(1), ZX(2), ZX(3), ZX(4), and ZX(5), and an INTEGER array K whose elements are K(−3), K(−2), K(−1), K(0), K(1), K(2), and K(3).

```
DIMENSION  ZX(0:5), K(-3:3)
```

Unless stated otherwise, we will assume that all array subscripts begin with the integer 1. There are situations, however, in which the range of subscripts logically starts with an integer other than 1. For instance, in the sample problem at the beginning of Chapter 5 we discussed a set of population values from the years 1880–1980. If this data were to be stored in an array, it might be very convenient to use the year to specify the corresponding population. We could specify such an array with the following statement:

```
INTEGER   POPUL(1880:1980)
```

In all compilers, values can be assigned to array elements in the same way that values are assigned to regular variables. The following are valid assignment statements:

```
J(1) = 36
J(5) = K*L
DIST(2) = 46.2 + SIN(X)
```

We will also find it extremely useful to use variables, instead of constants, as subscripts. The following loop will initialize all elements of the array J to the value 10:

```
DO 13 I=1,5
   J(I) = 10
13 CONTINUE
```

J(1)	10
J(2)	10
J(3)	10
J(4)	10
J(5)	10

The next loop initializes the array J to the values shown on the right:

```
DO 20 I=1,5
   J(I) = I
20 CONTINUE
```

J(1)	1
J(2)	2
J(3)	3
J(4)	4
J(5)	5

The values of the array DIST are initialized to real values with this set of statements:

```
DO 5 K=1,4
   DIST(K) = K*1.5
5 CONTINUE
```

DIST(1)	1.5
DIST(2)	3.0
DIST(3)	4.5
DIST(4)	6.0

The previous examples illustrate that a subscript can be an integer constant or an integer variable. Subscripts can also be integer expressions, as indicated in the following statements:

```
J(2*I) = 3
R(J) = R(J-1)
B1 = TR(2*I) + TR(2*I+1)
```

Whenever an expression is used as a subscript, be sure the value of the expression is between the starting and ending subscript, which is usually 1 to N, where N is the size of the array. If a subscript is outside the proper range, the program will not work correctly. With some compilers, a logic error message is given if a subscript is out of bounds, but other compilers will use an incorrect value for the invalid array reference, causing serious and difficult-to-detect errors.

6-2   DATA STATEMENT

The DATA statement is a specification statement and thus is nonexecutable. It can be very useful in initializing both simple variables and arrays. The general form of the DATA statement is:

DATA   *list of variable names /list of values/*

An example of a DATA statement to initialize simple variables is given below:

```
DATA  SUM, VEL, VOLT, LENGTH /0.0, 32.75, -10.0, 10/
```

The number of data values must match the number of variable names. The data values should also be in the correct type so that the computer does not have to convert them. The DATA statement above initializes the following variables:

SUM	0.0
VEL	32.75
VOLT	-10.0
LENGTH	10

Since the DATA statement is a specification statement, it must be before any executable statements. Thus, it is located near the beginning of your program, along with the REAL, INTEGER, and DIMENSION statements. Normally, it follows these other specification statements because any changes in the type of variables or the declaration of an array must be done before values are given to the corresponding memory locations.

When using the DATA statement, you should be cautious because the DATA statement initializes values only at the beginning of the program execution. This means that the DATA statement cannot be used in a loop to reinitialize variables. If it is necessary to reinitialize variables, you must use assignment statements.

If a number of values are to be repeated in the list of values, a constant followed by an asterisk indicates a repetition. Thus, the following statement initializes all four locations to zero:

```
DATA   A, B, C, D   /4*0.0/
```

The next two statements initialize the variables I, J, and K to 1, and X, Y, and Z to −0.5:

```
DATA   I, J, K, X, Y, Z /3*1, 3*-0.5/
```

or

```
DATA   I, X, J, Y, K, Z /3*(1, -0.5)/
```

A DATA statement can also be used to initialize one or more elements of an array, as follows:

```
DIMENSION   J(5), TIME(4)
DATA   J, TIME /5*0, 1.0, 2.0, 3.0, 4.0/
```

$$J \quad \boxed{0} \ \boxed{0} \ \boxed{0} \ \boxed{0} \ \boxed{0}$$

$$\text{TIME} \quad \boxed{1.0} \ \boxed{2.0} \ \boxed{3.0} \ \boxed{4.0}$$

or

```
DIMENSION   FREQ(5)
DATA   FREQ(1) /60.0/
```

$$\text{FREQ} \quad \boxed{60.0} \ \boxed{?} \ \boxed{?} \ \boxed{?} \ \boxed{?}$$

The question marks indicate that some array elements are not initialized by the data statement. A syntax error would occur if the subscript were left off the array reference FREQ(1) because the number of variables would then not match the number of data values. That is, FREQ represents five variables but FREQ(1) represents only one variable.

6-3 INPUT AND OUTPUT OF ONE-DIMENSIONAL ARRAYS

To read data into an array from a terminal or from cards, we can use the list-directed READ statement or the READ/FORMAT combination. If we wish to read an entire array, we can use the name of the array without subscripts. We can also specify specific elements in a READ statement. If the array A contains three elements, then the following two READ statements are equivalent. If the array A contains 8 elements, then the first READ statement will read values for all 8 elements and the second READ statement will read values for only the first 3 elements.

```
READ(5,1)A
READ(5,1)A(1), A(2), A(3)
```

Arrays may also be read with an *implied* DO loop. Implied DO loops use the indexing feature of the DO statement and may be used only on input and output statements and DATA statements. For example, if we wish to read the first 10 elements of the array A, we can use the following implied DO loop on the READ statement:

```
READ(5,1)(A(I), I=1,10)
```

Further examples illustrate the use of these techniques for reading data into an array.

EXAMPLE 6-1   Temperature Measurements

A set of 50 temperature measurements has been entered into a data file, one value per line, in columns 1–5 using an F5.1 format. The file is accessed with unit number 9. Give a set of statements to read this data into an array.

TEMP(1)	⟵	data file line 1
TEMP(2)	⟵	data file line 2
.		.
.		.
.		.
TEMP(50)	⟵	data file line 50

Solution 1

The READ statement in this solution reads one value, but the READ statement is in a loop executed 50 times and thus will read the entire array.

```
DIMENSION  TEMP(50)
    .
    .
    .
DO 10 I=1,50
    READ(9,2)TEMP(I)
2   FORMAT(F5.1)
10 CONTINUE
    .
    .
    .
```

Solution 2

The READ statement in this solution contains no subscript and hence will read the entire array. Since the format contains only one specification, each value will be read from a different data line.

```
DIMENSION  TEMP(50)
      .
      .
      .
      READ(9,2)TEMP
    2 FORMAT(F5.1)
      .
      .
      .
```

Solution 3

The READ statement in this solution contains an implied loop and is equivalent to a READ statement that listed TEMP(1), TEMP(2), ..., TEMP(50). Since the format contains only one specification, each value will be read from a different data line.

```
DIMENSION  TEMP(50)
      .
      .
      .
      READ(9,2)(TEMP(I), I=1,50)
    2 FORMAT(F5.1)
      .
      .
      .
```
◇

EXAMPLE 6-2 Snowfall Data

A set of 28 snowfall measurements are stored in a data file, with 1 week of data per line in a 7F5.2 format. The unit number is again assumed to be 9. Give statements to read this data into an array called SNOW.

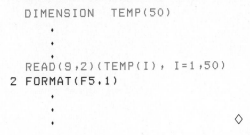

SNOW(1) SNOW(2) . . . SNOW(7)   ⟵   data file line 1
SNOW(8) SNOW(9) . . . SNOW(14)   ⟵   data file line 2
SNOW(15) SNOW(16) . . . SNOW(21)   ⟵   data file line 3
SNOW(22) SNOW(23) . . . SNOW(28)   ⟵   data file line 4

Correct Solution

The READ statement in this solution contains no subscript and hence will read the entire array. Since the format contains 7 specifications, 4 lines of data are required.

```
DIMENSION  SNOW(28)
      .
      .
      .
  READ(9,1)SNOW
1 FORMAT(7F5.2)
      .
      .
      .
```

Incorrect Solution

The READ statement in this solution reads one value, and the READ statement is in a loop executed 28 times. Thus, 28 lines of data are required. Since the data file is entered on 4 lines, an error will occur.

```
DIMENSION  SNOW(28)
      .
      .
      .
   DO 10 I=1,28
      READ(9,1)SNOW(I)
 1      FORMAT(7F5.2)
10 CONTINUE
      .
      .
      .                              ◇
```

Techniques to print the values in an array are similar to those used to read values into an array. The following examples will illustrate the use of DO loops and implied loops for arrays in WRITE statements.

EXAMPLE 6-3   Mass Measurements

A group of 30 mass measurements are stored in an array MASS. We want to print these values in the following tabulation:

MASS(1) = XXX KG   MASS(16) = XXX KG
MASS(2) = XXX KG   MASS(17) = XXX KG
        .   .
        .   .
        .   .
MASS(15) = XXX KG   MASS(30) = XXX KG

Solution

For each output line, we need to reference one value in the array, and then another value which is 15 values away from the first value. Thus, if I is a subscript for the first value, then I + 15 is the subscript desired for the second value. The values for I can be generated with a DO statement that has an index range of 1 through 15. The value for the other subscript, I + 15, can be computed with an arithmetic expression. The output format in this solution is important; go through it carefully to be sure you understand how it works.

```
DIMENSION  MASS(30)
     .
     .
     .
   DO 10 I=1,15
      WRITE(6,5)I, MASS(I), I + 15, MASS(I+15)
 5    FORMAT(' ',2('MASS(',I2,') = ',I3,1X,'KG',10X))
10 CONTINUE
     .
     .
     .
```

Incorrect Solution

This solution includes an implied loop that will print MASS(1), MASS(2), and their subscripts on the first line, MASS(3), MASS(4), and their subscripts on the second line, and so on. Clearly this is incorrect, since we wanted MASS(1) and MASS(15) on the first line.

```
DIMENSION  MASS(30)
     .
     .
     .
   WRITE(6,5)(I, MASS(I), I = 1,30)
 5 FORMAT(' ',2('MASS(',I2,') = ',I3,2X,'KG',10X))
     .
     .
     .
```

◇

EXAMPLE 6-4   Distance, Velocity, Acceleration

Arrays DIS, VEL, and ACC each contain 50 values. The first value in each array represents the distance, velocity, and acceleration of a test rocket at time equal to 1 second. The second set of values represent data for time equal to 2 seconds, and so on. Print the data in the following tabulation:

TIME (SEC)	DISTANCE (M)	VELOCITY (M/SEC)	ACCELERATION (M/SEC**2)
1	XXX.XX	XXX.XX	XXX.XX
2	XXX.XX	XXX.XX	XXX.XX
.	.	.	.
.	.	.	.
.	.	.	.
50	XXX.XX	XXX.XX	XXX.XX

Correct Solution 1

This solution uses an implied loop to specify the order of variables on the output statement. The subscript I is listed first, followed by the corresponding values in the arrays DIS, VEL, and ACC. This order is repeated as the subscript varies from 1 through 50. Since the format contains only 4 specifications for printing values, each set of 4 values [I, DIS(I), VEL(I), ACC(I)] is printed on a new line.

```
      DIMENSION  DIS(50), VEL(50), ACC(50)
         .
         .
         .
      WRITE(6,10)
10 FORMAT('1',,'TIME',10X,'DISTANCE',10X,'VELOCITY',
   +        10X,'ACCELERATION'/1X,'(SEC)',9X,'(M)',15X,
   +        '(M/SEC)',11X,'(M/SEC**2)'/)
      WRITE(6,15)(I, DIS(I), VEL(I), ACC(I), I=1,50)
15 FORMAT(' ',I3,12X,F6.2,12X,F6.2,14X,F6.2)
         .
         .
         .
```

Correct Solution 2

The only difference between this solution and the previous solution is that the implied loop has been replaced with a DO loop. Thus, this solution is the equivalent of 50 WRITE statements, each with 4 output variables.

```
      DIMENSION  DIS(50), VEL(50), ACC(50)
         .
         .
         .
      WRITE(6,10)
10 FORMAT('1',,'TIME',10X,'DISTANCE',10X,'VELOCITY',
   +        10X,'ACCELERATION'/1X,'(SEC)',9X,'(M)',15X,
   +        '(M/SEC)',11X,'(M/SEC**2)'/)
      DO 20 I=1,50
         WRITE(6,15)I, DIS(I), VEL(I), ACC(I)
15       FORMAT(' ',I3,12X,F6.2,12X,F6.2,14X,F6.2)
20 CONTINUE
         .
         .
         .
```

Incorrect Solution

```
   DIMENSION  DIS(50),  VEL(50),  ACC(50)
      .
      .
      .
   WRITE(6,10)
10 FORMAT('1','TIME',10X,'DISTANCE',10X,'VELOCITY',
  +        10X,'ACCELERATION',/1X,'(SEC)',9X,'(M)',15X,
  +        '(M/SEC)',11X,'(M/SEC**2)'/)
   DO 30 I=1,50
      WRITE(6,15)I, DIS, VEL, ACC
15    FORMAT(' ',I3,12X,F6.2,12X,F6.2,14X,F6.2)
30    CONTINUE
      .
      .
      .
```

This solution is incorrect for any format because each time through the loop, we are printing the index I, the *entire* array DIS (50 values), then the *entire* array VEL (50 values), and the *entire* array ACC (50 values). Thus, each time through the loop, we print 151 values! ◊

6-4 APPLICATION – National Park Snowfall Statistics

The following example will illustrate the use of a one-dimensional array to store data that needs to be accessed twice; first to find the average and then to compare each value to the average. For clarity, we include DIMENSION statements at the beginning of both refined pseudocode and refined flowcharts.

EXAMPLE 6-5 Snowfall Statistics

The snowfall for the month of January has been stored in a data file called JAN. Each data line contains a snowfall amount recorded in inches, in an F5.1 format. Line 1 contains the data for January 1st, line 2 contains the data for January 2nd, and so on. Determine the daily snowfall average for January and the number of days with snowfall above this daily average.

Solution

We will use an array to store the 31 snowfall values. The average is computed by dividing the total snowfall by the number of days. Then each of the 31 entries is compared to the average to see if it was above the average snowfall. If we needed only the average, an array would not be necessary. Instead, the same variable could be used to read each snowfall amount which would be added to a total amount. The total amount of snowfall would be divided by 31 to find the average. However, since the problem also requires that a count of the

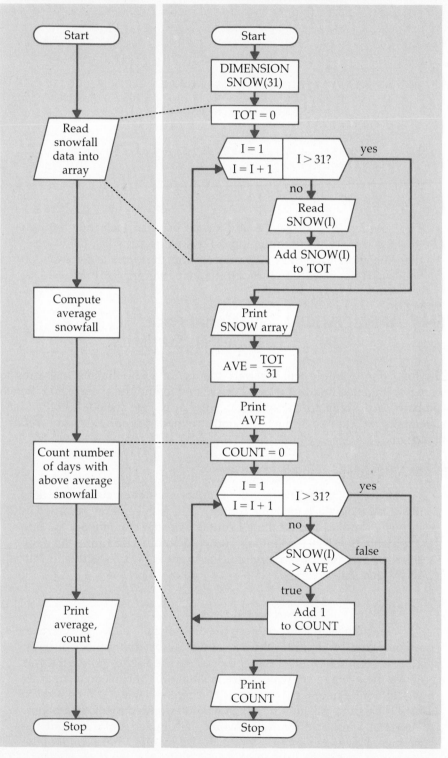

number of days with above-average snowfall be printed, the individual snowfall amounts are needed a second time. The refined flowchart on page 180 clearly shows the two separate loops needed. The snowfall array has also been printed to ensure that the array was read correctly.

FORTRAN Program

```
      PROGRAM  SNOFAL
C
C  THIS PROGRAM COMPUTES THE AVERAGE SNOWFALL
C  FOR JANUARY AND COUNTS THE NUMBER OF DAYS
C  WITH ABOVE AVERAGE SNOWFALL
C
      DIMENSION  SNOW(31)
      INTEGER   COUNT
C
      OPEN(UNIT=10, FILE='JAN', STATUS='OLD')
C
      TOT = 0.0
      DO 10 I=1,31
         READ(10,5)SNOW(I)
    5    FORMAT(F5.1)
         TOT = TOT + SNOW(I)
   10 CONTINUE
C
      WRITE(6,15)SNOW
   15 FORMAT(1X,5F6.1)
C
      AVE = TOT/31.0
C
      WRITE(6,18)AVE
   18 FORMAT('0','AVERAGE SNOWFALL IS',F6.1,' INCHES')
C
      COUNT = 0
      DO 20 I=1,31
         IF(SNOW(I).GT.AVE)COUNT = COUNT + 1
   20 CONTINUE
C
      WRITE(6,30)COUNT
   30 FORMAT('0',I3,' DAYS WITH ABOVE-AVERAGE SNOWFALL')
C
      STOP
      END
```

```
     5.2   38.0   26.4   15.5    8.2
    16.2    3.0    1.5    0.3    0.0
     0.0    0.0    0.3    1.2    5.7
     6.9    1.2    0.5    0.0    2.1
     6.1   10.4    9.5   14.9    1.6
     3.0    3.1    2.9    1.5    0.9
     0.7

   AVERAGE SNOWFALL IS   6.0 INCHES

   10 DAYS WITH ABOVE-AVERAGE SNOWFALL
```

◇

6-5 APPLICATION – Method of Least Squares

When working with experimental or *empirical* data, we are often interested in determining the equation of a straight line that represents a good fit to the data. If the data values represent a linear relationship, a corresponding linear equation can then be used to estimate values for which we have no data. For instance, suppose that the following data represents the load-deflection curve of a coil spring, where LENGTH is the length of the spring in inches and LOAD is the load or weight applied in pounds.

LOAD	LENGTH
0.28	6.62
0.50	5.93
0.67	4.46
0.93	4.25
1.15	3.30
1.38	3.15
1.60	2.43
1.98	1.46

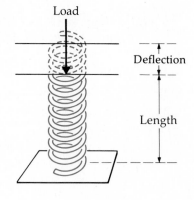

Given a linear equation that represents a good fit to the data, we could then estimate the initial length of the spring by substituting a value of zero for the load in the equation. Similarly, the load that causes the spring to have a length of 5 inches could also be calculated. The following plot contains the original data points plus an estimate of the position of the straight line that represents a good fit to the data.

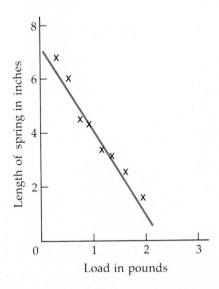

The *method of least squares* is a standard technique used for determining the equation of a straight line from a set of data. Recall that the equation of a straight line is:

$$y = m \cdot x + b$$

where m is the slope of the line and b is the y-intercept. Given a set of data, such as the load-versus-length values for the spring problem, the slope and y-intercept can be calculated using the following equations, which are derived from differential calculus. The symbol Σ represents summation. Therefore, given the set of points $\{(x_1,y_1), (x_2,y_2), \ldots, (x_n,y_n)\}$, let

$$\sum x = x_1 + x_2 + \cdots + x_n$$
$$\sum y = y_1 + y_2 + \cdots + y_n$$
$$\sum xy = x_1y_1 + x_2y_2 + \cdots + x_ny_n$$
$$\sum x^2 = x_1^2 + x_1^2 + \cdots + x_n^2$$

Then the slope and y-intercept can be calculated using these equations:

$$\text{slope} = \frac{\sum x \sum y - n \sum (x \cdot y)}{(\sum x)^2 - n \sum (x^2)}$$

$$y\text{-intercept} = \frac{\sum y - \text{slope} \cdot \sum x}{n}$$

Once the slope and y-intercept have been calculated, the equation of the line can be obtained.

If the data points and the straight line were drawn on a piece of graph paper, it would be possible to see how closely the line fits the data. Another way to see how well the line fits the data would be to take an x value and put it in the equation, thus calculating the y value. This new y value, designated $\hat{y}$, would be an estimate for the value of y when x is given. For example, suppose the least-squares technique yielded the following linear equation for a set of data:

$$y = 4.2x - 3.1$$

Then, for the data-point coordinate (1.0,.9), the estimate for y would be

$$\hat{y} = 4.2(1.0) - 3.1 = 1.1$$

The *residual* for a data point is the difference between the actual data value for y and its estimated value, $y - \hat{y}$. The residual for the data point above is (.9 − 1.1) or −0.2. If we sum the squares of the residuals, called the *residual sum*, we get an estimate of the quality of fit of the data to the linear equation without plotting the data. When the data is exactly linear, the residual sum is zero. As the residual sum becomes larger, the less the data is estimated by the linear equation.

EXAMPLE 6-6   Least-Squares Fit

Assume that the load-deflection data given at the beginning of this section is punched on two cards, all the x values (load) on one card and all the y values (length) on another card, in an 8F5.2 format. Compute the linear equation that best fits this data, using the least-squares method, and determine the corresponding residual sum.

Use the following output form:

THE LINEAR EQUATION IS
Y = xxx.x   X + xxx.x

ORIGINAL VALUES OF X	ORIGINAL VALUES OF Y	ESTIMATED VALUES OF Y	Y RESIDUALS
XX.XX	XX.XX	XX.XX	XX.XX
.	.	.	.
.	.	.	.
.	.	.	.

RESIDUAL SUM = XX.XX

Solution

We must use arrays for the x- and y-coordinates because we will need to access the individual data values after computing the slope and y-intercept in order to calculate the residual sum. Observe the changes in the pseudocode as we refine the general pseudocode into the more detailed pseudocode.

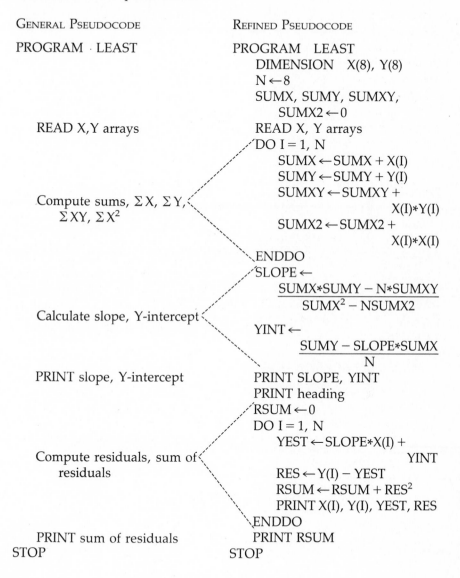

GENERAL PSEUDOCODE

PROGRAM · LEAST

READ X,Y arrays

Compute sums, ΣX, ΣY,
ΣXY, ΣX^2

Calculate slope, Y-intercept

PRINT slope, Y-intercept

Compute residuals, sum of
residuals

PRINT sum of residuals
STOP

REFINED PSEUDOCODE

PROGRAM   LEAST
DIMENSION   X(8), Y(8)
N ← 8
SUMX, SUMY, SUMXY,
    SUMX2 ← 0
READ X, Y arrays
DO I = 1, N
    SUMX ← SUMX + X(I)
    SUMY ← SUMY + Y(I)
    SUMXY ← SUMXY +
        X(I)*Y(I)
    SUMX2 ← SUMX2 +
        X(I)*X(I)
ENDDO
SLOPE ←
    $$\frac{SUMX*SUMY - N*SUMXY}{SUMX^2 - NSUMX2}$$
YINT ←
    $$\frac{SUMY - SLOPE*SUMX}{N}$$
PRINT SLOPE, YINT
PRINT heading
RSUM ← 0
DO I = 1, N
    YEST ← SLOPE*X(I) +
        YINT
    RES ← Y(I) − YEST
    RSUM ← RSUM + RES^2
    PRINT X(I), Y(I), YEST, RES
ENDDO
PRINT RSUM
STOP

FORTRAN Program

```
      PROGRAM  LEAST
C
C THIS PROGRAM COMPUTES A LINEAR EQUATION TO FIT
C A SET OF DATA. IT THEN COMPUTES A RESIDUAL SUM
C TO DETERMINE THE GOODNESS OF THE FIT.
C
      DIMENSION  X(8), Y(8)
      DATA  N, SUMX, SUMY, SUMXY, SUMX2 /8, 4*0.0/
C
      READ(5,1)X, Y
    1 FORMAT(8F5.2)
C
      DO 10 I=1,N
          SUMX = SUMX + X(I)
          SUMY = SUMY + Y(I)
          SUMXY = SUMXY + X(I)*Y(I)
          SUMX2 = SUMX2 + X(I)*X(I)
   10 CONTINUE
C
      SLOPE = (SUMX*SUMY - N*SUMXY)/
     +        (SUMX*SUMX - N*SUMX2)
      YINT =  (SUMY - SLOPE*SUMX)/N
C
      WRITE(6,20)SLOPE, YINT
   20 FORMAT(1X,17X,'THE LINEAR EQUATION IS'/1X,18X,'Y = ',
     +        F5.2,' X + ',F5.2)
C
      WRITE(6,25)
   25 FORMAT('0',' ORIGINAL',7X,'ORIGINAL',7X,
     +        'ESTIMATED',9X,'Y'/1X,'VALUES OF X',4X,
     +        'VALUES OF Y',4X,'VALUES OF Y',4X,
     +        'RESIDUALS'/)
C
      RSUM = 0.0
      DO 30 I=1,N
          YEST = SLOPE*X(I) + YINT
          RES = Y(I) - YEST
          RSUM = RSUM + RES*RES
          WRITE(6,28)X(I), Y(I), YEST, RES
   28     FORMAT(1X,3X,F5.2,10X,F5.2,10X,F5.2,9X,F5.2)
   30 CONTINUE
C
      WRITE(6,35)RSUM
   35 FORMAT('0',20X,'RESIDUAL SUM = ',F5.2)
C
      STOP
      END
```

```
             THE LINEAR EQUATION IS
              Y = -2.93 X +   7.06

   ORIGINAL          ORIGINAL          ESTIMATED            Y
 VALUES OF X       VALUES OF Y       VALUES OF Y       RESIDUALS

    0.28              6.62              6.24              0.38
    0.50              5.93              5.59              0.34
    0.67              4.46              5.10             -0.64
    0.93              4.25              4.33             -0.08
    1.15              3.30              3.69             -0.39
    1.38              3.15              3.02              0.13
    1.60              2.43              2.37              0.06
    1.98              1.46              1.26              0.20

              RESIDUAL SUM =   0.88
```

◊

6-6   STORAGE AND INITIALIZATION OF TWO-DIMENSIONAL ARRAYS

If we visualize a one-dimensional array as a single column of data, we can then visualize a group of columns, as illustrated below:

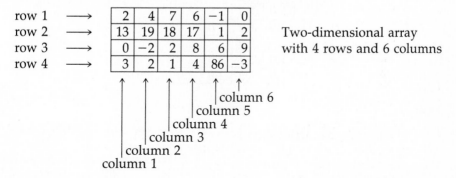

The diagram depicts an integer array with 24 elements. As in one-dimensional arrays, each of the 24 elements has the same array name. However, one subscript is not sufficient to specify an element in a two-dimensional array. For instance, if the array's name is M, it is not clear if M(3) should be the third element in the first row or the third element in the first column. To avoid any ambiguity, an element in a two-dimensional array will be referenced with two subscripts, one for the row number and one for the column number. The first subscript references the row and the second subscript references the column. Thus, M(2, 3) refers to the number in the second row and third column. In our diagram, M(2, 3) contains 18.

Two-dimensional arrays must be specified in a DIMENSION statement or a type statement, but not both. The DIMENSION statement below reserves storage for a one-dimensional real array B of 10 elements, a two-dimensional real array C with 3 rows and 5 columns, and a two-dimensional integer array J with 7 rows and 4 columns. The REAL statement reserves storage for a two-dimensional real array NUM with 5 rows and 2 columns. If the DIMENSION statement included NUM(5,2) along with the REAL statement, a compile error would occur.

```
DIMENSION  B(10), C(3,5), J(7,4)
REAL  NUM(5,2)
```

The statement

```
DIMENSION  R(0:2, -1:1)
```

reserves storage for array elements $R(0, -1)$, $R(0, 0)$, $R(0, 1)$, $R(1, -1)$, $R(1, 0)$, $R(1, 1)$, $R(2, -1)$, $R(2, 0)$, $R(2, 1)$.

Two-dimensional arrays can be initialized with assignment statements or with the DATA statement. If the name of the array is used without implied loops, the array will be filled in column order, as illustrated by the next example. When subscripts are used to access a two-dimensional array, it is common notation to use I for the row subscript and J for the column subscript.

EXAMPLE 6-7   Array Initialization, A(5, 4)

Fill the array A as shown:

1.0	1.0	2.0	2.0
1.0	1.0	2.0	2.0
1.0	1.0	2.0	2.0
1.0	1.0	2.0	2.0
1.0	1.0	2.0	2.0

Solution 1

```
DIMENSION  A(5,4)
DATA  A /10*1.0, 10*2.0/
     .
     .
     .
```

Solution 2

```
        DIMENSION  A(5,4)
            .
            .
            .
        DO 10 I=1,5
           A(I,1) = 1.0
           A(I,2) = 1.0
           A(I,3) = 2.0
           A(I,4) = 2.0
    10 CONTINUE
            .
            .
            .
```

Clearly the DATA statement presents the better solution for this example. ◇

EXAMPLE 6-8   Array Initialization, M(4, 3)

Fill the array M as shown:

1	1	1
2	2	2
3	3	3
4	4	4

Solution 1

If we observe that each element of the array contains its corresponding row number, then a solution is:

```
        DIMENSION  M(4,3)
            .
            .
            .
        DO 10 I=1,4
           DO 5 J=1,3
              M(I,J) = I
     5     CONTINUE
    10 CONTINUE
            .
            .
            .
```

Solution 2

The following DATA statement will also initialize the array correctly:

```
DIMENSION  M(4,3)
DATA  M /3*(1, 2, 3, 4)/
      .
      .
      .
```

Again, the DATA statement solution is preferable because only one statement is required. ◇

EXAMPLE 6-9   Identity Matrix

Fill the integer array TOTAL with 5 rows and 5 columns with 1's on the main diagonal and zeros elsewhere. This is called a 5×5 *identity matrix*. It is also a *square matrix* because it has the same number of rows and columns.

1	0	0	0	0
0	1	0	0	0
0	0	1	0	0
0	0	0	1	0
0	0	0	0	1

Solution

The positions that contain 1's are positions where the row number and column number are the same (TOTAL(1,1), TOTAL(2,2), TOTAL(3,3), TOTAL(4,4), TOTAL(5,5)).

```
        INTEGER  TOTAL(5,5)
           .
           .
           .
     DO 10 I=1,5
        DO 5 J=1,5
           IF(I.EQ.J)THEN
              TOTAL(I,J) = 1
           ELSE
              TOTAL(I,J) = 0
           ENDIF
  5       CONTINUE
 10 CONTINUE
           .
           .
           .                              ◇
```

6-7 INPUT AND OUTPUT OF TWO-DIMENSIONAL ARRAYS

The main difference between using values from a one-dimensional array and using values from a two-dimensional array is that two subscripts are required instead of one subscript. Hence most loops used in the reading or writing of two-dimensional arrays are usually nested loops.

EXAMPLE 6-10   Medical Data

Analysis of a medical experiment requires the use of a set of data containing the weight of 100 participants at the beginning of an experiment and at the end of the experiment. The data have been stored in a data file and will be accessed using unit number 13. Each line in the file contains the initial weight and final weight of a participant in a 2F7.2 format. Give statements to read the data into a two-dimensional array.

Solution 1

```
      DIMENSION  WEIGHT(100,2)
          .
          .
          .
      DO 10 I=1,100
          READ(13,5)WEIGHT(I,1), WEIGHT(I,2)
    5     FORMAT(2F7.2)
   10 CONTINUE
          .
          .
          .
```

Solution 2

```
   DIMENSION  WEIGHT(100,2)
       .
       .
       .
   READ(13,5)(WEIGHT(I,1), WEIGHT(I,2), I=1,100)
 5 FORMAT(2F7.2)
       .
       .
       .
```

◇

EXAMPLE 6-11   Terminal Inventory

A large technical firm keeps an inventory of the location of its computer terminals in a two-dimensional array. There are 4 types of terminals, represented by the 4 columns, and 20 laboratories using the terminals, represented by the 20 rows. Assume the data are stored in an array called LOCATE. Print the data on a new page in the following form:

	TERMINAL INVENTORY			
	TYPE 1	TYPE 2	TYPE 3	TYPE 4
LAB 1	XX	XX	XX	XX
LAB 2	XX	XX	XX	XX
.	.	.	.	.
.	.	.	.	.
.	.	.	.	.
LAB 20	XX	XX	XX	XX

Solution 1

This solution uses the index of a DO loop as the row subscript. Then the index of an implied loop on the WRITE statement supplies the column subscript. Hence, each time the WRITE statement is executed, one row of data is printed.

```
      DIMENSION  LOCATE(20,4)
         .
         .
         .
C
      WRITE(6,100)
  100 FORMAT('1',26X,'TERMINAL INVENTORY'/13X,'TYPE 1',
     +          8X,'TYPE 2',8X,'TYPE 3',8X,'TYPE 4')
C
      DO 200 I=1,20
         WRITE(6,150)(I, (LOCATE(I,J), J=1,4))
  150    FORMAT(' ','LAB',I3,4(9X,I2,3X))
  200 CONTINUE
         .
         .
         .
```

Solution 2

This solution uses nested implied loops to supply the row and column subscripts. It is the format that causes a new line of output to be printed for each row.

```
      DIMENSION  LOCATE(20,4)
            .
            .
            .
C
      WRITE(6,100)
  100 FORMAT('1',26X,'TERMINAL INVENTORY'/13X,'TYPE 1',
     +          8X,'TYPE 2',8X,'TYPE 3',8X,'TYPE 4')
C
      WRITE(6,150)(I, (LOCATE(I,J), J=1,4), I=1,20)
  150 FORMAT(' ','LAB',I3,4(9X,I2,3X))
```

◇

6-8 APPLICATION – Analysis of Power Plant Data

The following table of data represents typical power output in megawatts from a power plant over a period of 8 weeks. Each row represents 1 week's data; each column represents data taken from the same day of the week. The data is stored in a data file called POWER with 8 lines in a 7I4 format.

	Day 1	Day 2	Day 3	Day 4	Day 5	Day 6	Day 7
Week 1	207	301	222	302	22	167	125
Week 2	367	60	120	111	301	400	434
Week 3	211	72	441	102	21	203	317
Week 4	401	340	161	297	441	117	206
Week 5	448	111	370	220	264	444	207
Week 6	21	313	204	222	446	401	337
Week 7	213	208	444	321	320	335	313
Week 8	162	137	265	44	370	315	322

EXAMPLE 6-12   Power Plant Data

Write a program to read the information in the data file POWER and then print the following composite report:

COMPOSITE INFORMATION
AVERAGE DAILY POWER OUTPUT = XXX.X   MEGAWATTS
NUMBER OF DAYS WITH GREATER THAN AVERAGE POWER
    OUTPUT = XX
DAY(S) WITH MINIMUM POWER OUTPUT:

	WEEK	X	DAY	X
	WEEK	X	DAY	X
	.		.	
	.		.	
	.		.	
	WEEK	X	DAY	X

Solution

Begin analyzing this problem by first looking at each piece of output required:

1　The average daily power output will be calculated from a sum of all the power outputs divided by 56.

2　After the average is calculated, we can compare it to the individual power values to see how many are above average.

3　We will also need to find the minimum power output. The best way to accomplish this is to store the first power output in a new variable MIN. Then compare each power output to MIN, and, if a smaller value is found, replace the old value with this new power value. After comparing all values in the array to MIN in this manner, the smallest value will be in MIN.

4　We can determine the day and week numbers for those days having minimum output by comparing each power output to MIN and printing the subscripts of locations whose power output equals MIN.

Steps (1) and (3) can be done on the same pass through the data. Steps (2) and (4) will need to be done on separate passes through the data because of the order of the output required in the report. We now take these steps and combine them into pseudocode.

GENERAL PSEUDOCODE	REFINED PSEUDOCODE
PROGRAM PWRPLT	PROGRAM PWRPLT
	DIMENSION POWER(8,7)
READ POWER array	READ POWER
	TPOWER ← 0
	MIN ← POWER(1,1)
	DO I = 1,8
	DO J = 1,7
	TPOWER ←
	TPOWER + POWER(I,J)
Compute average power	IF POWER(I,J) < MIN
Find minimum power	THEN
	MIN ← POWER(I,J)
	ENDIF
	ENDDO
	ENDDO
	AVE ← TPOWER/56
PRINT average power	PRINT AVE
	OVERAV ← 0
	DO I = 1,8
	DO J = 1,7
Count days with above-	IF POWER (I,J) > AVE
average power	THEN
	OVERAV ←
	OVERAV + 1
	ENDIF
	ENDDO
	ENDDO
PRINT count of days with	PRINT OVERAV
above-average power	DO I = 1,8
	DO J = 1,7
PRINT days with minimum	IF POWER(I,J) = MIN
power	THEN
	WRITE I, J
	ENDIF
	ENDDO
	ENDDO
STOP	STOP

FORTRAN Program

```
      PROGRAM   PWRPLT
C
C  THIS PROGRAM COMPUTES AND PRINTS A COMPOSITE
C  REPORT COVERING 8 WEEKS FOR A POWER PLANT
C
      INTEGER   POWER(8,7), TPOWER, OVERAV
C
      OPEN(UNIT=10, FILE='POWER', STATUS='OLD')
C
      READ(10,10)((POWER(I,J), J=1,7), I=1,8)
   10 FORMAT(7I4)
C
      TPOWER = 0
      MIN = POWER(1,1)
      DO 100 I=1,8
         DO 50 J=1,7
            TPOWER = TPOWER + POWER(I,J)
            IF(POWER(I,J).LT.MIN)MIN = POWER(I,J)
   50    CONTINUE
  100 CONTINUE
C
      AVE = TPOWER/56.0
C
      WRITE(6,150)AVE
  150 FORMAT('1',18X,'COMPOSITE INFORMATION'/1X,
     +          'AVERAGE DAILY POWER OUTPUT = ',F5.1,
     +          ' MEGAWATTS')
C
      OVERAV = 0
      DO 300 I=1,8
         DO 200 J=1,7
            IF(POWER(I,J).GT.AVE)OVERAV = OVERAV + 1
  200    CONTINUE
  300 CONTINUE
C
      WRITE(6,350)OVERAV
  350 FORMAT(1X,'NUMBER OF DAYS WITH GREATER THAN ',
     +          'AVERAGE POWER OUTPUT = ',I2/1X,'DAY(S) ',
     +          'WITH MINIMUM POWER OUTPUT:')
C
      DO 400 I=1,8
         DO 375 J=1,7
            IF(POWER(I,J).EQ.MIN)WRITE(6,360)I, J
  360       FORMAT(14X,'WEEK',I2,2X,'DAY',I2)
  375    CONTINUE
  400 CONTINUE
C
      STOP
      END
```

```
                    COMPOSITE INFORMATION
AVERAGE DAILY POWER OUTPUT = 254.4 MEGAWATTS
NUMBER OF DAYS WITH GREATER THAN AVERAGE POWER OUTPUT = 29
DAY(S) WITH MINIMUM POWER OUTPUT:
            WEEK 3  DAY 5
            WEEK 6  DAY 1
```

◇

6-9 MULTI-DIMENSIONAL ARRAYS

FORTRAN allows as many as seven dimensions for arrays. We can easily visualize a three-dimensional array, such as a cube. We are also familiar with using three coordinates, X, Y, Z, to locate points. This idea extends into subscripts. The three-dimensional array below would be dimensioned T(3,4,4):

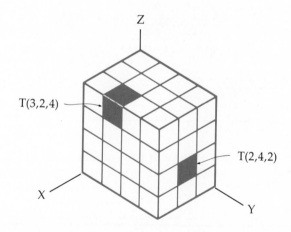

If we use the three-dimensional array name without subscripts, we access the array with the first subscript changing fastest, the second subscript changing next fastest, and the third subscript changing the slowest. Thus, using the array T of the previous diagram, the two statements below would be equivalent:

```
READ(5,1)T
READ(5,1)(((T(I,J,K), I=1,3), J=1,4), K=1,4)
```

It should be evident that three levels of nesting are often needed to access a three-dimensional array.

Most applications do not use arrays with more than three dimensions, probably because visualizing more than three dimensions seems to become abstract. However, here is a simple scheme that allows you to mentally picture even a seven-dimensional array:

Four-dimensional array: Picture a row of three-dimensional arrays. One subscript, the first, specifies a unique three-dimensional array. The other three subscripts specify a unique position in that array.

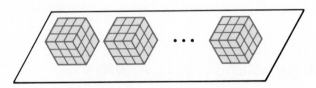

Five-dimensional array: Picture a block or grid of three-dimensional arrays. Two subscripts (first and second) specify a unique three-dimensional array. The other three subscripts specify a unique position in that array.

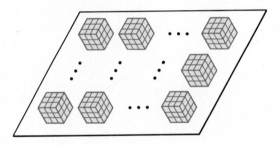

Six-dimensional array: Picture a row of blocks or grids. One subscript specifies the grid. The other five subscripts specify the unique position in the grid.

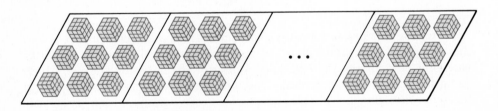

Seven-dimensional array: Picture a grid of grids or a grid of blocks. Two subscripts specify the grid. The other five subscripts specify the unique position in the grid.

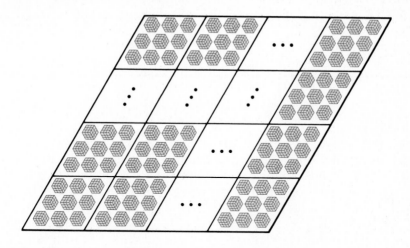

Now that you can visualize multi-dimensional arrays, a natural question is "what dimension array do I use for solving a problem?" There is no single answer. A problem that could be solved with a two-dimensional array of four rows and three columns could also be solved with 4 one-dimensional arrays of three elements each. Usually, the data fits one array form better than another. You should choose the form that will be the easiest for you to work with in your program. For example, if you have census data from 10 countries over the period 1950–1980, you would probably use an array with 10 rows and 31 columns, or 31 rows and 10 columns. If the data represents the populations of 5 cities from each of 10 countries for the period 1950–1980, a three-dimensional array would be most appropriate. The three subscripts would represent year, country, and city.

SUMMARY

In this chapter we learned how to use an array—a group of storage locations that all have a common name but are distinguished by one or more sub-scripts. Arrays prove to be one of the most powerful elements of FORTRAN because they allow us to keep large amounts of data easily accessible by our programs. The remaining chapters will rely heavily on arrays for storing and manipulating data.

KEY WORDS

array

DATA statement

DIMENSION statement

element

empirical data

implied DO loop

least squares

multi-dimensional array

one-dimensional array

subscript

two-dimensional array

DEBUGGING AIDS

Because arrays can be used so conveniently to handle large amounts of data, a natural tendency of new programmers is to use arrays for everything! Unfortunately, using arrays can also introduce new errors. As you debug programs that use arrays, therefore, analyze your decision to use each array. Ask yourself the questions "Do I need this data more than once?" and "Must this data be stored before I can use it?" If the answers to both questions are "No," then you should eliminate the array and replace it with simple variables. You will also probably be eliminating some loops and statements involving subscripts. These changes may not only reduce the number of errors in your program but will also reduce the overall complexity of your program.

If arrays are necessary, then consider each of the following items if your program is working incorrectly:

1 DIMENSION—The DIMENSION statement or a type statement must specify the maximum number of elements that are to be stored in the array. While you do not have to use all the elements of an array, you can never use more elements than specified in the DIMENSION statement or type statement.

2 SUBSCRIPT—Check each subscript to be sure that it represents an integer that falls within the proper range of values. Particularly check for subscript values that are one value too small (such as zero) or one value too large (such as $N + 1$).

3 INDEX—If you are using the index of a DO loop as a subscript, be sure you have used the same variable. That is, if the DO loop index is K, did you use I instead of K as a subscript?

4 REVERSE SUBSCRIPTS—When you are working with multi-dimensional arrays, be sure you have the subscripts in the proper order. Do you want B(K,J) or B(J,K)?

STYLE/TECHNIQUE GUIDES

As we mentioned in Debugging Aids, be sure that you really need an array before implementing an algorithm with an array. If you need arrays to solve your problem, take some time to decide the optimum size. Depending on the application, you may find that a two-dimensional array with 10 rows and 2 columns may be more direct and understandable than two separate arrays of 10 elements each. Choose the array structure that best suits the program.

Be consistent in your choice of subscript names. Common practice is to use the variable I for the first subscript, J for the second subscript, and K for the third subscript. If you follow the same pattern or a similar pattern, it is much easier to decide the nesting of loops and the values of DO loop parameters that are also used as subscripts.

PROBLEMS

In problems 1 though 9, draw the array and indicate the contents of each position in the array after executing the following sets of statements. Assume each set of statements is independent of the others. If no value is given to a particular position, fill it with a question mark.

```
1      DIMENSION  M(10)
       DO 5 I=1,10
          M(I) = I + 1
     5 CONTINUE

2      DIMENSION  M(10)
       DO 20 J=1,9
          M(J+1) = 2
    20 CONTINUE

3      DIMENSION  R(8)
       DO 15 KK=1,8
          R(KK) = 10 - KK
    15 CONTINUE

4      DIMENSION  LST(6)
       DO 1 K=1,6
          J = 7 - K
          LST(J) = K
     1 CONTINUE

5      DIMENSION  R(8)
       DO 10 I=1,8
          IF(I.LE.3)THEN
             R(I) = 2.5
          ELSE
             R(I) = -2.5
          ENDIF
    10 CONTINUE
```

```
6        DIMENSION  R(0:9)
         DO 10 I=1,8
            IF(I.GT.4)R(I) = 4.0
    10 CONTINUE

7        DIMENSION  CH(5,4)
         DO 5 I=1,5
            DO 4 J=1,4
               CH(I,J) = I*J
    4       CONTINUE
    5 CONTINUE

8        DIMENSION  K(5,4)
         DO 5 M=1,4
            DO 4 N=1,4
               K(M,N) = MOD(M+N,3)
    4       CONTINUE
    5 CONTINUE

9        DIMENSION  I(8,2)
         I(8,1) = 4
         I(8,2) = 5
         DO 6 L=1,7
            I(L,1) = 2
            I(L,2) = 3
    6 CONTINUE
```

In problems 10 through 13, assume that K, a one-dimensional array of 50 values, has already been filled with data.

10 Give FORTRAN statements to find and print the maximum value of K in the following form:

MAXIMUM VALUE IS XXXXX

11 Give FORTRAN statements to find and print the minimum value of K, and its position in the array, in the following form:

MINIMUM VALUE OF K IS
K(XX) = XXXXX

12 Give FORTRAN statements to count the number of positive values, zero values, and negative values in K. The output form should be:

XXX   POSITIVE VALUES
XXX   ZERO VALUES
XXX   NEGATIVE VALUES

13 Give FORTRAN statements to replace each value of K with its absolute value. Then print the array K, using 10 elements per line.

14 An array TIME contains 30 numbers. Give statements that will print every other value, beginning with the second value, in this form:

TIME(2) CONTAINS XXX.X   SECONDS
TIME(4) CONTAINS XXX.X   SECONDS
.
.
.
TIME(30) CONTAINS XXX.X   SECONDS

15 An array WIND of 70 integer values represents the average daily wind velocities in Chicago over a 10-week period. Assume the array with 10 rows and 7 columns has been filled. Give FORTRAN statements to print the data such that each week is on a separate line, in a 7I10 format.

CHICAGO WIND VELOCITY (MILES/HOUR)
WIND(1)   WIND(2)   . . .   WIND(7)
WIND(8)   WIND(9)   . . .   WIND(14)
.
.
.
WIND(64)   WIND(65) . . .   WIND(70)

16 Give FORTRAN statements to print the last 10 elements of an array M of size N. For instance, if M contains 25 elements, the output form is:

M(16) = XXX
M(17) = XXX
M(18) = XXX
.
.
.
M(25) = XXX

17 Give FORTRAN statements to interchange the 1st and 100th elements, the 2nd and 99th elements, and so on, of the array NUM which contains 100 values. See diagram that follows.

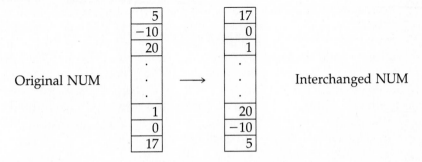

(*Hint:* You will need a temporary storage when you switch values.)

18   Give FORTRAN statements to compare each pair of adjacent values in an array NUM that contains 100 values. Let the subscript of the first value be J and the subscript of the second value be J + 1. If the (J + 1)th value is smaller than the Jth value, then switch the values. See the next diagram. Note that there will be 99 comparisons:

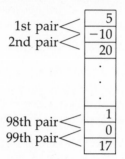

Observe that these statements will not sort the data, but they do cause the maximum value to be shifted to the bottom of the array, in position 100.

19   An array TEST contains test scores from 100 exams. Give the FORTRAN statements necessary to find the average of the first 50 exams and the second 50 exams. Print the following:

AVERAGES

1st 50 EXAMS 2nd 50 EXAMS

XXX.XX   XXX.XX

20   Write a complete program that will read as many as 20 integers from columns 1–4 of data cards. The last card will contain the integer 9999. Write the data in the reverse order from which it was read. Thus, the value 9999 will be the first value printed.

21   Sometimes, when an x-y plot is made from empirical data, the scatter of the data points is such that it is difficult to select a "best representative line" for the plot. In a case like this, the data can be adjusted to reduce the scatter by using a "moving average" mathematical method of finding the average of three points in succession and replacing the middle value with this average. Write a complete program to read an array X of 20 values from a file EXPR where the values are entered one per line in an F5.1 format. Build an array Y of 20 values where X is the array of adjusted values. That is, Y(2) is the average of X(1), X(2), and X(3); Y(3) is the average of X(2), X(3), and X(4); and so on. Notice that the first and last values of X cannot be adjusted and should be moved to Y without being changed. Do not destroy the original values in X. Print the original and the adjusted values next to each other in a table.

22 Three arrays are to be filled with data. ITEM is an array containing 20 item numbers. UNITPR is an array giving the corresponding 20 unit costs for the items in ITEM. INVEN is an array of warehouse inventory data that has 20 rows and 4 columns. Each row corresponds to a row in ITEM. That is, the third row of INVEN has warehouse information related to the item specified in ITEM(3). Each column of INVEN represents a warehouse.

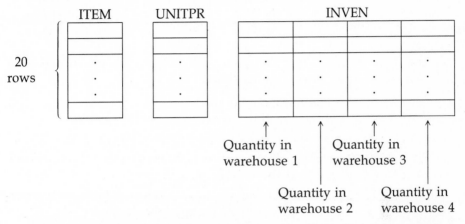

The data is stored in two files. The ITEMS file contains 20 lines, with each line containing an item number and its unit price in an I5,2X,F5.2 format. The INVNTR file contains the inventory information in 20 lines, in a 4I3 format. Write a complete program to read the arrays and then determine the monetary value of items in each warehouse. Print the following:

WAREHOUSE NUMBER	MONETARY VALUE
1	$ XXXXXX.
2	$ XXXXXX.
3	$ XXXXXX.
4	$ XXXXXX.
TOTAL	$XXXXXXX.

23 Write a complete program to read the data for the arrays of problem 22 from the files ITEMS and INVNTR. Then, read an item number from columns 1–3 of a data card. Then print the total number of items available in each warehouse:

        Item XXX: XXXXX UNITS IN WAREHOUSE 1
                    XXXXX UNITS IN WAREHOUSE 2
                    XXXXX UNITS IN WAREHOUSE 3
                    XXXXX UNITS IN WAREHOUSE 4

If the item number is not in the array ITEM, print an appropriate error message. Stop the program when an item number of 999 is read from the data cards.

24 A life insurance company has 12 salespersons. Each salesperson receives a commission on monthly sales that is dependent on what percentage of overall sales he or she sold. This commission is based on the following table:

Percent of Sales	Commission Rate
0.00– 24.99	.02
25.00– 74.99	.04
75.00–100.00	.06

The monthly sales, in dollars, for each salesperson is punched on a computer card in the following format:

Identification Number	cols 1–3
Total Monthly Sales	cols 10–14
(XXXXX)	

Write a complete program to read the data, convert each salesperson's sales to a percentage of the total sales, and compute his or her commission. Print the following report:

MONTHLY COMMISSION REPORT

	ID	SALES	PERCENT	COMMISSION
	XXX	$ XXXXX	XXX.X	$ XXXXX.XX
13 lines	.	.	.	.
	.	.	.	.
	.	.	.	.
	TOTALS	$ XXXXXX	XXX.X	$ XXXXXX.XX

Test your program with the following input data:

Id	Sales
002	9000
009	10050
012	550
016	1000
025	15000
036	20000
037	85000
040	4000
043	1250
044	0
045	400
046	850

25 Write a complete program that will read a two-dimensional array called RAIN containing 12 rows (one for each month) and 5 columns (one for each year 1978–1982). Each row is punched on a data card in a 5F6.2 format, beginning in column 1. Print the following table:

AVERAGE YEARLY RAINFALL
1978–XXX.XX
1979–XXX.XX
1980–XXX.XX
1981–XXX.XX
1982–XXX.XX

MAXIMUM RAINFALL
MONTH XX   YEAR XXXX

MINIMUM RAINFALL
MONTH XX   YEAR XXXX

26 Assume that the reservations for an airplane flight have been stored in a file called FLIGHT. The plane contains 38 rows with six seats in each row. The seats on each row are numbered one through six as follows:

1   Window seat, left side
2   Center seat, left side
3   Aisle seat, left side
4   Aisle seat, right side
5   Center seat, right side
6   Window seat, right side

The file FLIGHT contains 38 lines of information corresponding to the 38 rows. Each line contains six values in a 6I2 format, corresponding to the six seats. The value for any seat is either 0 or 1, representing either an empty or an occupied seat.

Write a complete program to read the FLIGHT information into a two-dimensional array called SEAT. Find and print all pairs of adjacent seats that are empty. Adjacent aisle seats should not be printed. If all three seats on one side of the plane are empty, then two pairs of adjacent seats should be printed. Print this information in the following manner:

AVAILABLE SEAT PAIRS

ROW   SEATS
XX   X, X
 .   .

 .   .
 .   .

XX   X, X

If no pairs are available, print an appropriate message.

27 Several buyers working for a large international corporation find themselves purchasing computer terminals from several warehouses. Although they can buy the terminals for roughly the same cost from any one warehouse, the shipping cost varies depending upon the location of both the buyer and the warehouse. Therefore, a complete computer program is needed to compute the costs of alternative purchase schemes in order to select the most economical purchase plan.

Assume the program initializes a table called COST for 5 warehouses and 6 buyers. Let columns represent the buyers and let rows represent the warehouses. The cost for shipping an item from a particular warehouse I to a particular buyer J is stored in COST(I,J). For example, if COST(3,2) = 15.0, then the cost for shipping each terminal from warehouse 3 to buyer 2 is $15. Use a DATA statement to initialize the following COST table in your program. Output the cost table in an easily understood format (include any necessary headings).

BUYER

W		1	2	3	4	5	6
A							
R	1	$12.00	$14.34	$13.45	$12.99	$17.31	$15.81
E	2	$18.23	$13.09	$21.01	$17.33	$17.76	$ 8.73
H	3	$ 9.12	$15.00	$14.67	$16.92	$14.03	$19.17
O	4	$23.23	$ 9.09	$15.87	$17.22	$12.33	$15.75
U	5	$16.81	$14.03	$21.32	$13.56	$16.63	$10.78
S							
E							

A possible purchasing order can be stored in another table called ORDER with 5 rows and 6 columns, where ORDER(I,J) represents the number of terminals from warehouse I that is bought by buyer J. Two possible purchase orders are stored in a file called PURCHS. Each line of the file corresponds to a row in the table ORDER and is read with a 6I2 format. Your program should read the first purchase order (5 lines) and compute and print the cost of the solution, along with the cost to each buyer, in the following manner:

SOLUTION 1

SHIPPING COST TO BUYER 1 = XXXXX.XX
SHIPPING COST TO BUYER 2 = XXXXX.XX
.
.
.
SHIPPING COST TO BUYER 6 = XXXXX.XX

TOTAL SHIPPING COST = $XXXXX.XX

Next, repeat the steps to evaluate and print the second solution. Then print a final line that specifies which solution (1 or 2) is more economical. For example, in a situation with 2 warehouses and 3 buyers, and if the COST and ORDER tables are those shown below, the cost to buyer 1 is 2*1 + 3*2 or $8, the cost to buyer 2 is 1*3 + 5*0 or $3, and the cost to buyer 3 is 10*0 + 4*4 or $16.

<table>
<tr><td colspan="4" align="center">COST</td><td colspan="4" align="center">ORDER</td></tr>
<tr><td></td><td>B1</td><td>B2</td><td>B3</td><td></td><td>B1</td><td>B2</td><td>B3</td></tr>
<tr><td>W1</td><td>$ 2</td><td>$ 1</td><td>$10</td><td>W1</td><td>1</td><td>3</td><td>0</td></tr>
<tr><td>W2</td><td>$ 3</td><td>$ 5</td><td>$ 4</td><td>W2</td><td>2</td><td>0</td><td>4</td></tr>
</table>

*28 Write a complete program to convert Gregorian dates in month-day-year form to a Julian date, which is the year followed by the number of the day in the year. For example, 010982 should be converted to 82009, and 052283 should be converted to 83142. Be sure to take leap years into account. (*Hint:* Use an array to store the number of days in each month.)

*29 Write a complete program to convert a Julian date, which is the year followed by the number of the day in the year, into the Gregorian date, which is month-day-year form. For example, 82009 should be converted to 010982, and 83142 should be converted to 052283. Be sure to take leap years into account. (*Hint:* Use an array to store the number of days in each month.)

*30 When a certain telephone company monitors local calls from a given phone, it punches a card containing the seven-digit number called. Write a complete program to read the cards and write each number called. If a number is called more than once, it should only be printed once. No more than 500 different numbers are ever dialed in one time period. The numbers are in columns 1–7 of the cards. The last card (trailer card) has the number 9999999.

Courtesy of New Mexico Tourism and Travel Division

SAMPLE PROBLEM – Oil-Well Production

A large oil-producing company uses computer programs to analyze the production of its oil wells and to predict future production. Write a routine that can be used with another computer program (also written in FORTRAN) that will compute, from the daily production data, the average daily production of barrels of oil from an individual well. (For solution, see Example 7-8, page 229.)

7.

SUBPROGRAMS

INTRODUCTION

As our programs become longer and more complicated, we frequently need to perform the same set of operations at more than one location in our programs. Rather than actually repeat the statements, we can write a special subprogram, either a *function* or a *subroutine*, that can be referred to as many times as needed by the program. Very commonly used routines, such as the trigonometric functions sine and cosine, are stored within the computer itself. The type of routine described in the sample problem is one which could be added to any program that needs to compute an average of some data values. Since this type of routine is independent of the programs that use it, a new structure is necessary.

7-1 PROGRAM MODULARITY

In Chapter 4 we stressed the importance of using structured programming techniques to achieve a top-down logic flow to our algorithms and programs. The WHILE loop is an essential ingredient in structured programming, but another key element in simplifying program logic is the use of *modules*. These modules, or functions and subroutines as we call them in FORTRAN, allow us to write programs composed of nearly independent segments or routines. You should begin to see the advantages immediately:

1 You can write and test one segment separate from the rest of the program.

2 Making changes in one segment will not require complete re-testing of other segments.

3 Segments can be used in other programs without rewriting.

4 Programs are more readable because of the module or *block* structure.

5 More than one programmer can work on a large program inde-pendently of other programmers.

6 Programs become simpler.

Before we go into the details of writing program modules in FORTRAN, let us look at an example and see how the use of modules simplifies its structure.

EXAMPLE 7-1   Average Production

Each week, an oil-producing company logs the production of its wells into a data file, OIL. The first line of the data file contains the date of the beginning of the week, in month-day-year form (MMDDYY). Thus, 092582 indicates that the data file contains data for one week beginning September 25, 1982. Each succeeding line in the data file contains an identification number for the oil well and then seven numbers representing the production for 7 consecutive days for that oil well in barrels. Each number (identification number and seven production numbers) contains seven digits with no decimals and is separated from the following number by a blank. Write a program that will read this data and then print the following report:

```
                                    PAGE XXXX
                    OIL WELL PRODUCTION
                    WEEK OF XX-XX-XX


        WELL ID              AVERAGE PRODUCTION

        XXXXXXX                  XXXXXXX.X
           .                         .
           .                         .
           .                         .
        XXXXXXX                  XXXXXXX.X

    OVERALL AVERAGE FOR XXX WELLS IS XXXXXXX.X
```

The output pages are to be numbered, and each page is to have the complete heading. Only 20 wells are to be listed per page. The final average is printed on the same page as the last well, even if the last well is the twentieth on the page.

Solution

We will not write all the code for this until the end of the chapter, but we can now discuss our approach to the problem and develop a solution that is broken into modules.

First, we need to decide if we need an array, and if so, what size array. Since we are computing averages, we do not need to store *all* the data—only 1 week's data at a time. Thus, we need an array to read each line of data and temporarily store that data with statements like:

```
        DIMENSION   OIL(7)
           .
           .
           .
        READ(8,5,END=99)ID, OIL
      5 FORMAT(I7,1X,7(F7.0,1X))
           .
           .
           .
```

We also need several counters in this program, such as:

NWELL—the number of individual wells

OILSUM—the accumulated average oil production from all the wells

PAGE—the page number

LINE—the number of lines that have been printed per page

Now that we have the names of the counters needed, we can begin to organize the steps in the problem solution.

The following flowchart begins to separate the program into sections that are independent of each other:

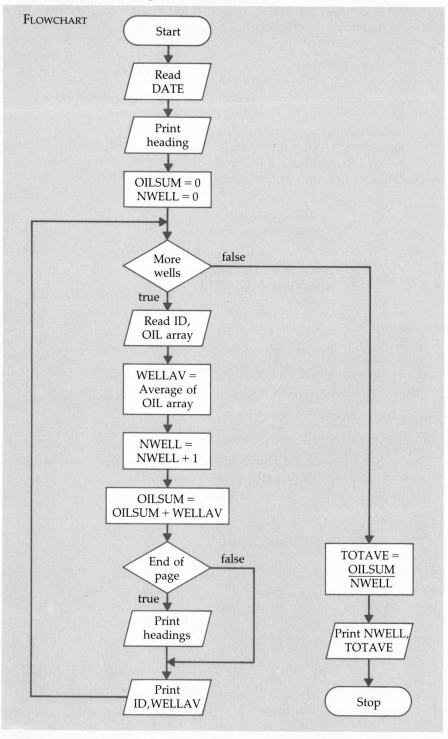

Flowchart

Start

Read DATE

Print heading

OILSUM = 0
NWELL = 0

More wells

false

true

Read ID, OIL array

WELLAV = Average of OIL array

NWELL = NWELL + 1

OILSUM = OILSUM + WELLAV

End of page

false

true

Print headings

Print ID,WELLAV

$$TOTAVE = \frac{OILSUM}{NWELL}$$

Print NWELL, TOTAVE

Stop

This general flowchart serves two purposes. First, it helps break the logic into smaller segments, or modules. Second, it allows a check of the natural flow of the program because we want to emphasize top-down coding and minimize branching. The following module will be of special interest later in this chapter because it involves a number of operations, such as incrementing the page number, resetting the line count to zero, and printing the headings with the correct date.

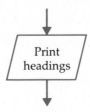

Another module of interest will be the following:

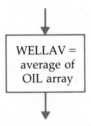

This module will be written to find the average of any one-dimensional array so that the module can be used in a variety of programs. This module is the one described in the sample program at the beginning of this chapter.   ◊

7-2   INTRINSIC FUNCTIONS

The first type of subprogram that we will study is the *function*, a subprogram whose name represents a value. You have already used functions, such as SIN, ABS, and SQRT. These functions are used so frequently that their code is included in the compiler as *intrinsic functions* or *library functions*. Appendix B contains a complete table of intrinsic functions and their definitions.

Although we introduced intrinsic functions in Chapter 2, we will summarize the main components of these functions again:

1   The function name and its input values (arguments) collectively represent a single value.

2   A function can never be used on the left side of an equal sign in an assignment statement.

3   The name of the intrinsic function usually determines the type of output from the function (i.e., if the function name begins with I→N, its value is an integer).

4   Generally, the arguments of a function are the same type as the function itself. However, there are a few exceptions; so refer to the list of intrinsic functions in Appendix B if you are not sure of the type of arguments used by a function.

5   The arguments of a function must be enclosed in parentheses.

6   The arguments of a function may be constants, variables, expressions, or other functions.

Generic functions accept arguments of any type and return a value of the same type as the argument. Thus, the generic function ABS will return an integer absolute value if its argument is an integer but will return a real absolute value if its argument is real. The table in Appendix B identifies generic functions.

7-3   WRITING FUNCTIONS

Since intrinsic functions are contained within a compiler, you may find that a function in one computer manufacturer's compiler is not available in another manufacturer's compiler. You may also find that you would like to use a function that is not available in any compiler. Both these problems can be solved by writing your own function.

FUNCTION SUBPROGRAM

A function subprogram, which is a program itself, will be separate from the *main program*. The function subprogram begins with a nonexecutable statement that identifies the function with a name and an argument list:

```
FUNCTION name(arguments)
```

Since a function is really a separate program, it must also end with an END statement. The following statements illustrate a main program followed by two functions.

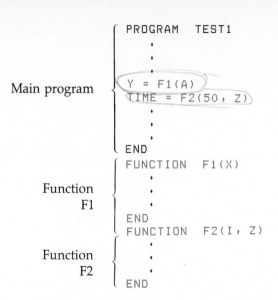

Main program

```
PROGRAM   TEST1
      .
      .
      .
   Y = F1(A)
   TIME = F2(50, Z)
      .
      .
      .
   END
```

Function F1

```
FUNCTION  F1(X)
      .
      .
      .
   END
```

Function F2

```
FUNCTION  F2(I, Z)
      .
      .
      .
   END
```

When writing a function, the following rules must be observed:

1 The arguments of the function must match, in type, the arguments used in the function reference from the main program.

2 If one of the arguments is an array, the size of the array should generally match the size of the array in the main program.

3 The value to be returned to the main program is stored in the function name.

4 When the function is ready to return control to the main program, an executable statement, RETURN, is used. A function may contain more than one RETURN statement whose general form is:

```
RETURN
```

5 A function can contain any statement except a function reference to itself.

6 A function subprogram is usually placed immediately after the main program, but it may also appear before the main program. In either case, the function is compiled as a separate program. If you have more than one function, the order of the functions does not matter as long as each function is completely separate from the other functions.

7 In timesharing systems, a main program and its subprograms can be stored together in the same file or they can be stored in separate files. If they are in separate files, it is necessary to merge them into one file using the system editor before the program can be run.

8   The same statement number may be used in both a function and the main program. No confusion occurs as to which statement is referenced, because the function and main program are completely separate, with only the argument list to link them together. Thus, a function and a main program could use the same variable name, such as SUM, to store different sums as long as the variable is not an argument to the function.

9   If you wish to change the type of value returned by a function, the name of the function must appear in a type statement in both the main program and the function. The following statements include a function AVE, which will return an integer value because it is identified as an INTEGER FUNCTION. The name of the function AVE must also appear in an INTEGER statement in the main program.

Main program
```
PROGRAM   TEST2
INTEGER   AVE
     .
     .
L = AVE(K)
     .
     .
     .
END
```

Function AVE
```
INTEGER FUNCTION   AVE(K)
     .
     .
     .
```

Note that the argument of the function AVE is also an integer.

EXAMPLE 7-2   Absolute Value

Suppose that you have a program that frequently uses an absolute value function, ABS, but the compiler you must use does not have an absolute value function. Write a function to be used with the main program to compute the absolute value.

Solution 1
```
        FUNCTION   ABS(X)
C
C   THIS FUNCTION RETURNS THE
C   ABSOLUTE VALUE OF X
C
        IF(X.LE.0.0)THEN
           ABS = -X
        ELSE
           ABS = X
        ENDIF
C
        RETURN
        END
```

Solution 2

```
          FUNCTION  ABS(A)
C
C    THIS FUNCTION RETURNS THE
C    ABSOLUTE VALUE OF X
C
          ABS = SQRT(A*A)
C
          RETURN
          END
```

Two possible solutions have been given. Arguments with different names, X and A, were used to emphasize that it does not matter what we call the argument, as long as the name represents a real value. Also note that the second solution uses the intrinsic function SQRT.

◇

When arrays are used as arguments in a function, they must be dimensioned in the function subprogram as well as the main program. Generally, the array will have the same size in the function as it does in the main program. There are situations, however, when the size of an array is an argument to the subprogram. This technique allows us to specify an array of variable size in the subprogram. The argument value then sets the size of the array when the subprogram is executed. This technique will be illustrated in the second solution to Example 7-3. The function name and arguments are specified at the beginning of pseudocode or flowcharts for clarity.

EXAMPLE 7-3   Array Average

Write a function that receives an array of seven real values. Compute the average of the array and return it as the function value.

Solution 1

PSEUDOCODE

```
FUNCTION AVE(Z)
    DIMENSION Z(7)
    SUM ← 0
    DO I = 1,7
        SUM ← SUM + Z(I)
    ENDDO
    AVE ← SUM/7.0
STOP
```

```
      FUNCTION  AVE(Z)
C
C THIS FUNCTION COMPUTES THE AVERAGE
C OF A REAL ARRAY WITH 7 ELEMENTS
C
      DIMENSION  Z(7)
C
      SUM = 0.0
      DO 10 I=1,7
         SUM = SUM + Z(I)
   10 CONTINUE
C
      AVE = SUM/7.0
C
      RETURN
      END
```

To use this approach in the oil-well-production example of Section 7-1, we would use:

```
      WELLAV = AVE(OIL)
```

in the main program. Also, since the function AVE is really a separate program, the variable SUM and statement number 10 could have been used in the main program independent of the function.

Solution 2

```
      FUNCTION  AVE(Z, N)
C
C THIS FUNCTION COMPUTES THE AVERAGE
C OF A REAL ARRAY WITH N ELEMENTS
C
      DIMENSION  Z(N)
C
      SUM = 0.0
      DO 10 I=1,N
         SUM = SUM + Z(I)
   10 CONTINUE
C
      AVE = SUM/N
C
      RETURN
      END
```

To use this solution in the oil-well-production example which computes weekly average production, we use:

```
      WELLAV = AVE(OIL, 7)
```

This solution uses *variable dimensioning* and, thus, can be used with any size array, making this solution more general.   ◊

ARITHMETIC STATEMENT FUNCTION

When a user-written function involves only an arithmetic computation that can be written in one statement, it is not necessary to write a function subprogram to incorporate this function in your main program. Instead, an *arithmetic statement function* can be used that will define the function at the beginning of the main program. For instance, we can write the absolute value function of solution 2, Example 7-2, as the arithmetic statement function

```
ABS(A) = SQRT(A*A)
```

An arithmetic statement function is nonexecutable and must be placed before any executable statement in the main program.

EXAMPLE 7-4   Triangle Area

The area of a triangle with angles ANGLEA, ANGLEB, and ANGLEC, and sides SIDEA, SIDEB, and SIDEC can be computed as shown below.

```
AREA = 0.5*SIDEA*SIDEB*SIN(ANGLEC)
```

where the triangle is labeled as shown:

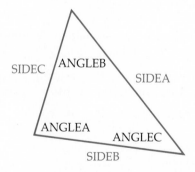

Write an arithmetic statement function that will compute the area of a triangle given two sides, SIDEA and SIDEB, and the angle between them, ANGLEC. Show where the arithmetic statement function is placed and give an example of how the arithmetic statement function is used by the main program.

Solution

```
Arithmetic      ⌈ PROGRAM   TEST3
statement  →    |  AREA(SIDEA,  SIDEB,  ANGLEC)  =  0.5*SIDEA*
 function       |  +          SIDEB*SIN(ANGLEC)
                |      ˙
                |      ˙
                |      ˙
                |  READ(5,1)SIDE1,  SIDE2,  ANGLE
     Main       |      ˙
   program  <   |      ˙
                |      ˙
                |  TRIA  =  AREA(SIDE1,  SIDE2,  ANGLE)
                |      ˙
                |      ˙
                |      ˙
                ⌊ END
```

This solution assumes that the angle will be in radians. If the angle is in degrees, the statement function would be:

```
AREA(SIDEA,  SIDEB,  ANGLEC)  =  0.5*SIDEA*SIDEB*
+          SIN(ANGLEC*(3.141593/180.0))   ◇
```

7-4   LIBRARY SUBROUTINES

Another type of subprogram is the *subroutine*. A subroutine differs from a function in several ways:

1   A subroutine does not represent a value as does a function, and thus the type of the name is irrelevant.

2   A subroutine is referenced with an executable statement, CALL, whose form is:

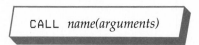

```
CALL  name(arguments)
```

3   A subroutine uses the argument list for not only inputs to the subprogram but also any output from the subprogram.

4   A subroutine may return one value, many values, or no value.

Some subroutines are prewritten and are part of a library of subprograms available to the computer system; however, there is not a common list of library subroutines available similar to the list of intrinsic functions. You will have to examine the documentation for your specific computer system to determine what library subroutines are available and what arguments are needed.

7-5 APPLICATION – Solution of Simultaneous Equations

Most computer systems have a library subroutine that will determine the solution of two simultaneous linear equations. We will describe a typical library subroutine SIMQ and its parameters. We then give an example that illustrates a main program that uses this library subroutine.

The subroutine SIMQ is accessed through the statement:

```
CALL SIMQ(A, B, N, IFLAG)
```

This subroutine will find the unique solution, if one exists, to a set of N simultaneous equations, each having N unknowns.

When $N = 2$, the two equations represent straight lines, and the solution is the point of intersection of the lines. When $N = 3$, the three equations represent planes, and the solution is the line of intersection of the planes. We can generalize the system of equations with the following form:

$$a_{11}x_N + a_{12}x_{N-1} + a_{13}x_{N-2} + \cdots + a_{1N}x_1 = b_1$$
$$a_{21}x_N + a_{22}x_{N-1} + a_{23}x_{N-2} + \cdots + a_{2N}x_1 = b_2$$
$$\vdots \qquad\qquad\qquad\qquad \vdots$$
$$a_{N1}x_N + a_{N2}x_{N-1} + a_{N3}x_{N-2} + \cdots + a_{NN}x_1 = b_N$$

The argument A represents the two-dimensional array of size $N \times N$ containing the coefficients from the left side of the equation set:

$$A = \begin{bmatrix} a_{11} & a_{12} & a_{13} & \cdots & a_{1N} \\ a_{21} & a_{22} & a_{23} & \cdots & a_{2N} \\ \cdot & & & & \cdot \\ \cdot & & & & \cdot \\ \cdot & & & & \cdot \\ a_{N1} & a_{N2} & a_{N3} & \cdots & a_{NN} \end{bmatrix}$$

The argument B represents the one-dimensional array with N elements containing the coefficients from the right side of the equation set:

$$B = \begin{bmatrix} b_1 \\ b_2 \\ \cdot \\ \cdot \\ \cdot \\ b_N \end{bmatrix}$$

The argument IFLAG is an error flag. If a unique solution exists to the set of equations, the error flag will contain a zero. If two or more of the equations represent the same line or surface, or parallel lines or surfaces, the error flag will contain a 1 to indicate that the results are invalid.

The original values of arrays A and B will be modified by the subroutine to find the solution. If a unique solution exists, the point common to all the equations will be returned in the array B.

EXAMPLE 7-5 Simultaneous Equations

Write a complete program that will read the coefficients of K pairs of linear equations. Print the original equations and give either the point of intersection or an error message. Use the following sets of equations to test the program:

$$\text{Set 1: } 2x + 3y = 13$$
$$5x - 2y = 4$$

$$\text{Set 2: } x + y = 8$$
$$x + y = 5$$

$$\text{Set 3: } x - y = 21$$
$$5x - 5y = 105$$

$$\text{Set 4: } x + y = 6$$
$$x - y = 1$$

Solution

GENERAL PSEUDOCODE

```
PROGRAM SIMEQN
   READ K
   DO I = 1,K
      READ coefficients
      PRINT coefficients
      CALL SIMQ
      IF ERROR = 0 THEN
         PRINT solution
      ELSE
         PRINT error message
      ENDIF
   ENDDO
STOP
```

REFINED PSEUDOCODE

```
PROGRAM SIMEQN
   DIMENSION A(2,2), B(2)
   READ K
   DO I = 1,K
      READ A, B
      PRINT A, B
      CALL SIMQ
      IF ERROR = 0 THEN
         PRINT solution
      ELSE
         PRINT error message
      ENDIF
   ENDDO
STOP
```

FORTRAN Program

```
      PROGRAM  SIMEQN
C
C  THIS PROGRAM SOLVES K SETS OF 2 X 2 SIMULTANEOUS
C  EQUATIONS USING A LIBRARY SUBROUTINE SIMQ
C
      DIMENSION  A(2,2), B(2)
      INTEGER  ERROR
C
      READ(5,2)K
    2 FORMAT(I2)
C
      DO 50 L=1,K
C
        READ(5,5)(A(I,1), A(I,2), B(I), I=1,2)
    5   FORMAT(3F6.0)
C
        WRITE(6,10)L, (A(J,1), A(J,2), B(J), J=1,2)
   10   FORMAT(/1X,'SET',I2,':',5X,F5.1,' X +',F5.1,
     +          ' Y = ',F7.1/1X,11X,F5.1,' X +',F5.1,
     +          ' Y = ',F7.1)
C
        CALL SIMQ(A, B, 2, ERROR)
C
        IF(ERROR.EQ.0)THEN
          WRITE(6,15)B
   15     FORMAT(/1X,5X,'INTERSECTION IS (',
     +            F5.1,',',F5.1,')')
        ELSE
          WRITE(6,20)
   20     FORMAT(/1X,5X,'NO UNIQUE SOLUTION')
C
        ENDIF
C
   50 CONTINUE
C
      STOP
      END
```

Input Data:

```
2.    3.    13.
5.   -2.    4.
1.    1.    8.
1.    1.    5.
1.   -1.    21.
5.   -5.    105.
1.    1.    6.
1.   -1.    1.
```

```
SET  1:          2.0 X +   3.0 Y =      13.0
                 5.0 X + -2.0 Y =       4.0

     INTERSECTION IS (   2.0,   3.0)

SET  2:          1.0 X +   1.0 Y =       8.0
                 1.0 X +   1.0 Y =       5.0

     NO UNIQUE SOLUTION

SET  3:          1.0 X + -1.0 Y =      21.0
                 5.0 X + -5.0 Y =     105.0

     NO UNIQUE SOLUTION

SET  4:          1.0 X +   1.0 Y =       6.0
                 1.0 X + -1.0 Y =,      1.0

     INTERSECTION IS (   3.5,   2.5)
```

◇

7-6 WRITING SUBROUTINES

User-written subroutines are accessed the same as a library subroutine. Writing a subroutine is much like writing a function, except that the first line in a subroutine is the following nonexecutable statement:

> SUBROUTINE *name(arguments)*

Also, the output of the subroutine is returned by the arguments rather than by the name as is done with a function.

Since the subroutine is a separate program, the arguments are the only link to the main program and the subroutine. Thus, the choice of statement numbers and variable names is independent of the choice of the statement numbers and variable names used in the main program.

The subroutine, like the function, requires:

1 A RETURN statement to return control to the main program.

2 An END statement because it is also a complete program module.

EXAMPLE 7-6 Average and Zero Count

Write a subroutine that receives a two-dimensional real array TEMP with N rows and M columns and returns the average value of the array and a count of the number of array elements whose value is zero. Show a typical sequence of calling instructions.

Solution

```
SUBROUTINE   ANALYZ(TEMP, N, M, AVE, ZEROCT)
   DIMENSION   TEMP(N,M)
   SUM ← 0.0
   ZEROCT ← 0
   DO I=1,N
      DO J=1,M
         SUM ← SUM + TEMP(I,J)
         IF TEMP(I,J) = 0.0 THEN
            ZEROCT ← ZEROCT + 1
         ENDIF
      ENDDO
   ENDDO
   AVE ← SUM/ (N*M)
RETURN
```

Main
program

```
        PROGRAM   TEST4
        DIMENSION   TEMP(5,5)
        READ(5,10)TEMP
           .
           .
           .
        CALL ANALYZ(TEMP, 5, 5, AVE, KTZERO)
           .
           .
           .
        WRITE(6,100)AVE, KTZERO
           .
           .
           .
        END
        SUBROUTINE   ANALYZ(TEMP, N, M, AVE, KTZERO)
C
C    THIS SUBROUTINE COMPUTES THE AVERAGE OF AN
C    ARRAY AND COUNTS THE NUMBER OF ZERO VALUES
C    IN THE ARRAY
C
        DIMENSION   TEMP(N,M)
C
        SUM = 0.0
        KTZERO = 0
        DO 10 I=1,N
           DO 5 J=1,M
              SUM = SUM + TEMP(I,J)
              IF(TEMP(I,J).EQ.0.0)KTZERO =
     +          KTZERO + 1
   5       CONTINUE
  10    CONTINUE
C
        AVE = SUM/(N*M)
C
        RETURN
        END   ◇
```

Subroutine
ANALYZ

EXAMPLE 7-7   Heading Report

In the oil-production analysis report program discussed in Section 7-1, a module was identified that would print the page headings at the top of each page of the report. This will require incrementing the page number and resetting the number of lines printed to zero. If the number of lines printed were not reset to zero, a new header would be printed for the 21st oil well, the 22nd oil well, and so on. We only want the heading printed after the 20th oil well, the 40th oil well, and so on.

Assume that PAGE has been initialized to 1 and LINE has been initialized to zero at the beginning of the main program and that DATE is an array already containing the month, day, and year. Write a subroutine that will be accessed with the following CALL:

```
      CALL HEADER(DATE, PAGE, LINE)
```

Recall that the heading format is to be the following, with 20 individual wells printed per page:

PAGE XXXX

OIL WELL PRODUCTION
WEEK OF XX-XX-XX

WELL ID   AVERAGE PRODUCTION

Solution

```
      SUBROUTINE  HEADER(DATE, PAGE, LINE)
C
C  THIS SUBROUTINE PRINTS A HEADING ON EACH NEW PAGE
C
      INTEGER  PAGE, DATE(3)
C
      WRITE(6,10)PAGE, DATE
   10 FORMAT('1',26X,'PAGE',I5/1X,3X,
     +         'OIL WELL PRODUCTION'/1X,5X,'WEEK OF ',
     +         I2,'-',I2,'-',I2/'0',
     +         'WELL ID     AVERAGE PRODUCTION'/)
C
      PAGE = PAGE + 1
      LINE = 1
C
      RETURN
      END  ◊
```

7-7 APPLICATION – Formal Report on Oil-Well Production

We are now ready to write the complete code for the main program that uses a function for computation of an array average (Example 7-3) and a header subroutine (Example 7-7) to solve the problems presented in Example 7-1. Using the flowchart developed in Section 7-1 as a guide, we can develop the following main program, which would be accompanied by the two subprograms developed in previous examples.

In a flowchart, we reference an operation to be performed by a subprogram with the following symbol:

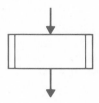

In pseudocode, we reference a function by its name and argument list, and we reference a subroutine by a CALL statement. The subprogram algorithms are then included in separate flowcharts or pseudocode.

EXAMPLE 7-8 Average Oil-Well Production

Write a complete program to use the data file OIL and print the corresponding report described in Example 7-1.

Solution

From the general flowchart developed in Example 7-1, we can develop the refined flowchart shown on page 230.

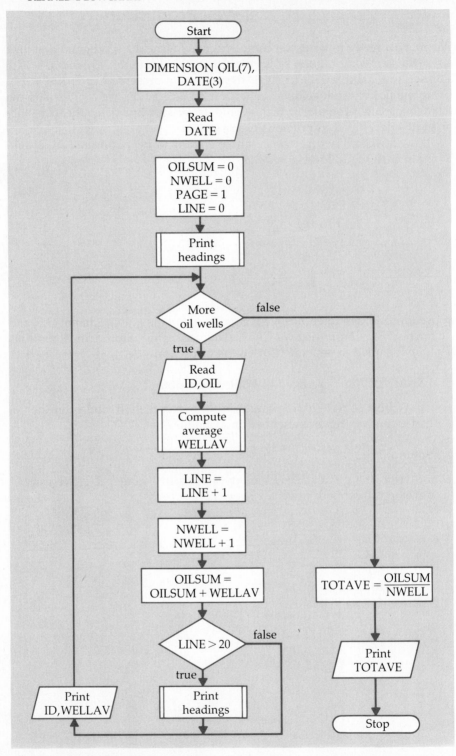

FORTRAN Program

```
        PROGRAM   WELL
C
C  THIS PROGRAM ANALYZES THE OIL PRODUCTION
C  FROM A GROUP OF OIL WELLS
C
        DIMENSION  OIL(7)
        INTEGER  PAGE, DATE(3)
C
        OPEN(UNIT=10, FILE='OIL', STATUS='OLD')
C
        READ(10,10)DATE
     10 FORMAT(3I2)
C
        OILSUM = 0
        NWELL = 0
        PAGE = 1
C
        CALL HEADER(DATE, PAGE, LINE)
        LINE = 0
C
     20 READ(10,25,END=99)ID, OIL
     25 FORMAT(I7,1X,7(F7.0,1X))
C
          WELLAV = AVE(OIL)
C
          LINE = LINE + 1
          NWELL = NWELL + 1
          OILSUM = OILSUM + WELLAV
C
          IF(LINE.GT.20)CALL HEADER(DATE, PAGE, LINE)
C
          WRITE(6,30)ID, WELLAV
     30     FORMAT(1X,I7,10X,F9.1)
C
        GO TO 20
C
     99 TOTAVE = OILSUM/NWELL
C
        WRITE(6,105)NWELL, TOTAVE
    105 FORMAT(//,1X,'OVERALL AVERAGE FOR',I4,' WELLS IS',
       +          F10.1)
C
        STOP
        END
```

(Function AVE and subroutine HEADER go here.)

Input Data

050681

52	87	136	0	54	60	82	51
63	54	73	88	105	20	21	105
24	67	98	177	35	65	98	0
8	23	34	52	67	180	80	3
64	33	55	79	108	118	130	20
66	40	44	63	89	36	54	36
67	20	35	76	87	154	98	80
55	10	13	34	23	43	12	0
3	34	56	187	34	202	23	34
2	98	98	87	34	54	100	20
25	29	43	54	65	12	15	17
18	45	65	202	205	100	99	98
14	36	34	98	34	43	23	9
13	0	9	8	4	3	2	10
36	23	88	99	65	77	45	35
38	23	100	134	122	111	211	0
81	23	34	54	98	5	93	82
89	29	58	39	20	50	30	47
99	100	12	43	98	34	23	9
45	23	93	75	93	2	34	8
88	23	301	23	83	23	9	20
77	28	12	43	43	92	83	98
39	98	43	12	23	54	23	98
12	43	54	92	84	75	72	91
48	83	138	189	73	27	49	10

```
                              PAGE     1
     OIL WELL PRODUCTION
        WEEK OF   5- 6-81

WELL ID        AVERAGE PRODUCTION

      52                  67.1
      63                  66.6
      24                  77.1
       8                  62.7
      64                  77.6
      66                  51.7
      67                  78.6
      55                  19.3
       3                  81.4
       2                  70.1
      25                  39.6
      18                 116.3
      14                  33.6
      13                   5.1
      36                  61.7
      38                 100.1
      81                  55.6
      89                  39.0
      99                  45.6
      45                  46.9
------------------------------------------------
                              PAGE     2
     OIL WELL PRODUCTION
        WEEK OF   5- 6-81

WELL ID        AVERAGE PRODUCTION

      88                  68.9
      77                  57.0
      39                  50.1
      12                  73.0
      48                  81.3

OVERALL AVERAGE FOR 25 WELLS IS        61.0
```

◇

7-8 APPLICATION – Test Scores Sort Routine

In this section we write a subroutine to sort a one-dimensional array into an *ascending*, or low-to-high, order. With minor changes, the subroutine can be changed to one that sorts an array into descending order. The topic of sorting techniques is the subject of entire textbooks; so this text will not attempt to present all the important aspects of sorting. A simple, multi-pass sort that is straightforward to code will be presented.

The basic step to this sort routine will be a single pass through the array, comparing adjacent elements in the array. If a pair of adjacent elements is in the correct order (that is, the first value less than or equal to the second value), then we go to the next pair. If the pair is out of order, we must switch the values and then go to the next pair.

The single pass through the array can be performed in a DO loop with index I. Each pair of adjacent values will be referred to by the subscripts I and I+1. If there are N elements in the array, we will make N−1 comparisons. Thus, the loop will need to be performed N−1 times. When the value of the index is N−1, the last pair of adjacent values will still be referenced by I and I+1, but the actual values of I and I+1 will be (N−1) and N, respectively.

The switch of two adjacent values will require three steps, not two as might first be imagined. Consider the statements below:

```
A(I)   = A(I+1)
A(I+1) = A(I)
```

Suppose A(I) contained the value 3 and A(I+1) contained the value −1. The first statement will change the contents of A(I) from the value 3 to the value−1. The second statement will move the value in A(I) to A(I+1), and then both locations contain −1. A correct way to switch the two values is shown below:

```
TEMP   = A(I)
A(I)   = A(I+1)
A(I+1) = TEMP
```

Follow the execution of these three statements using a pair of values to convince yourself that the switch is made correctly.

A single pass through a one-dimensional array, switching adjacent elements which are out of order, is not guaranteed to sort the values. Consider a single pass through the following example array:

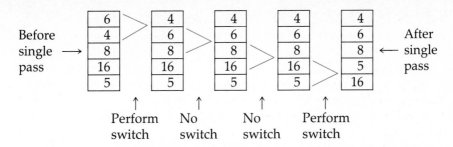

Before single pass →									After single pass ←
6		4		4		4		4	
4		6		6		6		6	
8		8		8		8		8	
16		16		16		16		5	
5		5		5		5		16	

↑	↑	↑	↑
Perform switch	No switch	No switch	Perform switch

It will take two more complete passes before the array is sorted into ascending order. A maximum of $N-1$ passes may be necessary to sort an array with this technique. If no switches are made during a single pass through the array, however, it is in ascending order. Thus, our algorithm for sorting a one-dimensional array will be to perform single passes through the array making switches until no elements are out of order. In developing the pseudocode, we use a variable SORTED that is initialized to zero at the beginning of each pass through the data array. If any values are out of order, we switch the values and change the value of SORTED to 1. Thus, at the end of a pass through the data, if the value of SORTED is still zero, the array is in ascending order.

GENERAL PSEUDOCODE

```
SUBROUTINE  SORT(A, N)
    DIMENSION  A(N)
    WHILE A is not in
        ascending order DO
        perform single pass
        through A switching
        adjacent elements that
        are out of order
    ENDWHILE
RETURN
```

REFINED PSEUDOCODE

```
SUBROUTINE  SORT(A, N)
    DIMENSION A(N)
    SORTED ← 1
    WHILE SORTED = 1 DO
        SORTED ← 0
        DO I=1,N−1
            IF A(I) > A(I+1) THEN
                TEMP ← A(I)
                A(I) ← A(I+1)
                A(I+1) ← TEMP
                SORTED ← 1
            ENDIF
        ENDDO
    ENDWHILE
RETURN
```

EXAMPLE 7-9   Test Scores Sort

An engineering professor would like a subroutine that will sort a one-dimensional array to use in sorting test scores. After printing the test scores in ascending order, it will be easier for the professor to establish a curve based on the test grades. Write a subroutine to sort a one-dimensional integer array whose size is also an input parameter. Then write a main program that will read test scores, one per data line, in an I3 format from a file GRADES. Assume that the number of test scores will not exceed 75.

Solution

PSEUDOCODE

```
PROGRAM   SCORES
    DIMENSION   TEST(75)
    N ← 1
    WHILE more test scores DO
        READ TEST(N)
        N ← N + 1
    ENDWHILE
    CALL SORT(TEST, N − 1)
    PRINT TEST
STOP
```

FORTRAN Program

```
                  PROGRAM  SCORES
C
C  THIS PROGRAM WILL READ A SET OF TEST
C  SCORES, CALL A SUBROUTINE TO SORT
C  THEM, AND THEN PRINT THE SORTED SCORES
C
       INTEGER  TEST(75)
C
       OPEN(UNIT=9, FILE='GRADES',
      +          STATUS='OLD')
C
       NUM = 1
     1 READ(9,5,END=20)TEST(NUM)
     5 FORMAT(I3)
         NUM = NUM + 1
       GO TO 1
C
       N = NUM - 1
C
    20 CALL SORT(TEST, N)
C
       WRITE(6,30)(TEST(I), I=1,N)
    30 FORMAT(1X,I3)
C
       STOP
       END
       SUBROUTINE  SORT(L, N)
C
C  THIS SUBROUTINE SORTS AN INTEGER ARRAY
C  OF N ELEMENTS INTO ASCENDING ORDER
C
       DIMENSION L(N)
       INTEGER  SORTED, TEMP
C
       SORTED = 0
C
     3 IF(SORTED.EQ.1)THEN
         SORTED = 0
C
         DO 5 I=1,N-1
           IF(L(I).GT.L(I+1))THEN
              TEMP = L(I)
              L(I) = L(I+1)
              L(I+1) = TEMP
              SORTED = 1
           ENDIF
     5     CONTINUE
C
         GO TO 3
       ENDIF
C
       RETURN
       END
```

Main program {

Subroutine SORT {

87
92
71
100
86
52
65
93
84
69
87

COMPUTER OUTPUT

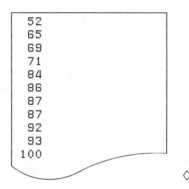

```
52
65
69
71
84
86
87
87
92
93
100
```

◇

7-9   COMMON BLOCKS AND BLOCK DATA SUBPROGRAMS

As you modularize your programs, you will find that the argument lists can sometimes get long as you pass more and more data to functions and subprograms. FORTRAN allows you to set up a block of storage that is accessible, or common, to the main program and all its subprograms, called a *common block*. The variables in this block of storage do not have to be passed through argument lists. Unless extremely large amounts of data must be passed to subprograms, the use of common blocks is discouraged because they weaken the independence of modules. If you change a variable in a common block, it could conceivably affect all modules using data in the common block.

BLANK COMMON

Blank common is set up with the nonexecutable specification statement

```
COMMON  variable list
```

that goes before any executable statements. Each subprogram that uses data in this common block must also contain a COMMON statement. While the data names do not have to be the same in every subprogram, the order of the names is important. Consider these COMMON statements from a main program and a subprogram, respectively:

```
COMMON  A, J, B
COMMON  TEMP, KTOT, SUM
```

Here, A and TEMP represent the same value, J and KTOT represent the same value, and B and SUM represent the same value.

Arrays may be dimensioned in either the DIMENSION statement, the COMMON statement, or a type statement, but not in more than one. Variables in common blocks cannot be used as arguments in subprograms. Finally, variables in common cannot be initialized with DATA statements.

NAMED COMMON

Named common is established if the list of variable names in the COMMON statement is preceded by a name set in slashes:

```
COMMON  /name/ variable list
```

The purpose of establishing different blocks of common with unique names is to allow subprograms to refer to the named common block with which they wish to share data without listing all the other variables in the other common blocks. Named common is also referred to as *labeled common*.

BLOCK DATA SUBPROGRAM

Variables in common can be initialized with a special subprogram called a BLOCK DATA subprogram. This subprogram is not executable and serves only to assign initial values to variables in a common block. An example of a block data subprogram that will initialize two named common blocks is given below:

```
BLOCK   DATA
COMMON  /EXPER1/ TEMP(100)
COMMON  /EXPER2/ TIME, DIST, VEL(10)
DATA TEMP, TIME, DIST, VEL /100*0.0, 50.5, 0.5, 10*0.0/
END
```

SUMMARY

Structured programming requires that long programs be separated into modules. The modules (functions and subroutines) can then be joined with a main program to form the problem solution. Long programs are easier to write, modify, test, and document when they are broken into meaningful blocks or modules.

KEY WORDS

argument
arithmetic statement function
ascending order
blank common
BLOCK DATA statement
COMMON statement
common block
descending order
function
FUNCTION statement
generic function
intrinsic function

library function
library subroutine
main program
module
named common
RETURN statement
sort
structured programming
subprogram
subroutine
SUBROUTINE statement
variable dimensioning

DEBUGGING AIDS

Because subprograms are independent with respect to each other, you can test and debug them separately. In fact, it is really not a good idea to put the main program and all its subprograms together for initial testing. Instead, use a very simple main program (called a *driver*) to initialize the input to the specific subprogram that you are testing. After executing your subprogram, the driving program should print the output of the subprogram. Only after testing each subprogram should you begin combining the complete main program with the subprograms, one subprogram at a time.

The described procedure for testing a main program and its subprograms may seem unnecessarily long. It requires writing some extra driver programs and it requires a specific order to the test. This procedure, however, is very effective in minimizing serious errors in larger programs. A finished subprogram can also be tested before the rest of the modules have been written.

The testing of an individual module is actually the testing of a complete program and generally follows the guidelines that have been summarized at the end of the previous chapters. We list here some specific guides to use regarding the communication link between the subprogram and its main program or driver.

FUNCTIONS

1   Be sure the name of the function reflects the type of value that you want returned. If necessary, use a type statement, REAL or INTEGER.

2   Be sure that each path to a RETURN provides a value for the function.

SUBROUTINES

3   Be sure all output variables receive new values.

BOTH TYPES OF SUBPROGRAMS

4   Be sure the variables listed in the main program match the arguments in the subprogram statement. Check the corresponding variables for correct order *and* correct type.

5   Print the values of all variables just before using the subprogram and just after returning from the subprogram as you debug the subprogram.

6   Test several sets of inputs with each subprogram.

7   You can put extra WRITE statements (checkpoints) in subprograms just like you can in a main program to help isolate trouble spots.

8   In general, try to use arrays of the same size in both the main programs and subprograms. If $A(10)$ is an argument, it refers to the tenth element of the array, not the first 10 elements of the array A or an array A of 10 elements.

COMMON

9   If your variables in COMMON are not being computed correctly, minimize the number of variables that you keep in COMMON. Change variables in common to regular subprogram arguments or use labeled common in order to use smaller blocks.

10 Pay particular attention to the order of the variables on all COMMON statements. Also look for omitted variables. If a variable is left out of a COMMON statement in a subprogram, incorrect values will be used for all variables following it in the COMMON statement.

11 Look for misspelled variable names in the COMMON statements.

STYLE/TECHNIQUE GUIDES

Separating a long program into modules that transfer control smoothly from one to another becomes easier with practice. While different sets of modules may solve the same problem, some choices will probably be more logical and readable than others; these are the solutions that you want to be able to develop. Once you have selected a segment that is to be made into a module, you must decide whether it is to be a function or a subroutine. Does it have only one value to return? If so, it should probably be a function. But also look at the larger picture. If a loop is used to process each element of an array with a function, it might be better to transfer the whole array to a subroutine, process it in a loop in the subroutine, and return the entire modified array to the main program.

As we mentioned earlier, minimize the use of COMMON. If you must use it, use small blocks of labeled COMMON.

We will now list a few style suggestions for writing subprograms:

1 Choose descriptive names for the subprograms themselves.

2 Use comment lines in the subprograms as you would in the main program. Particularly use comments at the beginning of a subprogram to describe its purpose and define the arguments if necessary.

3 For clarity, use the same variables in the argument list of the subprogram as will be used in the main program if possible. If not, use completely different argument names.

4 List input arguments before output arguments in subroutine argument lists.

PROBLEMS

In problems 1 through 4, give the value of the following function. Assume that $A = -5$, $B = -6.2$, $C = 0.1$, and $D = 16.2$.

```
      FUNCTION   TEST(X, Y, Z)
C
C   THIS FUNCTION RETURNS EITHER 0.5 OR -0.5
C   BASED ON THE VALUES OF X, Y, Z
C
      IF(X.GT.Y.OR.Y.GT.Z)THEN
         TEST = 0.5
      ELSE
         TEST = -0.5
      RETURN
      END
```

1   TEST(5.2, 5.3, 5.6)

2   TEST(B, C, A)

3   TEST(ABS(A), C, D)

4   TEST(C, C, D*D)

For problems 5 through 8, assume that you have a function subprogram DENOM to compute

$$x^2 + \sqrt{1 + 2x + 3x^2}$$

with the input value x. Write the section of a main program that uses this function subprogram to compute and print each of the following:

5   ALPHA $= \dfrac{6.9 + y}{y^2 + \sqrt{1 + 2y + 3y^2}}$

6   BETA $= \dfrac{2.3z + z^4}{z^2 + \sqrt{1 + 2z + 3z^2}}$

7   GAMMA $= \dfrac{\sin y}{y^4 + \sqrt{1 + 2y^2 + 3y^4}}$

8   DELTA $= \dfrac{1}{\sin^2 y + \sqrt{1 + 2\sin y + 3\sin^2 y}}$

In problems 9 through 13, write the function subprogram whose return value is described below. The input to the function is an integer array K of 100 elements.

9   MAXA(K), the maximum value of the array K

10   MINA(K), the minimum value of the array K

11   NPOS(K), the number of values greater than or equal to zero in the array K

12 NNEG(K), the number of values less than zero in the array K

13 NZERO(K), the number of values equal to zero in the array K

In problems 14 through 18, write arithmetic statement functions to compute the following:

14 Area of a circle, $A = \pi r^2$

15 Radians from degrees, $rad = \dfrac{180}{\pi} (degrees)$

16 Degrees from radians, $deg = \dfrac{\pi}{180} (radians)$

17 Kinetic energy equation, $T = \dfrac{mw^2a^2s}{4}$

18 Radius of a circle, $r = \sqrt{x^2 + y^2}$

In problems 19 through 22, give the values returned in the arguments after each of the following subroutine calls to the subroutine ANSWER. Assume that $N(1) = 5$, $N(2) = 4$, $N(3) = 1$.

```
          SUBROUTINE  ANSWER(N, K, L)
       C
       C   THIS SUBROUTINE RETURNS
       C   A VALUE FOR L BASED ON N AND K
       C
              DIMENSION  N(3)
              IF(K.LT.0)THEN
                 L = K
              ELSE
                 L = 0
                 DO 10 I=1,3
                    L = L + N(I)
       10        CONTINUE
              ENDIF
       C
              RETURN
              END
```

19 CALL ANSWER(N, 0, L)

20 CALL ANSWER(N, 18, NUM)

21 CALL ANSWER(N, -2, L)

22 CALL ANSWER(N, N(1), N(2))

In problems 23 through 26, write the subroutines described below. The input to each subroutine is a two-dimensional array Z of size 5×4. The output is another array W of the same size.

23 SUBROUTINE ABSOL(Z, W), where each element of W contains the absolute value of the corresponding element in Z.

24 SUBROUTINE SIGNS(Z, W), where each element of W contains a value based on the corresponding element in Z, where

$$W(I,J) = 0.0 \quad \text{if} \quad Z(I,J) = 0$$
$$W(I,J) = -1.0 \quad \text{if} \quad Z(I,J) < 0$$
$$W(I,J) = 1.0 \quad \text{if} \quad Z(I,J) > 0$$

25 SUBROUTINE GREAT(Z, W), where W contains the same values of Z unless the corresponding value was greater than the average value of Z. In these cases, the corresponding value of W should contain the average value.

26 SUBROUTINE ROUND(Z, W), where each element of W is the corresponding value of Z rounded up to the next multiple of 10. Thus, 10.76 rounds to 20.0, 18.7 rounds to 20.0, 0.05 rounds to 10.0, 10.0 rounds to 10.0, and −5.76 rounds to 0.0.

27 Write a function whose input is a two-digit number. The function is to return a two-digit number whose digits are reversed from the input number. Thus, if 17 is the input to the function, 71 will be the output.

28 Write a subroutine that will read a group of test scores until it finds a card with a test score of −1 in columns 1 and 2. The subroutine should return the number of test scores read before the −1 was encountered and the average of the test scores.

29 Write a function FACT that receives an integer value and returns the factorial of the value. Recall, the definition of a factorial is

$$n! = n \cdot (n-1)(n-2) \cdots 1; \; n > 0$$
$$0! = 1$$

If $n < 0$, the function should return a value of zero.

30 Write a subroutine that will compute the average $\overline{X}$, the variance σ^2, and the standard deviation σ of an array of 100 real values. Use the following formulas:

$$\overline{X} = \frac{\sum\limits_{i=1}^{100} X_i}{100}$$

$$\sigma^2 = \frac{\sum\limits_{i=1}^{100} (\overline{X} - X_i)^2}{99}$$

$$\sigma = \sqrt{\sigma^2}$$

31 Rewrite the subroutine of problem 30 so that it will compute the average, variance, and standard deviation for an array of size N. The denominator of the expression for σ^2 should then be $N - 1$.

32 Write a subroutine called BIAS that is invoked with the following statement:

$$\text{CALL BIAS(X, Y, N)}$$

X is an input array of N values. Y is an output array whose values are the values of X with the minimum value of the X array subtracted from each value in the array. For example,

if $\quad X = \boxed{\begin{matrix} 10 \\ 2 \\ 36 \\ 8 \end{matrix}}$, $\quad$ then $\quad Y = \boxed{\begin{matrix} 8 \\ 0 \\ 34 \\ 6 \end{matrix}}$

Thus, the minimum value of Y is always 0. This operation is referred to as *adjusting for bias in X*.

33 Write a function ITOT that will convert three arguments representing hours, minutes, and seconds to a grand total of seconds. For example, ITOT(3, 2, 5) should return the value 10,925.

34 An array SSN is dimensioned to hold 1000 social security numbers. The array is sorted from smallest to largest. When a new employee is hired, his or her social security number is added to the sorted list with the following call:

$$\text{CALL ADD(SSN, NEW)}$$

Assume that there are less than 1000 values in the SSN array and that all unused elements at the end of the array have been set to 999999999. Write the subroutine ADD that finds the proper place in the array, inserts NEW, and pushes the rest of the values down one position in the SSN array.

35 An array SSN is dimensioned to hold 1000 social security numbers. The array is sorted from smallest to largest. When an employee retires, his or her social security number is deleted from the list with the following call:

$$\text{CALL DROP(SSN, OLD)}$$

Any unused elements at the end of the array are set to 999999999. Write the subroutine DROP that finds the proper place in the array, deletes OLD, and moves the rest of the values up one position in the SSN array.

36 A certain application requires use of a main program and three subprograms SUBA, SUBB, SUBC. To facilitate communication between these modules, a common block will be used. The desired correspondence of variables is given below. Write the necessary COMMON statements for the main program and the subprograms.

	Main	SUBA	SUBB	SUBC	
	V1		BV1		
	V2	AV1	BV2	CV1	
Single variables	V3			CV2	
		AV2	BV3		
	V5		BV4	CV3	
					Dimension
	A1			CA1	20
Arrays	A2		BA1		13
		AA1	BA2		15

*37 The cosine of an angle may be computed from the series

$$\cos x = 1 - \frac{x^2}{2!} + \frac{x^4}{4!} - \frac{x^6}{6!} + \cdots$$

where x is measured in radians. Write a function whose input is an angle in radians. The function should compute the first 10 terms of series and return that approximation of the cosine. Use the factorial function of problem 29. [*Hint:* The alternating sign can be obtained by computing $(-1)^k$. When k is even, $(-1)^k = +1$; when k is odd, $(-1)^k = -1$.]

*38 Rewrite the function in problem 37 as a subroutine such that it computes the cosine with as many terms of the series as necessary to ensure that the absolute value of the last term used is less than 0.000001. That is, use N terms where

$$|\text{term}_N| < 0.000001$$

The subroutine should return the approximation to the cosine as well as the number of terms, N.

*39 Write a main program that will produce a table with three columns. The first column should contain angles, x, beginning with 0 radian and incrementing through 3.1 radians in increments of 0.1 radian. The second column should contain the cosine of the angle x as computed by the intrinsic function. The third column should contain the cosine as computed by the function in problem 37. Print the cosine values with an F9.7 format.

SAMPLE PROBLEM – Hot Air Balloons

The Federal Aviation Agency (FAA) assigns a unique registration number to all aircraft, including hot air balloons. This number, which begins with the letter N, is assigned to an aircraft for its lifetime. A new registration system for balloons has been proposed that would use the characters following the letter N to represent information such as the balloon's manufacturer, year of manufacture, and balloon type. The various balloon types, and associated code letters, are:

1   P = propane-heated hot air balloons.

2   S = solar-heated hot air balloons.

3   H = gas balloons filled with helium or hydrogen.

Assuming a data file is available containing these new registration numbers, count the number of propane-filled balloons. (For solution, see Example 8-1, page 255.)

INTRODUCTION

We have used only integers and real numbers as data up to this point. Data often comes in other forms, however, as we will see in this chapter and the next. In this chapter, we will learn how to use *character information* that may contain numbers, letters, and special characters. The processing of these *character strings* is called *text processing* or *word processing*.

8-1 COMPUTER REPRESENTATION OF CHARACTERS

In Chapter 1 we learned that computers internally use a language composed of 0's and 1's, called *binary language*. Integers and real numbers are converted into binary numbers when they are used in a computer. If you study computer hardware or computer architecture, you will learn how to convert values such as 56 and −13.25 into binary numbers. To use FORTRAN, however, it is not necessary to learn how to convert numbers from our decimal number system to a binary number system. When characters are used in the computer, they must also be converted into a binary form, or a *binary string*. There are several codes for converting character information into binary strings, but most computers use *EBCDIC* (Extended Binary-Coded-Decimal Interchange Code) or *ASCII* (American Standard Code for Information Interchange). In these codes, each character can be represented by a binary string. Table 8-1 contains a few characters and their EBCDIC and ASCII equivalents.

TABLE 8-1 Binary Character Codes

CHARACTER	ASCII	EBCDIC
A	1000001	11000001
H	1001000	11001000
Y	1011001	11101000
3	0110011	11110011
+	0101011	01001110
$	0100100	01011011
=	0111101	01111110

Just as you did not need to memorize the punched card code for characters, you do not need to memorize the binary code for characters in order to use the characters in your FORTRAN programs. You do need, however, to be aware of the fact that the computer will store characters differently than numbers that are to be used in arithmetic computations. That is, the integer number 5 and the character 5 will not be stored the same. Thus, it is not possible to use arithmetic operations with character data even if the characters represent numbers.

8-2 CHARACTER STRING CONSTANTS AND VARIABLES

Using character strings in FORTRAN is similar in many respects to using numeric data. We can have character string constants that will always represent the same information. Character string variables will have names and represent character strings that may remain constant or may change. Generally, these character string constants and variables should contain characters from the *FORTRAN character set*, which is composed of the 26 alphabetic letters, the 10 numeric digits, a blank, and the following 12 symbols:

$$+ \quad - \quad * \quad / \quad = \quad (\quad) \quad , \quad . \quad ' \quad \$ \quad :$$

If other symbols are used, a program may not execute the same on one computer as it does on another computer.

Character constants are always enclosed in apostrophes. These apostrophes are not counted when determining the *length* or number of characters in a constant. If two consecutive apostrophes (not a double quote) are encountered within a character constant they represent a single apostrophe. Thus, the character constant for the word LET'S is 'LET''S'. The list below gives several examples of character constants and their corresponding lengths:

'SOLUTION'	8 characters
'TIME AND DISTANCE'	17 characters
'ABC'	3 characters
'CHANNEL 9'	9 characters
' $ AMT.'	7 characters
'84.56−13.7'	10 characters
'THREE '	6 characters
'CAN''T'	5 characters
''''''	2 characters

A character string variable must always be specified in a nonexecutable specification statement whose form is:

$$\boxed{\text{CHARACTER} * n \quad \textit{variable list}}$$

where n represents the number of characters in the variable string. For instance, the following statement,

```
CHARACTER*8   CODE, NAME
```

identifies CODE and NAME as variables containing eight characters each. There is no significance to the first letter of the name of a character variable. Character strings of different lengths can be specified on separate statements, or on the same statement with the following form:

```
CHARACTER   TITLE*10, NAME*15
```

A character string array can also be specified with the CHARACTER statement, as in:

```
CHARACTER*4   REG(50)
```

This statement identifies an array of 50 character strings, each containing 4 characters.

8-3   OPERATIONS WITH CHARACTER STRINGS

While character strings cannot be used in arithmetic computations, we can assign values to character strings, compare two character strings, extract a subset of a character string, and combine two character strings into one longer character string. Each of these four operations involving character strings is discussed separately.

ASSIGN VALUES

Values can be assigned to character variables with the assignment statement and a character constant. Thus, the statements below initialize a character string array RANK with the five abbreviations for freshman, sophomore, junior, senior, and graduate.

```
CHARACTER*2  RANK(5)
RANK(1) = 'FR'
RANK(2) = 'SO'
RANK(3) = 'JR'
RANK(4) = 'SR'
RANK(5) = 'GR'
```

If a character constant in an assignment statement is shorter in length than the character variable, blanks will be added to the right of the constant. Thus, if the following statement was executed, RANK(1) would contain letter F followed by a blank.

```
RANK(1) = 'F'
```

That is, an equivalent statement would be the following:

```
RANK(1) = 'F '
```

If a character constant in an assignment statement is larger than the character variable, the excess characters on the right will be ignored. Thus, the following statement,

```
RANK(1) = 'FRESHMAN'
```

would store the letters FR in the character array element RANK(1). The two examples emphasize the importance of using character strings that are the same length as the variables used to store them; otherwise, the statements can be very misleading.

One character string variable can also be used to initialize another character string variable as shown in the following statements:

```
CHARACTER*4  GRADE1, GRADE2
GRADE1 = 'GOOD'
GRADE2 = GRADE1
```

Both variables, GRADE1 and GRADE2, contain the character string 'GOOD'. Character strings may also be initialized with the DATA statement.

COMPARE VALUES

An IF statement can be used to compare character strings. Assuming that the variable DEPT and the array CH are character strings, the following are valid statements:

```
IF(DEPT.EQ.'EECE')KT = KT + 1
IF(CH(I).GT.CH(I+1))THEN
    CALL SWITCH(I)
    CALL PRINT(CH)
ENDIF
```

To evaluate a logical expression using character strings, you must first look at the length of the two strings. If one string is shorter than the other, add blanks to the right of the shorter string so that you can proceed with the evaluation using strings of equal length.

The comparison of two character strings of the same length is made from left to right, one character at a time. Two strings must have exactly the same characters in the same order to be equal.

A *collating sequence* lists characters from the lowest to the highest value. Partial collating sequences for EBCDIC and ASCII are given in Table 8-2. While the ordering is not exactly the same, there are some similarities that include:

1 Capital letters are in order from A to Z.

2 Digits are in order from 0 to 9.

3 Capital letters and digits do not overlap; digits either precede letters, or letters precede digits.

4 The blank character is less than any letter or number.

TABLE 8-2 Partial Collating Sequences for Characters

ASCII
ƀ " # $ % & ( ) * + , − . /
0 1 2 3 4 5 6 7 8 9
: ; = ? @
A B C D E F G H I J K L M N O P Q R S T U V W X Y Z

EBCDIC
ƀ . (+ & $ *) ; − / , % ? : # @ = "
A B C D E F G H I J K L M N O P Q R S T U V W X Y Z
0 1 2 3 4 5 6 7 8 9

Several pairs of character strings are now listed, along with their correct relationships.

$$'A1' < 'A2'$$
$$'JOHN' < 'JOHNSTON'$$
$$'176' < '177'$$
$$'THREE' < 'TWO'$$
$$'\$' < 'DOLLAR'$$

If character strings contain only letters, then their order is the same as that which is used in a dictionary. This ordering according to the dictionary is called a *lexicographic ordering*.

EXTRACT SUBSTRING

A *substring* of a character string is any string that represents a subset of the original string and maintains the original order. The following list contains substrings of the string 'FORTRAN'.

'F'	'FO'	'FOR'	'FORT'	'FORTR'	'FORTRA'	'FORTRAN'
'O'	'OR'	'ORT'	'ORTR'	'ORTRA'	'ORTRAN'	
'R'	'RT'	'RTR'	'RTRA'	'RTRAN'		
'T'	'TR'	'TRA'	'TRAN'			
'R'	'RA'	'RAN'				
'A'	'AN'					
'N'						

Substrings are referenced by using the name of the character string followed by two integer expressions in parentheses separated by a colon. The first expression in parentheses is evaluated to give the position in the original string of the beginning of the substring, and the second expression gives the position of the end of the substring. Thus, if the string 'FORTRAN' is stored in a variable LANG, then some of its substring references are shown as follows:

REFERENCE	SUBSTRING
LANG(1:1)	'F'
LANG(1:7)	'FORTRAN'
LANG(2:3)	'OR'
LANG(7:7)	'N'

If the first expression in the parentheses is omitted, the substring begins at the beginning of the string. Thus, LANG(:4) refers to the substring 'FORT'. If the second expression in the parentheses is omitted, the substring ends at the end of the string. Thus, LANG(5:) refers to the substring 'RAN'.

The substring operation will not operate correctly if the beginning and ending positions are not integers, are negative, or contain values greater than the number of characters in the substring. The ending position must also be greater than or equal to the beginning position of the substring.

The substring operator is a very powerful tool, as the next two examples will illustrate.

EXAMPLE 8-1   Propane-Filled Balloons

Assume that a character array REGNUM contains the registration numbers of 500 hot air balloons. Each registration number is a character string of seven characters. The fifth character specifies balloon type: P, for propane filled; S, for solar heated; and H, for helium or hydrogen filled. Write a segment of FORTRAN code that counts the number of propane-filled hot air balloons.

Solution

```
      CHARACTER*7  REGNUM(500)
      INTEGER  COUNTP
         .
         .
         .
      COUNTP = 0
C
      DO 10 I=1,500
         IF(REGNUM(I)(5:5).EQ.'P')COUNTP = COUNTP + 1
   10 CONTINUE
         .
         .
         .
```
◇

EXAMPLE 8-2   Character Count

A character string CODE of 50 characters contains coded information. The number of occurrences of the letter S represents a special piece of information. Write the loop that will count the number of occurrences of the letter S in CODE.

Solution

```
      CHARACTER*50  CODE
      INTEGER  COUNTS
         .
         .
         .
      COUNTS = 0
C
      DO 20 I=1,50
         IF(CODE(I:I).EQ.'S')COUNTS = COUNTS + 1
   20 CONTINUE
         .
         .
         .
```
◇

A reference to a substring can be used anywhere that a string can be used. For instance, if LANG contains the character string 'FORTRAN', the following statement will change the value of LANG to 'FORMATS':

```
LANG(4:7) = 'MATS'
```

If LANG contains 'FORMATS', then the following statement will change the value of LANG to 'FORMASS':

```
LANG(6:6) = LANG(7:7)
```

When modifying a substring of a character string with a substring of the same character string, the substrings must not overlap. That is, do not use LANG(2:4) to replace LANG(3:5). Also, recall that, if a substring is being moved into a smaller string, only as many characters as needed to replace the smaller string will be moved from left to right. If the substring is being moved into a larger string, the extra positions on the right will be filled with blanks.

COMBINE STRINGS

Concatenation is the operation of combining two or more character strings into one character string and is indicated by two slashes between the character strings to be combined. Thus, the next expression concatenates the constants 'WORK' and 'ED' into one string constant 'WORKED':

```
'WORK'//'ED'
```

The next statement combines the contents of three character string variables MO, DA, and YR into one character string and then moves the combined string into a variable called DATE:

```
DATE = MO//DA//YR
```

If MO = '05', DA = '15', and YR = '84', then DATE = '051584'. Since concatenation represents an operation, it cannot appear on the left of an equal sign.

8-4   INPUT AND OUTPUT OF CHARACTER STRINGS

When a character string is used in a list-directed output statement, the entire character string will be printed. When a character string variable is used in a list-directed input statement, the corresponding data value must be enclosed in apostrophes. When a character string is used in formatted output, Aw is used as the specification. If w is omitted, the entire string will be printed. If w is less than the length of the character string, the first w positions of the character string will be printed. If w is greater than the length of the character string, the extra positions will be filled with blanks on the left of the string.

When the specification Aw for formatted input is used, if w is less than the length of the character string, the rightmost positions in memory will be filled with blanks. If w is greater than the length of the character string, only the first w characters will be stored. If w is omitted, the length of the string will be used to determine the number of positions to read.

To illustrate the rules for output, assume that the character string variable NAME contains 'JOHN A. SMITH', and that the following statement has been executed:

```
CHARACTER*13   NAME
       .
       .
       .
WRITE(6,10)NAME
```

Beside each of the following format statements is the corresponding output.

FORMAT		CORRESPONDING OUTPUT
10	FORMAT(1X,A)	JOHN A. SMITH
10	FORMAT(1X,A13)	JOHN A. SMITH
10	FORMAT(1X,A4)	JOHN
10	FORMAT(1X,A10)	JOHN A. SM
10	FORMAT(1X,A15)	bbJOHN A. SMITH

To further illustrate the rules for input, assume that ADDR is a character string with length 15. If a computer card contained 962 E.MAIN ST., in columns 1–15, then the execution of the following READ statement would yield the results shown:

```
CHARACTER*15   ADDR
       .
       .
       .
READ(5,20)ADDR
       .
       .
       .
```

FORMAT		CONTENTS OF ADDR
20	FORMAT(A)	962 E. MAIN ST.
20	FORMAT(A15)	962 E. MAIN ST.
20	FORMAT(A11)	962 E. MAIN bbbb
20	FORMAT(A3)	962 bbbbbbbbbbbb
20	FORMAT(A20)	962 E. MAIN ST.

8-5 APPLICATION – Printer Plot of Interference Patterns

Information is often more understandable if it can be represented graphically. A plotting device is usually the device preferred for preparing graphical output because of its versatility and its good resolution. Not every computer system, however, has a plotting device attached to it, and the extra resolution of a plotter may not be necessary to observe trends in the data. Therefore, in this section we will present a type of graph that is used in *printer plotting*.

In this application, we are interested in studying the interference pattern produced by two sinusoidal wave generators operating in phase. These signal sources might be two speakers driven by the same amplifier or two radio antennas powered by the same transmitter. We assume that we have a function that defines a displacement Z that describes the interference of the sources. If we are dealing with surface waves, Z would be the actual displacement of the surface, which could be water. If we are talking about sound waves, Z could refer to pressure. Let R1 and R2 be the straight line distances from the two sources to the same point (x, y). We will consider the interference pattern, where the displacement can be computed with the function

$$Z = \cos(R1) + \cos(R2)$$

Figure 8-1 contains a three-dimensional graph of this interference pattern, which was produced by a pen plotter. The black squares represent the signal sources. The printer-plot program will be a two-dimensional representation of the surface.

The output of our printer-plot program will be a group of 61 character strings, each containing 101 characters. This will produce a square graph, whose x-axis and y-axis will vary from -10 units to 10 units. Figure 8-2 contains a diagram of this output.

From Figure 8-2, it can be seen that the change in Y from one row to the next is

$$\Delta Y = 20/60 = 1/3$$

and the change in X from one column to the next is

$$\Delta X = 20/100 = 1/5$$

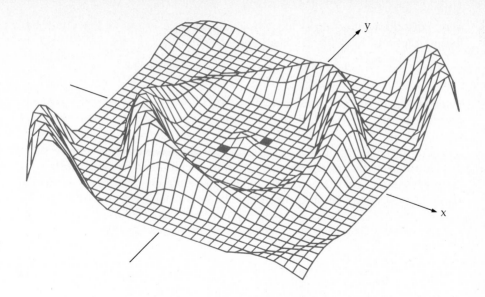

FIGURE 8-1   Pen plot of sinusoidal interference pattern.

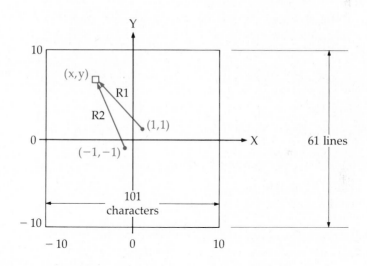

FIGURE 8-2   Printer-plot output diagram.

Also, with the wave sources located at positions (1, 1) and (−1, −1), we can compute R1 and R2 with the following equations:

```
R1 = SQRT((X-1)**2 + (Y-1)**2)
R2 = SQRT((X+1)**2 + (Y+1)**2)
```

Thus, for each print position in our square grid, we first compute the *x*- and *y*-coordinates in the given units, and then we compute the straight line distances, R1 and R2, from the print position to the sources. Finally, we then compute the displacement Z of the print position. We want to represent the displacement with characters such that the character becomes darker as the displacement increases. Some of the following characters are not in the standard FORTRAN set and thus may not be available on all systems.

VALUE OF Z	CHARACTER REPRESENTATION
$Z \le 0.0$	'
$0.0 < Z \le 0.5$	+
$0.5 < Z \le 1.0$	%
$1.0 < Z \le 1.5$	@
$1.5 < Z \le 2.0$	#

The origin will be located by the intersection of the X and Y axes. The X axis will be represented by '−' and will represent values where

$$|Y| \le 0.001$$

The Y axis will be represented by '!' and will represent values where

$$|X| \le 0.001$$

The axis symbol will take precedence over the other character representations.

EXAMPLE 8-3 Interference Pattern

Write a complete program that will produce a plot of the displacement Z, where

$$Z = \cos(R1) + \cos(R2)$$

and the wave sources are located at positions (1,1) and (−1,−1). The plot should be 61 lines long, with 101 characters on each line. Use a single character string, not an array of character strings.

Solution

Let ROW be a character string of 101 characters that will be used for printing each line of output.

General Pseudocode	Refined Pseudocode
PROGRAM GRAPH	PROGRAM GRAPH
CHARACTER*101 ROW	CHARACTER*101 ROW
	XDELT $\leftarrow 1/5$
	YDELT $\leftarrow 1/3$
Initialize Y	Y $\leftarrow 10.0$
DO I=1,61	DO I=1,61
Initialize X	X $\leftarrow -10.0$
DO J=1,101	DO J=1,101
Compute distances	R1 $\leftarrow \sqrt{(X-1)^2 + (Y-1)^2}$
R1, R2 from point	R2 $\leftarrow \sqrt{(X+1)^2 + (Y+1)^2}$
(X,Y)	Z $\leftarrow \text{COS(R1)} + \text{COS(R2)}$
Compute	IF Z ≤ 0.0 THEN
displacement Z	ROW(J:J) $\leftarrow$
	apostrophe
	ELSE
	IF Z ≤ 1.0 THEN
	IF Z ≤ 0.5 THEN
	ROW(J:J) $\leftarrow$ '+'
	ELSE
	ROW(J:J) $\leftarrow$ '%'
	ENDIF
ROW(J:J) $\leftarrow$	ELSE
appropriate	IF Z ≤ 1.5 THEN
character	ROW(J:J) $\leftarrow$ '@'
dependent on Z	ELSE
	ROW(J:J) $\leftarrow$ '#'
	ENDIF
	ENDIF
	ENDIF
	IF $|Y| \leq 0.001$ THEN
	ROW(J:J) $\leftarrow$ '$-$'
	IF $|X| \leq 0.001$ THEN
	ROW(J:J) $\leftarrow$ '!'
Increment X	X $\leftarrow$ X + XDELT
ENDDO	ENDDO
Increment Y	Y $\leftarrow$ Y + YDELT
PRINT ROW	PRINT ROW
ENDDO	ENDDO
STOP	STOP

```
      PROGRAM   GRAPH
C
C   THIS PROGRAM PRODUCES AN INTERFERENCE
C   GRAPH FOR SINUSOIDAL SIGNALS
C
      CHARACTER*101  ROW
C
      WRITE(6,1)
    1 FORMAT('1')
C
      XDELT = 0.2
      YDELT = 1.0/3.0
      Y = 10.0
C
      DO 20 I=1,61
         X = -10.0
         DO 10 J=1,101
C
            R1 = SQRT((X - 1.0)**2 + (Y - 1.0)**2)
            R2 = SQRT((X + 1.0)**2 + (Y + 1.0)**2)
            Z = COS(R1) + COS(R2)
C
            IF(Z.LE.0.0)THEN
               ROW(J:J) = ''''
            ELSE
               IF(Z.LE.1.0)THEN
                  IF(Z.LE.0.5)THEN
                     ROW(J:J) = '+'
                  ELSE
                     ROW(J:J) = '%'
                  ENDIF
               ELSE
                  IF(Z.LE.1.5)THEN
                     ROW(J:J) = '@'
                  ELSE
                     ROW(J:J) = '#'
                  ENDIF
               ENDIF
            ENDIF
C
            IF(ABS(Y).LE.0.001)ROW(J:J) = '-'
            IF(ABS(X).LE.0.001)ROW(J:J) = '!'
C
            X = X + XDELT
   10    CONTINUE
         Y = Y - YDELT
         WRITE(6,15)ROW
   15    FORMAT(5X,A101)
   20 CONTINUE
C
      STOP
      END
```

8-6 CHARACTER STRING SUBPROGRAMS

There are two intrinsic functions, INDEX and LEN, that are commonly used with character strings. INDEX is used to locate substrings within a specified string, while LEN is used to determine the length of a string.

INDEX

The INDEX function has two arguments, both character strings. The function returns an integer value giving the position in the first string of the second string. Thus, if STRGA contained the phrase 'TO BE OR NOT TO BE', INDEX(STRGA,'BE') would return the value 4, which points to the first occurrence of the string 'BE'. To find the second occurrence of the string, we could use the following statements:

```
CHARACTER*18   STRGA
    .
    .
    .
K = INDEX(STRGA,'BE')
J = INDEX(STRGA(K+1:),'BE') + K
```

After execution of these statements, K would contain the value 4 and J would contain the value 17. Note that we had to add K to the second reference of INDEX in order to get the correct position because the second use of INDEX referred to the substring 'E OR NOT TO BE'. Thus, the second INDEX reference would return a value of 13, not 17. The value of INDEX(STRGA,'AND') would be zero because the second string 'AND' does not occur in the first string STRGA.

LEN

The input to the function LEN is a character string, and the output is an integer that contains the length of the character string. This function is particularly useful in a subprogram that accepts character strings of any length, but needs the actual length within the subprogram. The statement in the subprogram that allows a character string to be used with any length is

```
CHARACTER*(*) A, B, STRGA
```

This form can be used only in subprograms. The next example will use both the LEN function and the variable string length parameter in a subprogram.

EXAMPLE 8-4   Frequency of Blanks

Write a function subprogram that accepts a character string and returns a count of the number of blanks in the string.

Solution

```
      INTEGER  FUNCTION  BLANKS(X)
C
C  THIS FUNCTION COUNTS THE NUMBER
C  OF BLANKS IN A CHARACTER STRING X
C
      CHARACTER*(*)  X
C
      BLANKS = 0
C
      DO 10 I=1,LEN(X)
         IF(X(I:I).EQ.' ')BLANKS = BLANKS + 1
   10 CONTINUE
C
      RETURN
      END                                          ◊
```

Character strings may also be used in user-written subroutines. In the next example, we will write a subroutine that combines input character strings into an output character string.

EXAMPLE 8-5   Name Editing

Write a subroutine that will receive 3 character strings, FIRST, MIDDLE, and LAST, each containing 15 characters. The output of the subroutine is to be a character string 35 characters long that contains the first name followed by one blank, the middle initial followed by a period and one blank, and finally the last name. Assume that FIRST, MIDDLE, and LAST have no leading blanks and no embedded blanks. Thus:

> FIRST = 'JOSEPH   '
> MIDDLE = 'CHARLES   '
> LAST = 'LAWTON   '
> NAME = 'JOSEPH C. LAWTON   '

Solution

The solution to this problem is simplified by the use of the substring operation that allows us to look at individual characters, and the INDEX function that is used to find the end of the first name. We move to NAME the characters in FIRST, then a bl nk, the middle initial, a period, another blank, and the last name. As you go through the solution, observe the use of the concatenation operation. Also, note that the move of the first name fills the rest of the character string NAME with blanks because FIRST is smaller than the field to which it is moved.

FORTRAN Subprogram

```
      SUBROUTINE  EDIT(FIRST, MIDDLE, LAST, NAME)
C
C  THIS SUBROUTINE EDITS A NAME TO THE FORM
C  FIRST, MIDDLE INITIAL, LAST
C
      CHARACTER*15  FIRST, MIDDLE, LAST
      CHARACTER*35  NAME
C
C  MOVE FIRST NAME
C
      NAME = FIRST
C
C  MOVE MIDDLE INITIAL
C
      L = INDEX(FIRST,' ')
      NAME(L:L+3) = ' '//MIDDLE(1:1)//', '
C
C  MOVE LAST NAME
C
      NAME(L+4:) = LAST
C
      RETURN
      END                                              ◇
```

8-7 APPLICATION – Bar Graph of Construction Data

Bar graphs are frequently used to graphically compare a group of values. In this section, we will develop a subroutine that will print a bar graph scaled to fit different sizes of computer paper. The subroutine will be general enough to be used in many circumstances.

EXAMPLE 8-6 Bar Graph Plot

Write a subroutine that receives an array of N values and prints a bar graph for the values that has a line size LINE. We will present two solutions, the first being a simple and quick solution and the second being a more complicated but more attractive solution.

Solution 1

We will assume that this subroutine will be called with a statement of the form

```
CALL BARGR1(DATA, N, LINE)
```

where DATA is the array of N data values. The bar graph is to be scaled such that the maximum number of characters in each line is LINE. In order to determine the scaling needed, we need to know the maximum and minimum values in DATA. These can be computed in the subroutine, or other subprograms can be used to compute these values, which we will call DMAX and DMIN. We will want the value DMAX to be represented by a full line, one with LINE characters, and DMIN to be represented by a line with one character. The number of characters K in a line representing an arbitrary value DATA(I) can be computed using proportions.

Using Figure 8-3, we see that

$$\frac{K - 1}{LINE - 1} = \frac{DATA(I) - DMIN}{DMAX - DMIN}$$

Hence, we can then solve for K,

$$K = \left(\frac{DATA(I) - DMIN}{DMAX - DMIN}\right)\left(LINE - 1\right) + 1$$

If we let DATA(I) equal DMAX, you can see that K is computed to be LINE, as desired. If we let DATA(I) equal DMIN, K is computed to be 1, again as desired. Values between DMIN and DMAX will have proportional values between 1 and LINE. The pseudocode, subroutine, sample data, and output are given on pages 268–270.

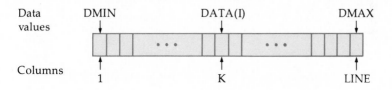

Data values   DMIN   DATA(I)   DMAX

Columns   1   K   LINE

FIGURE 8-3 Calculation of bar length, K.

General Pseudocode	Refined Pseudocode
SUBROUTINE BARGR1 (DATA, N, LINE) DIMENSION DATA(N)	SUBROUTINE BARGR1(DATA, N, LINE) DIMENSION DATA(N) CHARACTER*130 COL

IF LINE > 130 THEN
PRINT error message
RETURN
ENDIF
	IF LINE > 130 THEN
	PRINT error message
	RETURN
	ENDIF
	DO I=1,LINE
	COL(I:I) = '*'
	ENDDO
	DMAX ← DATA(1)
	DMIN ← DATA(1)

DMIN ←
minimum data value
DMAX ←
maximum data value
	DO I=2,N
	IF DATA(I) < DMIN THEN
	DMIN ← DATA(I)
	IF DATA(I) > DMAX THEN
	DMAX ← DATA(I)
	ENDDO

DO I=1,N Compute bar length K using DATA(I), DMIN, DMAX, LINE PRINT K asterisks ENDDO RETURN	DO I=1,N $K \leftarrow \left(\dfrac{DATA(I) - DMIN}{DMAX - DMIN}\right) \cdot \left(LINE - 1\right) + 1$ PRINT COL(1:K) ENDDO RETURN

```fortran
      SUBROUTINE  BARGR1(DATA, N, LINE)
C
C THIS SUBROUTINE PRINTS A BAR GRAPH
C USING THE VALUES IN THE ARRAY DATA
C
      DIMENSION  DATA(N)
      CHARACTER*130  COL
C
C ERROR RETURN
C
      IF(LINE.GT.130)THEN
         WRITE(6,5)LINE
   5     FORMAT(1X,'LINE = ',I4/1X,
     +          'MUST BE LESS THAN 130')
         RETURN
      ENDIF
C
C FILL CHARACTER STRING WITH ASTERISKS
C
      DO 10 I=1,LINE
         COL(I:I) = '*'
  10  CONTINUE
C
C FIND MAX AND MIN
C
      DMAX = DATA(1)
      DMIN = DATA(1)
      DO 20 I=2,N
         IF(DATA(I).LT.DMIN)DMIN = DATA(I)
         IF(DATA(I).GT.DMAX)DMAX = DATA(I)
  20  CONTINUE
C
C PRINT BAR GRAPH
C
      DO 30 I=1,N
         K = (DATA(I) - DMIN)/
     +       (DMAX - DMIN)*(LINE - 1) + 1
         WRITE(6,25)COL(1:K)
  25     FORMAT(1X,A)
  30  CONTINUE
C
      RETURN
      END
```

DATA 21.0   N 10   LINE 30
      33.0
      44.0
      34.0
      71.0
      18.0
      46.0
      26.0
      38.0
      45.0

COMPUTER OUTPUT

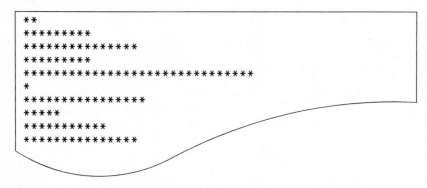

```
**
*********
***************
*********
******************************
*
****************
*****
***********
**************
```

Solution 2

We can improve the appearance of the bar graph in the following ways:

1 Add a heading and vertical scales.

2 Each bar will be made up of one line of spaces and three lines of asterisks.

3 The middle line of asterisks for each bar will also have a title printed with it.

4 A line of dashes will be printed at the end of the bar graph.

5 Allow the user to specify the beginning value and ending values to be used on the bar scale. Thus, instead of the first character in the bar representing the minimum value, it could be set to represent another value, such as zero.

The new variables to be added to the argument list and their definitions are now listed.

MTITLE—Main title of chart, 40 characters

  HX—Heading of X axis, 20 characters

HY—Heading of Y axis, 20 characters

TITLEB—Array of bar titles, N elements, 20 characters each

DMIN—Minimum value on bar scale

DMAX—Maximum value on bar scale

We now include pseudocode, a main program (driver) to test BARGR2, the subroutine BARGR2, sample data that represents the reduction in building construction, and sample output.

GENERAL PSEUDOCODE	REFINED PSEUDOCODE

SUBROUTINE BARGR2
    (MTITLE, HX, HY,
    TITLEB, DATA, N,
    LINE, DMIN, DMAX)
	SUBROUTINE BARGR2
	    (MTITLE, HX, HY, TITLEB,
	    DATA, N, LINE, DMIN,
	    DMAX)
	CHARACTER*40 MTITLE
	CHARACTER*20 HX, HY,
	    TITLEB(N)
	CHARACTER*130 COL, DASH

GENERAL PSEUDOCODE

```
DIMENSION  DATA(N)
IF LINE > 130 THEN
    PRINT error message
    RETURN
ENDIF




PRINT headings, scale,
    Y axis






DO I=1,N
    Compute bar length K
        using DATA(I),
        DMIN, DMAX, LINE
    PRINT bar title and
        bar of K asterisks
ENDDO

PRINT Y axis

RETURN
```

REFINED PSEUDOCODE

```
DIMENSION  DATA(N)
IF LINE > 130 THEN
    PRINT error message
    RETURN
ENDIF
DO I=1,LINE
    COL(I:I) ← '*'
    DASH(I:I) ← '−'
ENDDO
PRINT MTITLE, HY, HX
DASH(1:1) ← '+'
DASH(LINE:LINE) ← '+'
PRINT DASH(1:LINE)
DO I=1,N
    PRINT '!'
```

$$K \leftarrow \left(\frac{DATA(I) - DMIN}{DMAX - DMIN}\right) \cdot \left(LINE - 1\right) + 1$$

```
    PRINT COL(1:K)
    PRINT TITLEB(I), COL(1:K)
    PRINT COL(1:K)
ENDDO
PRINT '!'
PRINT DASH(1:LINE)
RETURN
```

FORTRAN Program

```
      PROGRAM  DRIVER
C
C  THIS IS A DRIVER PROGRAM TO TEST THE SUBROUTINE BARGR2
C
      CHARACTER*40  MTITLE
      CHARACTER*20  HX, HY, TITLEB(10)
      DIMENSION  DATA(10)
C
      OPEN(UNIT=9, FILE='CONST', STATUS='OLD')
C
C  READ HEADER INFORMATION
C
      READ(9,50)MTITLE, HX, HY
   50 FORMAT(A)
C
C  READ BAR TITLES AND DATA ARRAY,
C  FIND MAXIMUM DATA VALUE
C
      DMAX = 0.0
      DO 100 I=1,10
         READ(9,52)TITLEB(I), DATA(I)
   52    FORMAT(A20,1X,F10.0)
         IF(DMAX.LT.DATA(I))DMAX = DATA(I)
  100 CONTINUE
C
C  CALL SUBROUTINE TO PRINT BAR GRAPH
C
      CALL BARGR2(MTITLE, HX, HY, TITLEB, DATA, 10, 52,
     +         0.0, DMAX)
C
      STOP
      END
```

FORTRAN Subprogram

```
      SUBROUTINE BARGR2(MTITLE, HX, HY, TITLEB, DATA, N,
         LINE, DMIN, DMAX)
C
C  THIS SUBROUTINE PRINTS AN IMPROVED BAR GRAPH
C     MTITLE = MAIN TITLE
C     HX, HY = X, Y HEADINGS
C     TITLEB = BAR TITLE ARRAY, SIZE N
C     DATA = DATA ARRAY, SIZE N
C     LINE = NUMBER OF CHARACTERS PER LINE
C     DMIN, DMAX = MIN, MAX VALUES FOR BAR GRAPH
C
      CHARACTER*40  MTITLE
      CHARACTER*20  HX, HY, TITLEB(N)
      CHARACTER*130  COL, DASH
      DIMENSION  DATA(N)
```

```
C
C   ERROR RETURN
C
      IF(LINE.GT.130)THEN
         WRITE(6,5)LINE
    5    FORMAT(1X,'LINE = ',I4/1X,
   +           'MUST BE LESS THAN 130')
         RETURN
      ENDIF
C
C   FILL CHARACTER STRING COL WITH ASTERISKS
C   FILL CHARACTER STRING DASH WITH DASHES
C
      DO 10 I=1,LINE
         COL(I:I) = '*'
         DASH(I:I) = '-'
   10 CONTINUE
C
C   PRINT HEADINGS AND SCALE
C
      WRITE(6,25)MTITLE
   25 FORMAT('1',A)
      WRITE(6,30)HY
   30 FORMAT('0',25X,A)
      WRITE(6,35)HX
   35 FORMAT(1X,A)
C
C   SET UP AND PRINT Y AXIS
C
      DASH(1:1) = '+'
      DASH(LINE:LINE) = '+'
      WRITE(6,40)DASH(1:LINE)
   40 FORMAT(21X,A)
C
C   PRINT BAR GRAPH
C
      DO 100 I=1,N
         WRITE(6,50)'!'
   50    FORMAT(21X,A)
         K = (DATA(I) - DMIN)/
   +         (DMAX - DMIN)*(LINE - 1) + 1
         WRITE(6,50)COL(1:K)
         WRITE(6,60)TITLEB(I), COL(1:K)
   60    FORMAT(1X,A20,A)
         WRITE(6,50)COL(1:K)
  100 CONTINUE
C
C   PRINT LINE OF DASHES
C
      WRITE(6,50)'!'
      WRITE(6,40)DASH(1:LINE)
C
      RETURN
      END
```

REDUCTION IN CONSTRUCTION VALUE

CITY

CITY	VALUE
NEW YORK, NY	21.0
CHICAGO, IL	33.0
DETROIT, MI	44.0
PHILADELPHIA, PA	34.0
WASHINGTON, DC	71.0
LOS ANGELES, CA	18.0
BALTIMORE, MD	46.0
DAYTON, OH	26.0
CLEVELAND, OH	38.0
NEW ORLEANS, LA	45.0

COMPUTER OUTPUT

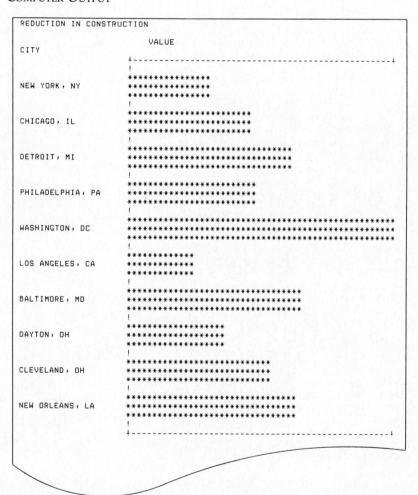

8-8 APPLICATION – Average Word Length of Text Material

Text processing is necessary in many computerized applications in engineering and science. The text processing may be the fundamental part of the program, as in *cryptography* (the encoding and decoding of secret messages), or text processing may be used to improve the form of the output, as in editing and report generation. The application of text processing presented in this section will be one that analyzes the content of text material.

EXAMPLE 8-7 Average Word Length

Text material is sometimes analyzed very carefully to determine quantities such as average word length. A quantity such as average word length can be used to recommend the level of reading ability necessary to read the text. Average word length can even be used to help determine authorship of a literary work and has been applied to the works of Shakespeare in an attempt to suggest whether or not Sir Francis Bacon may have authored some of the plays attributed to Shakespeare. Write a function that receives a character string and returns the average word length of the string. Assume that all words are separated from adjacent words by at least one blank. The first and last characters may or may not be blanks.

Solution

Sometimes the best way to get started on a problem is to work a few cases by hand. Assume that the text is 18 characters long. Then the following strings can be analyzed as shown:

'TO BE OR NOT TO BE'
> 6 words, 13 letters, 2.17 average word length

'   HELLO   '
> 1 word, 5 letters, 5.0 average word length

'IDIOSYNCRATICALLY! '
> 1 word, 18 letters, 18.0 average word length

'MR. JOHN P. BUD   '
> 4 words, 12 letters, 3.0 average word length

'   '
> 0 words, 0 letters, 0.0 average word length

From these cases, we see that the text could have no blanks or be all blanks. The words may be separated by one or more blanks, and the text may or may not begin and end with a blank. The key part of the algorithm will be recognizing words—where they begin and end. One solution is presented in the following discussion. Test the solution by hand on the example strings given earlier before proceeding to the FORTRAN code. You should always be convinced that your algorithm works before you start to code it.

We will use NWORDS to store the number of words and NLETRS to store the number of letters. Both of these variables will be initialized to zero. Note that we are counting any nonblank character as a letter. We begin by looking through the text (TEXT) for the first nonblank character, using the substring notation. If we do not find a nonblank character, we will return an average word length of zero. If we do find a nonblank character, call the appropriate position FIRST. Then look for the first blank character in the substring beginning at position FIRST and call this new position NEXTBL. If there are no blanks after FIRST, set NEXTBL to the first position after the end of the string. The number of characters in the word would be NEXTBL − 1. We add this value to NLETRS and 1 to NWORDS. We move the value of NEXTBL to FIRST, and repeat the process until we reach the end of the string. At that point, we compute the average word length, being careful not to lose the fractional portion, and return to the main program.

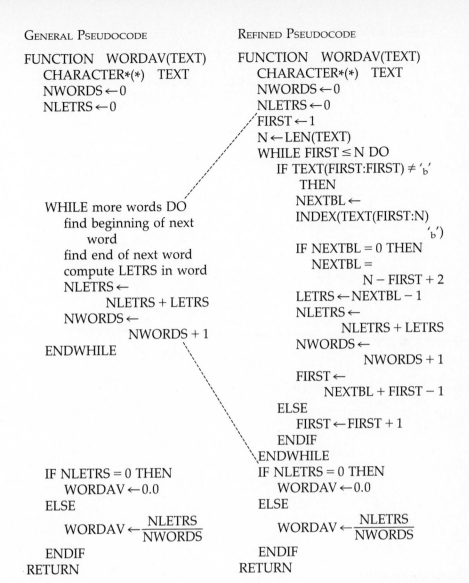

General Pseudocode:

```
FUNCTION  WORDAV(TEXT)
   CHARACTER*(*)  TEXT
   NWORDS ← 0
   NLETRS ← 0




   WHILE more words DO
      find beginning of next
         word
      find end of next word
      compute LETRS in word
      NLETRS ←
            NLETRS + LETRS
      NWORDS ←
            NWORDS + 1
   ENDWHILE



   IF NLETRS = 0 THEN
      WORDAV ← 0.0
   ELSE
      WORDAV ← NLETRS
               ───────
               NWORDS
   ENDIF
   RETURN
```

Refined Pseudocode:

```
FUNCTION  WORDAV(TEXT)
   CHARACTER*(*)  TEXT
   NWORDS ← 0
   NLETRS ← 0
   FIRST ← 1
   N ← LEN(TEXT)
   WHILE FIRST ≤ N DO
      IF TEXT(FIRST:FIRST) ≠ 'ᵦ'
         THEN
         NEXTBL ←
         INDEX(TEXT(FIRST:N)
                            'ᵦ')
         IF NEXTBL = 0 THEN
            NEXTBL =
                  N − FIRST + 2
         LETRS ← NEXTBL − 1
         NLETRS ←
               NLETRS + LETRS
         NWORDS ←
               NWORDS + 1
         FIRST ←
               NEXTBL + FIRST − 1
      ELSE
         FIRST ← FIRST + 1
      ENDIF
   ENDWHILE
   IF NLETRS = 0 THEN
      WORDAV ← 0.0
   ELSE
      WORDAV ← NLETRS
               ───────
               NWORDS
   ENDIF
   RETURN
```

FORTRAN Subprogram

```
      FUNCTION  WORDAV(TEXT)
C
C  THIS FUNCTION COMPUTES THE AVERAGE WORD
C  LENGTH OF THE CHARACTER STRING TEXT
C
      CHARACTER*(*)  TEXT
      INTEGER  FIRST
C
      NWORDS = 0
      NLETRS = 0
      FIRST = 1
      N = LEN(TEXT)
C
   10 IF (FIRST.LE.N)THEN

         IF (TEXT(FIRST:FIRST).NE.' ')THEN
            NEXTBL = INDEX(TEXT(FIRST:N),' ')
            IF(NEXTBL.EQ.0)NEXTBL = N - FIRST + 2
            LETRS = NEXTBL - 1
            NLETRS = NLETRS + LETRS
            NWORDS = NWORDS + 1
            FIRST = NEXTBL + FIRST - 1
         ELSE
            FIRST = FIRST + 1
         ENDIF
         GO TO 10
C
      ENDIF
C
      IF(NLETRS.EQ.0)THEN
         WORDAV = 0.0
      ELSE
         WORDAV = NLETRS/REAL(NWORDS)
      ENDIF
C
      RETURN
      END                                                ◇
```

SUMMARY

The processing of character strings plays an ever-increasing role in the analysis and presentation of information. We no longer have to assume that answers to problems must always be numbers. With character string operations, we can creatively display our solutions, whether numeric or not, in ways that communicate more effectively with both computer users and noncomputer users.

KEY WORDS

ASCII
binary string
character string
collating sequence
concatenation
EBCDIC

FORTRAN character set
lexicographical order
printer plotting
substring
text processing
word processing

DEBUGGING AIDS

Many errors in character string manipulations occur because the character string is used incorrectly with numeric data. Some typical examples are:

Arithmetic expressions—Even if a character string contains numeric digits, it cannot be used in an arithmetic operation.

Comparisons—Character strings should always be compared to other character strings and not to a numeric constant or variable.

Subprogram arguments—A character string used as an argument to a subprogram must be identified in CHARACTER statements in both the main program and the subprogram.

Another source of errors may be introduced when moving or comparing strings of unequal length. For comparisons, the shorter string will be compared as if it had enough blanks on the right to be equal in length to the longer string. Character strings are always moved character by character from left to right, until the receiving string is filled. If there are not enough characters in the sending string, blanks will be moved into the right-most characters of the receiving string.

A final caution on the substring operation: Invalid results will occur if the beginning or ending positions of the substring reference are outside the original string itself.

STYLE/TECHNIQUE GUIDES

A programmer who is comfortable and proficient with character string manipulations will find them to be extremely useful. The ability to display information clearly and simply is very valuable in communicating with people, and the use of character strings adds a new dimension to the method of both reading and displaying information.

Some guides for using character strings in your programs are now listed:

1 Use character strings of the same length where possible.

2 Use the function INDEX instead of writing your own routines to find substrings in a string.

3 Become proficient with the substring and concatenation operators. These are powerful tools in manipulating and analyzing character strings.

4 Take advantage of the printer-plotting techniques that are described in this chapter and in the problems at the end of the chapter.

PROBLEMS

In problems 1 through 12, a character string of length 25 called TITLE is initialized with the statements,

```
CHARACTER*25  TITLE
TITLE = 'CONSERVATION OF ENERGY'
     .
     .
     .
```

Tell what substrings are referred to in the following references:

1 TITLE(1:25)   **2** TITLE(1:12)

3 TITLE(13:23)   **4** TITLE(16:16)

5 TITLE(8:8)   **6** TITLE(17:)

7 TITLE(:12)   **8** TITLE(:)

9 TITLE//'LAW'

10 TITLE(1:12)//' IS '//'A'//' LAW'

11 TITLE(1:7)//'E'//TITLE(16:)

12 ''''//TITLE(1:4)//'ID'//TITLE(19:20)//'ATE'//''''

In problems 13 through 18, WORD is a character string of length 6. What is stored in WORD after each of the following statements?

13 WORD = 'DENSITY'   **14** WORD = 'AREA'

15 WORD = 'CAN''T'   **16** WORD = '''''''!'

17 WORD = 'FT'//''//'/SEC'   **18** WORD = ' VOLUME'

In problems 19 through 24, tell whether each of the logical expressions is "true" or "false." Assume EBCDIC as the internal code.

19 'ABC'.EQ.'ABC '   **20** 'ADAM'.LT.'ABLE'

21 '**'.LT.'* *'   **22** 'TWO'.GE.'TWOSOME'

23 '138.5'.LE.'138.50'   **24** ' JOE'.NE.'JOE'

In problems 25 through 30, the character string PHRASE contains 40 characters and has been initialized with the following statement:

```
CHARACTER*40   PHRASE
      .
      .
      .
PHRASE = 'ELECTRONS, NEUTRONS, PROTONS'
```

What value is returned by the following intrinsic functions?

25 LEN(PHRASE)

26 LEN(PHRASE(12:))

27 INDEX(PHRASE,'ON')

28 INDEX(PHRASE(12:),'ING')

29 INDEX(PHRASE(22:),PHRASE(1:1))

30 INDEX(PHRASE(:21),' ')

For problems 31 through 34, assume that a data line contains the following characters, beginning in the first position,

ENERGY ALTERNATIVE AND SOURCES

and the line is read with these statements:

```
CHARACTER*20   TITLE
      .
      .
      .
READ(10,5)TITLE
```

Give the contents of TITLE for each of the following formats:

31 5 FORMAT(A)	**32** 5 FORMAT(A20)
33 5 FORMAT(A5)	**34** 5 FORMAT(A25)

In problems 35 through 38, what is written by the following statements with the different formats indicated?

```
CHARACTER*10   UNIT
      .
      .
      .
UNIT = 'METERS'
      .
      .
      .
WRITE(6,20)UNIT
```

35 20 FORMAT(1X,A)	**36** 20 FORMAT(1X,A10)
37 20 FORMAT(1X,A15)	**38** 20 FORMAT(1X,A5)

39 Write a complete program that will read 50 sets of cards containing names and addresses as shown below:

Card 1:	First	Middle	Last
	Name	Name	Name
	col 1–10	col 15–20	col 25–45

Card 2:	Address	City	State	ZIP
	col 1–25	col 30–39	col 45–46	col 50–54

Print the information in the following label form:

> First Initial.   Middle Initial. Last Name
> Address
> City, State   ZIP

Skip four lines between labels. The city should not contain any blanks before the comma that follows it. A typical label might be:

> J. D. DOE
> 117 MAIN ST.
> TAOS, NM   87186

For simplicity, assume no embedded blanks in the individual data values. That is, San Jose is punched SANJOSE,, not SAN JOSE.

40 Write a subroutine PACK that receives a character string IN of 50 characters and returns a character string OUT that has no adjacent blanks except at the end of the string. Thus, if IN was composed of 'ᵦHELLObbbTHERE' followed by 36 blanks, then the output OUT from the subroutine PACK should be ' HELLO THERE' followed by 38 blanks.

41 Write a subroutine DELETE that has an argument list composed of a character string TEXT of 100 characters and a pointer PTR. The subroutine should delete the character in position PTR. The characters in the positions following PTR should be moved one position to the left. A blank should then be added at the end of TEXT to keep the length of TEXT consistent at 100 characters.

42 Write a subroutine INSERT that has an argument list composed of a character string TEXT of 100 characters, a point PTR, and a single character CHAR. The subroutine should insert CHAR in the position pointed to by PTR. The rest of the characters should be moved one position to the right, with the last character truncated to keep the length of TEXT at 100 characters.

43 A data file called CARS contains the license plate number and the number of gallons of gas that can be put into the car for each car in the state of California. The license plate is composed of three characters, followed by three digits, in columns 1–6. The gallons amount is in columns 9–12 and has one decimal position. The last line in the file has a license number of ZZZ999 and is not a valid data line. Write a complete program that will analyze the feasibility of gas rationing based on whether the license plate number is odd or even. The data to be computed and printed is the following:

	GALLONS	%
SUM OF GAS FOR ODD CARS	XXXXX.X	XX.X
SUM OF GAS FOR EVEN CARS	XXXXX.X	XX.X
TOTAL	XXXXXX.X	XXX.X

44 A *palindrome* is a word or piece of text that is spelled the same forward and backward. The word 'RADAR' is an example of a palindrome, but ' RADAR' is not a palindrome because of the unmatched blank. 'ABLE ELBA' is another palindrome. Write a function PALIND that receives a character string X of variable length and returns a 1 if X is a palindrome and a 0 if X is not a palindrome.

45 Write a subroutine ALPHA that receives an array of 50 names, NAME, each 4 characters long. The subroutine should sort the names into an alphabetized list and return this list in the array ANAME.

46 Write a subroutine whose input is a character string of length 50. Change all punctuation marks (commas, periods, exclamation points, and question marks) to blanks and return this new string in the same character string. Assume that the main program accesses the subroutine with the following statement:

```
CALL EDIT(STRING)
```

47 Write a subroutine that receives a piece of text called PROSE that contains 200 characters. The subroutine should print the text in lines of 30 characters each. Do not split words between two lines. Do not print any lines that are completely blank.

48 Write a function CONSNT that receives an array CHAR of 100 elements. Each element contains one character. Count the number of consonants and return that number to the main program. (It might be easiest to count the number of vowels and subtract that number from 100.)

49 Write a subroutine that receives an array of N real values and prints a printer X-Y plot. Use a line of 101 characters. Scale the line from the negative absolute maximum value to the positive absolute maximum value. The first line of output should be 101 periods representing the Y axis. All the following lines should contain a period in column 51 to represent the origin and the letter X to represent the position of each data point, as shown in the following diagram:

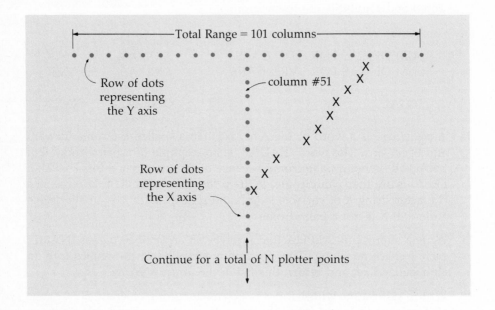

50 Write a main program that will use the subroutine in problem 49 to prepare an X-Y plot of the current A(t) of the following circuit:

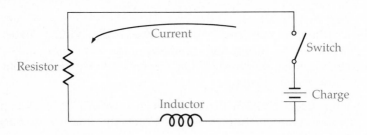

Here,

$$A(t) = AMAX \cdot e^{-250 \cdot t} \cdot \cos(7061.4 \cdot t)$$

with AMAX = 0.07176 and a time increment of 0.1697E−04 seconds. Start with t = 0, and plot 200 points of the function.

51 Modify the function of Example 8-7 so that punctuation characters are not included in the calculation of average word length. Punctuation characters include:

$$. \quad , \quad ; \quad : \quad ! \quad ?$$

*52 Write a complete program that reads and stores the following array of 9 character strings, each string containing 6 characters.

ATIDEB
LENGTH
ECPLOT
DDUEFS
OUTPUT
CGDAER
HIRXJI
KATIMN
BHPARG

Now read the 11 strings listed below and find the same string in the array above. Print the positions of characters of these hidden words that may appear forward, backward, up, down, or diagonally. For instance, the word EDIT is located in positions 1:5, 1:4, 1:3, and 1:2.

Hidden Words

PLOT	STRING
CODE	TEXT
EDIT	READ
LENGTH	GRAPH
INPUT	BAR
OUTPUT	

*53 Modify the subroutine of problem 47 such that the length of the output line is an argument to the subroutine. Distribute any blanks at the beginning of a line and the end of a line between words in the line so that every line begins and ends with a nonblank character. Thus, if the character string PROSE contained a portion of the Gettysburg Address, and the line length were 23, then the first few lines of output should be:

FOUR   SCORE   AND   SEVEN
YEARS   AGO   OUR   FATHERS
BROUGHT   FORTH   UPON   THIS

SAMPLE PROBLEM – Laser Mirror Alignment

The alignment of curved mirrors in a laser system is a very precise operation. The calculations may include computing the *sag* of the spherical mirror surface, which can be computed with the following equation:

$$\text{sag} = \frac{rs^2}{1 + \sqrt{1 - r^2 s^2}}$$

Here, r is the radius of the spherical mirror and s is the distance from the center of the spherical mirror to its tangent plane.

Compute the sag of a spherical mirror, given the corresponding values of r and s, to 10 digits of accuracy. Assume that computations with real numbers have only 7 digits of accuracy. (For solution, see Example 9-1, page 290.)

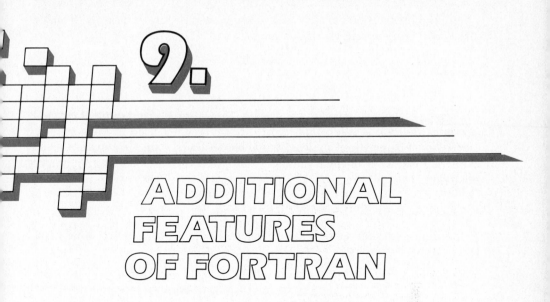

INTRODUCTION

This chapter summarizes a number of features of FORTRAN that are not introduced in the earlier chapters but should be included for completeness. While these topics are not used frequently, they may be extremely helpful, and even necessary, in some applications. We shall discuss three new types of variables, three new specification statements, additional format features, and some additional features of subprograms and files.

9-1   DOUBLE PRECISION VALUES

In some applications, more precision is needed than is available through real variables. In these cases, a special type of *double precision* variable or constant is used. Typically, this type of constant or variable has more than twice as many digits of accuracy as available for real variables. If 7 digits of accuracy correspond to real values, then usually 16 digits of accuracy correspond to double precision values.

DOUBLE PRECISION CONSTANTS

A double precision constant is written in an exponential form, with a D in place of E. Some examples of double precision constants are:

$$0.378926542D+04$$
$$1.4762D-02$$
$$0.25D+00$$

Always use the exponential form with the letter D for double precision constants, even if seven or less digits of accuracy are used in the constant. Otherwise, you may lose some accuracy because a fractional value that can be expressed evenly in decimal notation may not be evenly expressed in binary notation.

DOUBLE PRECISION VARIABLES

Double precision variables are specified with a specification statement, whose general form is:

```
DOUBLE PRECISION   variable names
```

A double precision array is specified as shown below:

```
DOUBLE PRECISION   DTEMP(50)
```

While there are no specific rules for assigning a name to a double precision variable, it is common practice to begin the name with the letter D to emphasize that the variable represents a double precision value.

INPUT AND OUTPUT

A double precision value can be used in list-directed output similar to a real value. The only distinction will be that more digits of accuracy can be stored in a double precision value, and thus more digits of accuracy can be written from a double precision value.

In formatted input and output, double precision values may be referenced with the F or E format specifications. A new specification, Dw.d, may also be used. It functions essentially like the E specification but the D emphasizes that it is being used with a double precision value. In output, the value in exponential form is printed with a D instead of an E. Thus, if the following statements were executed,

```
          DOUBLE PRECISION  DX
                  .
                  .
                  .
          DX = 1.66587514521D+00
          WRITE(6,10)DX
       10 FORMAT(1X,D17.10)
                  .
                  .
                  .
```

the output would contain the value,

$$0.1665875145D+01$$

DOUBLE PRECISION EXPRESSIONS

When an arithmetic operation is performed with two double precision values, the result will be double precision. If an operation involves a double precision value and a single precision value or an integer, the result will be a double precision result. In such a mixed-mode operation, do not assume that the other value is converted to double precision. Instead, think of the other value as being extended in length with zeros. To illustrate this point, the first two assignment statements below will yield exactly the same values. The third assignment statement, however, adds a double precision constant to DX and yields the most accurate result of three statements.

```
          DOUBLE PRECISION  DX, DY1, DY2, DY3
               .
               .
               .
          DY1 = DX + 0.3872
          DY2 = DX + 0.3872000000000
          DY3 = DX + 0.3872D+00
               .
               .
               .
```

The most accurate way to obtain a constant that cannot be written in a fixed number of decimal places is to perform an operation in double precision that will yield the desired value. For instance, to obtain the double precision constant one-third, use the following expression:

$$1.0D+00/3.0D+00$$

DOUBLE PRECISION FUNCTIONS

If a double precision argument is used in a generic function, the function value will also be double precision. Many of the common intrinsic functions for real numbers can be converted to double precision functions by preceding the name with the letter D. For instance, DSQRT, DABS, DMOD, DSIN, DEXP, DLOG, and DLOG10 all require double precision arguments and yield double precision values. Double precision functions can also be used to compute constants with double precision accuracy. For instance, the following statements compute π with double precision accuracy:

```
DOUBLE PRECISION  DPI
     .
     .
     .
DPI = 4.0D+00*DATAN(1.0D+00)
```

While Appendix B contains a complete list of the functions that relate to double precision values, there are two functions, DBLE and DPROD, that are specifically designed for use with double precision variables. DBLE converts a REAL argument to a double precision value. DPROD has two REAL arguments and returns the double precision product of the two arguments.

EXAMPLE 9-1   Spherical Mirror Sag

Assume that DR and DS represent double precision values for the radius (DR) of the spherical mirror and the distance (DS) from the center of the spherical mirror to its tangent plane. These two values have already been computed in a program. Write the section of code to compute the sag to at least 10 digits of accuracy (assuming real values have 7 digits of accuracy), where

$$\text{sag} = \frac{rs^2}{1 + \sqrt{1 - r^2 s^2}}$$

Solution

```
DOUBLE PRECISION  DR, DS, DSAG
   .
   .
   .
DSAG = DR*DS*DS/(1.0D+00 + DSQRT(1.0D+00 - DR*DR*DS*DS))
   .
   .
   .
```

$\diamond$

9-2   COMPLEX VALUES

Since *complex numbers* are needed to solve many problems in science and engineering, particularly in physics and electrical engineering, FORTRAN includes a special type for these complex variables and constants. These complex values are stored as an ordered pair of real values, the real portion of the value and the imaginary portion of the value.

COMPLEX CONSTANTS

A complex constant is specified by two real constants separated by a comma and enclosed in parentheses. The first constant represents the real part of the complex value, and the second constant represents the imaginary part of the complex value. Thus, the complex constant $3.0 - i1.5$, where i represents $\sqrt{-1}$, is written in FORTRAN as the complex constant $(3.0, -1.5)$.

COMPLEX VARIABLES

Complex variables are specified with a specification statement, whose general form is:

```
COMPLEX    variable names
```

A complex array is specified as shown below:

```
COMPLEX    CX(100)
```

It is common practice to begin the name of a complex variable with the letter C to emphasize that the variable represents a complex value.

INPUT AND OUTPUT

A complex value in list-directed output will be printed as two real values separated by a comma and enclosed in parentheses. Also, two real values will be read for each complex value in a list-directed input statement.

In formatted input, a complex value is read with two real specifications. For output, a complex value is printed with two real specifications. The real part of the complex value will be read or printed before the imaginary portion. It is good practice to enclose the two parts printed in parentheses and separate them by a comma, or print them in the $a + ib$ form. Both of these forms are illustrated in the statements below:

```
COMPLEX    CX, CY
     .
     .
     .
  CX = (1.5, 4.0)
  CY = (0.0, 2.4)
  WRITE(6,5)CX, CY
5 FORMAT(1X,'(',F4.1,',',F4.1,')'/1X,F4.1,' + I',F4.1)
```

The output from the write statement would be:

$$(1.5, 4.0)$$
$$0.0 + I\ 2.4$$

COMPLEX EXPRESSIONS

When an arithmetic operation is performed between two complex values, the result will also be a complex value. Expressions containing both complex values and double precision values are not allowed. In an expression containing a complex value and a real or integer value, the real or integer value is converted to a complex value whose imaginary part is zero.

The rules of complex arithmetic are not as familiar as those for integers or real values; so we list below the results of basic operations on two complex numbers C_1 and C_2, where $C_1 = a_1 + ib_1$ and $C_2 = a_2 + ib_2$:

$$C_1 + C_2 = (a_1 + a_2) + i(b_1 + b_2)$$
$$C_1 - C_2 = (a_1 - a_2) + i(b_1 - b_2)$$
$$C_1 * C_2 = (a_1 a_2 - b_1 b_2) + i(a_1 b_2 + a_1 b_2)$$
$$\frac{C_1}{C_2} = \frac{a_1 a_2 + b_1 b_2}{a_2{}^2 + b_2{}^2} + i\,\frac{a_2 b_1 - b_2 a_1}{a_2{}^2 + b_2{}^2}$$
$$|C_1| = \sqrt{a_1{}^2 + b_1{}^2}$$
$$e^{C_1} = e^{a_1} \cos b_1 + i e^{a_1} \sin b_1$$
$$\cos C_1 = 1 - \frac{C_1{}^3}{3!} + \frac{C_1{}^5}{5!} - \frac{C_1{}^7}{7!} + \cdots$$

COMPLEX FUNCTIONS

If a complex value is used in one of the generic functions, such as SQRT, ABS, SIN, COS, EXP, or LOG, the function value will also be complex. The functions, CSQRT, CABS, CSIN, CCOS, CEXP, and CLOG, are all intrinsic functions with complex arguments. These function names begin with the letter C to emphasize that they are complex functions.

While Appendix B contains a complete list of the functions that relate to complex values, there are four functions, REAL, AIMAG, CONJ, and CMPLX, that are specifically designed for use with complex variables. REAL yields the real part of its complex argument and AIMAG yields the imaginary part of its complex argument. CONJ converts a complex number to its conjugate, where the conjugate of $a + ib$ is $a - ib$. CMPLX is a function that converts two real arguments, a and b, into a complex value $a + ib$.

9-3 LOGICAL VALUES

The final new type of variable allowed in FORTRAN is a *logical variable*. We have worked with logical expressions in IF statements and we can now extend these ideas to a new type of constant and variable.

LOGICAL CONSTANTS

There are only two logical constants, .TRUE. and .FALSE..

LOGICAL VARIABLES

Logical variables are specified with a specification statement, whose general form is:

```
LOGICAL   variable names
```

A logical array is specified as shown below:

```
LOGICAL   LX(100)
```

It is common practice to begin the name of logical variables with the letter L to emphasize that the variable represents a logical value.

INPUT AND OUTPUT

A logical value in list-directed output will be printed as the letter T or the letter F, depending on whether the value is .TRUE. or .FALSE.. For list-directed input, the value for a logical variable must be a character string whose first nonblank letter is T or F, depending on whether the value is .TRUE. or .FALSE..

In formatted input, a logical value is read with the specification Lw, where w represents the width of the input field. The first nonblank character in the field must be T or F. In formatted output, the Lw specification is also used. All w positions will be blanks except the rightmost position, which will contain T or F, depending on the value of the logical variable.

As an example of the formatted input and output, consider the following segment from a program:

```
LOGICAL   LX
      .
      .
      .
    READ(5,1)LX
  1 FORMAT(L5)
    WRITE(6,2)LX
  2 FORMAT(1X,L5)
      .
      .
      .
```

If the data card read with this segment contained the word FALSE in columns 1–5, the value of LX would be .FALSE.. The corresponding output line would contain four blanks followed by the letter F.

LOGICAL EXPRESSIONS

A logical variable, like the other variable types, can be initialized with the DATA statement, a read statement, or an assignment statement. Some examples of initialization with assignment statements are as follows:

```
LOGICAL  LX, LY, LZ, LQ
     .
     .
     .
LX = .TRUE.
LY = LX.OR.LZ
LQ = A.GT.B
     .
     .
     .
```

A logical variable can be used where a logical expression is valid, as in an IF-THEN-ENDIF structure

```
LOGICAL  SORTED
     .
     .
     .
IF(.NOT.SORTED)THEN
    CALL SORT(Z, N)
    SORTED = .TRUE.
    WRITE(*,*)Z
ENDIF
     .
     .
     .
```

It is invalid to compare two logical variables with the relation .EQ. or .NE.. Instead, two new relations, .EQV. and .NEQV., are used to represent equivalent and not equivalent. Thus, if we wish to compare two logical variables LX and LY, we can use statements such as:

```
IF(LX.EQV.LY)LX = .NOT.LX

IF(LY.NEQV..FALSE.)KTR = 0
```

Whenever arithmetic operators, relational operators, and logical operators are in the same expression, the arithmetic operations are performed first, then the relational operators are applied to yield .TRUE. or .FALSE. values, and these are evaluated with the logical operators whose precedence is .NOT., .AND., .OR.. The relations .EQV. and .NEQV. are evaluated last, as illustrated in the following logical expression:

A + B.LT.C.EQV..NOT.LX

9-4 IMPLICIT, PARAMETER, AND EQUIVALENCE STATEMENTS

Three specification statements, and thus nonexecutable statements, have not yet been covered. The IMPLICIT statement is used to specify the beginning letters of variable names that are to be associated with a particular type, such as REAL, or CHARACTER. The PARAMETER statement is used to initialize constants. The EQUIVALENCE statement allows the sharing of data storage.

IMPLICIT STATEMENT

We have discussed six different specification statements: INTEGER, REAL, CHARACTER, DOUBLE PRECISION, COMPLEX, and LOGICAL. Only two of these statements, INTEGER and REAL, have default values. That is, variable names beginning with letters I→N specify integer variables by default, and all other variable names specify real variables by default. The IMPLICIT statement allows us to specify defaults for variables of all types. Its general form is:

> IMPLICIT   *type1(default), type2(default), . . .*

For instance, if a program contained only integers, you might want to specify that any variable is an integer, with this statement:

        IMPLICIT   INTEGER(A-Z)

Or, you might want to specify that the first half of the alphabet should represent beginning letters of integer names and the last half should represent real values:

        IMPLICIT   INTEGER(A-M), REAL(N-Z)

If you are following the convention of beginning all double precision variable names with the letter D, instead of listing all the names in a DOUBLE PRECISION statement, you could use the following:

        IMPLICIT   DOUBLE PRECISION(D)

An implicit declaration can be overridden with a specification statement, as shown below:

        IMPLICIT   COMPLEX(C), LOGICAL(L)
        CHARACTER*10   CHAR

The variable CHAR should be a complex variable according to the IMPLICIT statement, but instead it is defined to be a character string by the CHARACTER statement.

PARAMETER STATEMENT

The PARAMETER statement is a specification statement used to assign constant values to variable names, with the following general form:

> PARAMETER   (name1=expression, name2=expression, . . .)

The expression after the equal sign typically is a constant, but it may be an expression that contains variables that have already been defined in a DATA statement or a PARAMETER statement. A specific example of the PARAMETER statement is:

```
PARAMETER   (PI=3.14159, N=75)
```

This statement cannot be used in a subprogram.

The DATA statement and PARAMETER statement can both be used to initialize variables, but there are some differences between the two statements. A variable defined in a PARAMETER statement cannot be redefined in another statement such as a READ or an assignment. However, a variable defined in a PARAMETER statement can be used anywhere in a program that a constant is used except in FORMAT statements. It is particularly useful in conjunction with other specification statements, as seen in the following pair of statements:

```
PARAMETER   (M=50)
DIMENSION   TEMP(M,M)
```

If a variable is to be initialized with a PARAMETER statement, any other specification statements that affect the variable must precede the PARAMETER statement. For example, if a PARAMETER statement is used to initialize a character string, the CHARACTER statement must precede the PARAMETER statement.

```
CHARACTER*6   DATE
PARAMETER   (DATE='010184')
```

EQUIVALENCE STATEMENT

The EQUIVALENCE statement, a specification statement that permits data storage to be shared by several variables, has the following general form:

> EQUIVALENCE   (variable list 1), (variable list 2), . . .

The variable list may contain variable names, array names, and character substring names. The EQUIVALENCE statement causes all the names enclosed in a set of parentheses to reference the same storage location. Character variables cannot be equivalenced with noncharacter variables. In fact, it is best to use the same type in all equivalence lists. When array elements are equivalenced, the entire arrays are involved, as will be shown in the next example, because an array is always stored sequentially in memory. Two variables in a common block or in two different common blocks cannot be made equivalent, and two variables in the same array cannot be made equivalent.

Consider the following EQUIVALENCE statements:

```
DIMENSION  A(5), B(9), C(2,2)
EQUIVALENCE  (HEIGHT,DIST), (A(1),B(4),C(1,1))
```

The first variable list specifies that HEIGHT and DIST are to occupy the same location that is referenced by either variable name. The equivalence of storage locations specified by the second variable list is best explained using the following diagram of computer memory:

	B(1)	
	B(2)	
	B(3)	
A(1)	B(4)	C(1,1)
A(2)	B(5)	C(2,1)
A(3)	B(6)	C(1,2)
A(4)	B(7)	C(2,2)
A(5)	B(8)	
	B(9)	

⟵ All three variables share the same storage location

By specifying that A(1) and B(4) share the same location, we also have implicitly specified that A(2) and B(5) share the same location, and so on through A(5) and B(8). Furthermore, we have equated the location that stores A(1) and B(4) with C(1,1), and hence other implicit equivalences, have been specified as shown in the diagram. When using two-dimensional arrays in equivalence statements, it is important to remember that they are stored by columns.

9-5 APPLICATION – Temperature Distribution in Metal Plate

In this application we consider the temperature distribution in a thin metal plate as it reaches a point of thermal equilibrium. The plate is constructed so that each edge is *isothermal*, or maintained at a constant temperature. The temperature of an interior point on the plate is a function of the temperature of the surrounding material. If we consider the plate to be similar to a grid, then a two-dimensional array could be used to store the temperatures of the corresponding points on the plate. Figure 9-1 contains an array that is used to store the temperatures of a plate that is being analyzed with 5 temperature measurements along the sides and 10 temperature measurements along the top and bottom. A total of 50 temperature values will be stored.

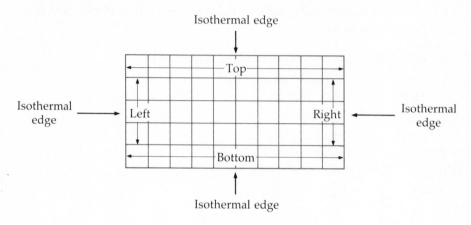

Figure 9-1 Metal plate temperature grid.

The isothermal temperatures at the top, bottom, left, and right would be given. The interior points are initially set to some arbitrary temperature, usually zero. The new temperature of each interior point is calculated as the average of its four surrounding points, as shown in the diagram below.

$$T_0 = \frac{T_1 + T_2 + T_3 + T_4}{4}$$

After computing the new temperatures for each interior point, the difference between the old temperatures and the new temperatures is computed. If the magnitude of a temperature change is greater than some specified tolerance value, the plate is not yet in thermal equilibrium, and the entire process is repeated.

Since we will use only one array for the temperatures, as we change one temperature, this new value will affect the change in adjacent temperatures. The final results will also be slightly different depending on whether the changes are made across the rows or down the columns. To be sure that you understand the process, we will go through a simple case, looking at each iteration. The array contains 4 rows and 4 columns. The isothermal temperatures are these:

$$Top \longrightarrow 100.0$$
$$Bottom \longrightarrow 200.0$$
$$Left\ Side \longrightarrow 100.0$$
$$Right\ Side \longrightarrow 200.0$$

The internal points are initialized to zero, and the tolerance value is 0.1.

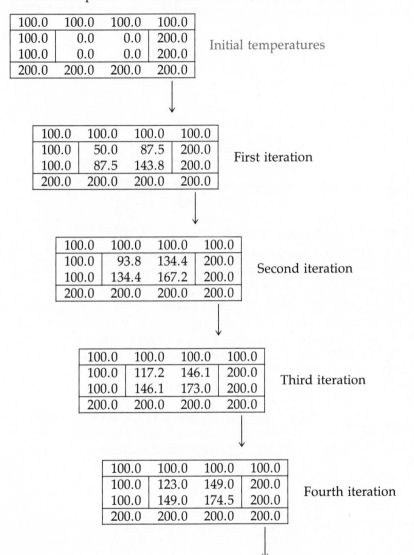

100.0	100.0	100.0	100.0
100.0	0.0	0.0	200.0
100.0	0.0	0.0	200.0
200.0	200.0	200.0	200.0

Initial temperatures

100.0	100.0	100.0	100.0
100.0	50.0	87.5	200.0
100.0	87.5	143.8	200.0
200.0	200.0	200.0	200.0

First iteration

100.0	100.0	100.0	100.0
100.0	93.8	134.4	200.0
100.0	134.4	167.2	200.0
200.0	200.0	200.0	200.0

Second iteration

100.0	100.0	100.0	100.0
100.0	117.2	146.1	200.0
100.0	146.1	173.0	200.0
200.0	200.0	200.0	200.0

Third iteration

100.0	100.0	100.0	100.0
100.0	123.0	149.0	200.0
100.0	149.0	174.5	200.0
200.0	200.0	200.0	200.0

Fourth iteration

$\downarrow$

100.0	100.0	100.0	100.0
100.0	124.5	149.8	200.0
100.0	149.8	174.9	200.0
200.0	200.0	200.0	200.0

Fifth iteration

$\downarrow$

100.0	100.0	100.0	100.0
100.0	124.9	149.9	200.0
100.0	149.9	175.0	200.0
200.0	200.0	200.0	200.0

Sixth iteration

$\downarrow$

Equilibrium

100.0	100.0	100.0	100.0
100.0	125.0	150.0	200.0
100.0	150.0	175.0	200.0
200.0	200.0	200.0	200.0

EXAMPLE 9-2   Temperature Distribution

Write a program that will initialize the number of rows and number of columns with a PARAMETER statement. The four iso-thermal temperatures and the tolerance value will be initialized with a DATA statement. The program should initialize a two-dimensional array with the edge temperatures as specified in the DATA statement and with zero internal temperatures. Use a logical variable EQUILB in the test for equilibrium. Print the initial plate temperatures and the final plate temperatures after equilibrium has been reached. Print the temperatures in a grid format. Assume a maximum of 10 rows and 10 columns.

The general flowchart on page 301 contains the order of steps necessary to find the equilibrium temperatures in the metal plate. One of these steps, "perform update of internal temperatures," is refined on page 302 into a WHILE loop with a nested loop structure inside it.

Solution

GENERAL FLOWCHART

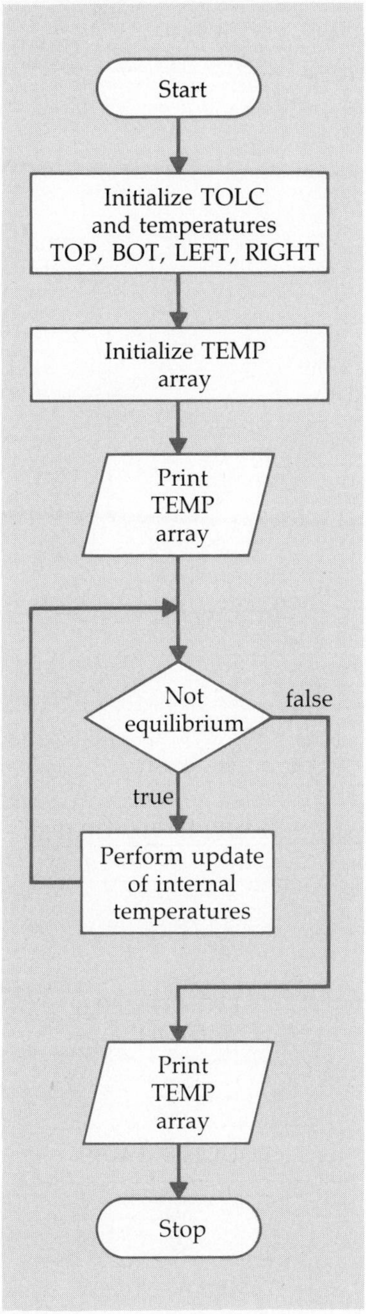

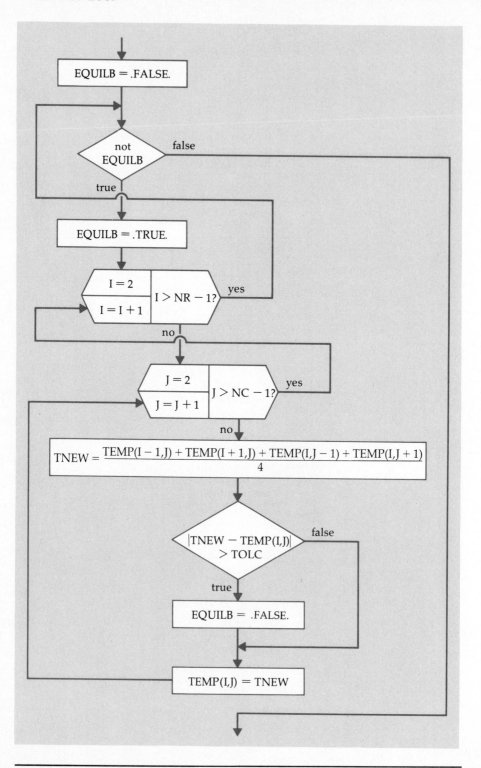

```
C
      PROGRAM   PLATE
C
C  THIS PROGRAM INITIALIZES THE TEMPERATURES IN A METAL
C  PLATE AND DETERMINES THE EQUILIBRIUM TEMPERATURES
C  BASED ON A TOLERANCE VALUE
C
      PARAMETER  (NR=6, NC=6)
      DIMENSION  TEMP(NR,NC)
      LOGICAL  EQUILB
      REAL  LEFT
      DATA  TOP, BOT, LEFT, RIGHT, TOLC
     +      /100.0, 100.0, 350.0, 350.0, 0.2/
C
C  INITIALIZE TEMPERATURE ARRAY
C
      DO 10 J=1,NC
         TEMP(1,J) = TOP
         TEMP(NR,J) = BOT
   10 CONTINUE
      DO 20 I=2,NR-1
         TEMP(I,1) = LEFT
         TEMP(I,NC) = RIGHT
         DO 15 J=2,NC-1
            TEMP(I,J)=0.0
   15    CONTINUE
   20 CONTINUE
C
C  PRINT INITIAL TEMPERATURE ARRAY
C
      WRITE(6,50)
   50 FORMAT('1',' INITIAL TEMPERATURES'/)
      DO 60 I=1,NR
         WRITE(6,55)(TEMP(I,J), J=1,NC)
   55    FORMAT(' ',12(F6.1,1X))
   60 CONTINUE
C
C  CALCULATE NEW TEMPERATURES AND TEST TOLERANCE
C
      EQUILB = .FALSE.
   70 IF(.NOT.EQUILB)THEN
         EQUILB = .TRUE.
         DO 80 I=2,NR-1
            DO 75 J=2,NC-1
               TNEW = (TEMP(I-1,J) + TEMP(I+1,J)
     +                 + TEMP(I,J-1) + TEMP(I,J+1))/4.0
               IF(ABS(TNEW-TEMP(I,J)).GT.TOLC)
     +                 EQUILB = .FALSE.
               TEMP(I,J) = TNEW
   75       CONTINUE
   80    CONTINUE
         GO TO 70
      ENDIF
C
C  PRINT EQUILIBRIUM TEMPERATURE ARRAY
C
      WRITE(6,100)
  100 FORMAT(/,1X,' EQUILIBRIUM TEMPERATURES'/)
      DO 110 I=1,NR
         WRITE(6,55)(TEMP(I,J), J=1,NC)
  110 CONTINUE
C
      STOP
      END
```

```
INITIAL TEMPERATURES

100.0   100.0   100.0   100.0   100.0   100.0
350.0     0.0     0.0     0.0     0.0   350.0
350.0     0.0     0.0     0.0     0.0   350.0
350.0     0.0     0.0     0.0     0.0   350.0
350.0     0.0     0.0     0.0     0.0   350.0
100.0   100.0   100.0   100.0   100.0   100.0

EQUILIBRIUM TEMPERATURES

100.0   100.0   100.0   100.0   100.0   100.0
350.0   224.8   183.1   183.1   224.9   350.0
350.0   266.4   224.7   224.7   266.5   350.0
350.0   266.5   224.7   224.8   266.6   350.0
350.0   224.9   183.2   183.2   224.9   350.0
100.0   100.0   100.0   100.0   100.0   100.0
```

◇

9-6 ADDITIONAL SUBPROGRAM FEATURES

This section discusses additional features of FORTRAN that relate to subprograms. The SAVE, INTRINSIC, and EXTERNAL statements are not frequently used but can be very useful, as pointed out in the discussions following. The ENTRY statement and alternate return point from a subprogram are covered in order that the coverage of FORTRAN 77 be complete, but their usage is discouraged because they do not support a structured, *one-way-in, one-way-out* concept.

SAVE

Local variables are those used in a subprogram that are not arguments. Thus, they tend to be totals, loop indexes, and counters. The values of these local variables are generally lost when a RETURN statement is executed. However, a SAVE specification statement will save the values of local variables so that they will contain the same values as they had at the end of the previous reference. This nonexecutable statement appears only in the subprogram. The general form of the SAVE statement is:

SAVE   *variable list*

If the list of variables is omitted, the values of all local variables will be saved.

To illustrate the use of the SAVE statement, suppose you wanted to know how many times a subprogram was accessed. The following statements would initialize the counter COUNTR to zero at the beginning of the program and increment COUNTR each time the subprogram was used. Recall that the DATA statement does not reinitialize COUNTR each time the function is used.

```
FUNCTION  AVE(X, Y)
INTEGER  COUNTR
SAVE  COUNTR
DATA  COUNTR /0/
   .
   .
   .
COUNTR = COUNTR + 1
   .
   .
   .
END
```

INTRINSIC, EXTERNAL

The INTRINSIC and EXTERNAL statements are specification statements used when subprogram names are to be used as arguments in another subprogram. The general forms of these nonexecutable statements are:

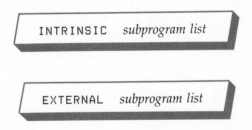

```
INTRINSIC   subprogram list
```

```
EXTERNAL   subprogram list
```

These statements appear only in the module that sends the arguments representing the subprogram names. If the argument is an intrinsic function, use the INTRINSIC statement. If the argument is a user-written function or a subroutine, use the EXTERNAL statement.

In the following statements, we reference a subroutine twice. With one reference, the subroutine replaces each value in an array with its natural logarithm. The other reference replaces each value in an array with its logarithm, using base 10.

Main program
```
          PROGRAM  TEST5
          DIMENSION  X(10), TIME(10)
          INTRINSIC  ALOG, ALOG10
            .
            .
            .
          CALL COMPUT(X, ALOG)
            .
            .
            .
          CALL COMPUT(TIME, ALOG10)
            .
            .
            .
          END
```

Subroutine COMPUT
```
          SUBROUTINE  COMPUT(R, F)
     C
     C    THIS SUBROUTINE APPLIES A
     C    FUNCTION TO THE ARRAY R
     C
          DIMENSION  R(10)
     C
          DO 10 I=1,10
             R(I) = F(R(I))
     10 CONTINUE
     C
          RETURN
          END
```

ENTRY

The ENTRY statement is used to define entry points into a subprogram other than the entry point at the beginning of the subprogram. The general form of the statement is:

ENTRY *entry name (argument list)*

The ENTRY statement is placed at the point in the subprogram that is to be an alternative entry. The argument list does not have to be the same as that for the original entry point. The ENTRY statement is nonexecutable and will not affect execution of the subprogram if it is in the statements being executed from a previous entry point.

The following statements illustrate references to a subroutine through two different entry points.

Main program
```
PROGRAM   TEST6
    .
    .
    .
CALL  SUBAA(X)
    .
    .
    .
CALL  SUBAB(X, K)
    .
    .
    .
END
```

Subroutine SUBAA
```
SUBROUTINE   SUBAA(T)
    .
    .
    .
ENTRY    SUBAB(T, J)
    .
    .
    .
END
```

One of the fundamental advantages of structured programming lies in the simplicity of linkages between modules. The use of multiple entry points to a subprogram complicates that linkage, and thus their usage is generally not recommended.

ALTERNATE RETURNS

Normally, the execution of a RETURN statement in a subroutine returns control to the first statement below the CALL statement. A return point, however, can be specified with an argument in the subroutine. The dummy argument list contains asterisks in the locations of arguments that are the alternate return points. The RETURN statement has this expanded general form:

RETURN   *integer expression*

If the value of the integer expression is 1, the return point is the statement number that corresponds to the first asterisk in the argument list. If the value of the integer expression is 2, the return point is the statement number that corresponds to the second asterisk, and so on. The following statements will help clarify this process:

```
                 PROGRAM   TEST7
                    ·
                    ·
                    ·
                 CALL   SUB1(A, B, *20, *50)
                    ·
                    ·
                    ·
Main program     20  WRITE(6,5)A
                    ·
                    ·
                    ·
                 50  COUNT = COUNT + 1
                    ·
                    ·
                    ·
                 END
                 SUBROUTINE   SUB1(X, Y, *, *)
                    ·
Subroutine          ·
  SUB1              ·
                 RETURN I
                 END
```

If the value of I is 1 in the subroutine, then control will return to statement 20. If the value I = 2, then control returns to statement 50. An error occurs if the value of I is not 1 or 2.

Multiple return points also complicate the linkage between modules and generally should be avoided.

9-7   ADDITIONAL FORMAT FEATURES

In addition to several new FORMAT specifications and extensions, we introduce a technique called *variable formatting* that permits you to use a character string as a list of FORMAT specifications.

FORMAT SPECIFICATIONS

The following FORMAT specifications are not routinely used, but occassionally these specifications will simplify the input and output steps in a program.

Gw.d—The G format code is a generalized code used to transmit real data. The width w specifies the number of positions in the input or output that are used. Input data can be entered in an F or E format. The real advantage of the G format is in output formats. If the exponent of the data value is negative or larger than d, the output is performed with an Ew.d specification. If the exponent is between 0 and d, the output is performed with an $(F(w-4).d, 4X)$ specification. Thus, very large or small values are automatically printed with an E format, and values of reasonable size are printed with an F format. For example, if the G specification is G10.3, then the value 26.8 is printed as 26.800_{bbbb} while the value 1248.1 is printed as $_b0.125_bE04$.

wH—Literal data can be specified in an output format with an H, or Hollerith, specification. The width w specifies the total number of positions in the literal, and the literal itself immediately follows the H. The following two formats are equivalent:

```
10 FORMAT(1X,'EXPERIMENT NO. 1')

10 FORMAT(1X,16HEXPERIMENT NO. 1)
```

Specifying literals with apostrophes is easier because we do not need to count the characters in the literal, and hence H formats are rarely used.

TLn and TRn—While the Tn specification that we introduced in Chapter 3 tabbed to position n in the input or output record, TLn and TRn specifications tab left or tab right for n positions from the current position. The following formats are thus equivalent:

```
85 FORMAT(1X,25X,'HEIGHT',5X,'WEIGHT')

85 FORMAT(T27,'HEIGHT',TR5,'WEIGHT')
```

The tab specifications are particularly useful in aligning column headings and data.

FORMAT EXTENSIONS

The following FORMAT extensions are not specifications that correspond to a variable, but instead are modifiers that affect the performance of the specifications already presented.

Ew.dEe and Gw.dEe—The addition of Ee to an exponential or generalized format specifies that e positions are to be printed in the exponent. The Ee affects only output specifications.

nP—The addition of nP to an F, E, D, or G format code specifies a scale factor n that is applied to subsequent specifications until another scale factor is encountered. The actual value stored will be multiplied by 10**n to give the number read or printed when the scale factor n is in effect. For instance, if the following READ statement is executed,

```
     READ(*,5)A, B
   5 FORMAT(2PF4.1,F5.1)
```

and the data line read is,

12.1362.4

then the value stored in A is 0.121 and the value stored in B is 3.624. Thus, any computations with A and B use the values 0.121 and 3.624. The output statement

```
      WRITE(*,10)A, B
   10 FORMAT(1X,F4.1,1X,F5.1)
```

generates the following data line

00.1$_{bbb}$3.6

The scale factor might be useful in applications that use percentages. The input could be in the form XX.X but the internal values used in calculations and the output would use the form .XXX. If a scale factor is used, document its use carefully in the program.

S, SP, and SS—These options affect I, F, E, G, and D specifications during the execution of output statements. If a numerical value is negative, the minus sign is printed in the first position to the left of the data value. If the numerical value is positive, the printing of the plus sign is system-dependent. If SP precedes a specification, in the value to be printed and all subsequent values, a sign will be printed, whether the value is positive or negative. If SS precedes a specification, in the value to be printed and all subsequent values, only a minus sign will be printed. If S precedes a specification, the system designation of producing signs is restored. The following example illustrates the use of the SP modifier. If these statements are executed,

```
      A = 36.2
      WRITE(*,5)A, A, A
   5 FORMAT(1X,F5.1,1X,SPF5.1,1X,F5.1)
```

the output line is

$_b$36.2$_b$+36.2 +36.2

BN and BZ—The BN and BZ modifiers specify the interpretation of nonleading blanks in numeric data fields during the execution of input statements. Normally, leading and nonleading blanks are converted to zeros in numeric input fields. The modifier BN, however, specifies that blanks be considered to be null characters or ignored in the current and all succeeding specifications. The

BZ modifier restores the interpretation of all blanks as zeros in numeric fields. If the data line

$$_b21_{bb}21_b$$

is read with the statement

```
      READ(*,15)I, J
  15 FORMAT(I4,BNI4),
```

the value stored in I is 210 and the value stored in J is 21.

Colon—A colon terminates the format if there are no more items in the input or output list. The following statements and their corresponding output illustrate the usefulness of this feature.

```
      MAX = 20
      MIN = -5
      WRITE(*,10)MAX
      WRITE(*,10)MAX, MIN
  10 FORMAT(1X,'MAX = ',I3,:,2X,'MIN = ',I3)
```

The output from the first WRITE statement is

$$MAX_b = {}_b20$$

while the output from the second WRITE statement is

$$MAX_b = {}_b20_{bb}MIN_b = {}_b-5$$

Without the colon, the output from the first WRITE statement would be

$$MAX_b = {}_b20_{bb}MIN_b =$$

VARIABLE FORMATTING

The format identifier in input and output statements up to this point has always been a statement number reference. However, this format identifier can also be an integer variable that has been initialized by an assign statement with the number of the desired FORMAT statement. The format identifier can also be a character constant, character array element, character array, or character expression. The power of variable formatting with character strings is illustrated in the following WRITE statements:

```
CHARACTER*20  CHAR
   .
   .
   .
IF(COUNTR.EQ.1)THEN
   CHAR = '(1X,''X = '',F4.1)'
ELSE
   CHAR = '(1X,4X,F4.1)'
ENDIF
WRITE(*,CHAR)X
```

If the value of COUNTR is 1, then the output line will include the literal 'X = '. All other lines will include only data values, allowing us to use the same WRITE statement to obtain reports of the following form:

```
X =    1.5
      17.2
      -8.6
       8.1
```

9-8 ADDITIONAL FILE CONCEPTS

In the previous chapters, we have had limited contact with data files. A READ statement automatically referred to input from a terminal or a card reader. A WRITE statement automatically referred to output on the terminal or line printer. These two files are automatically connected to your program. Using the OPEN statement introduced in Chapter 3, we also used other files. All these types of files are called *external files* because they are external to the CPU.

A number of additional statements are used for file access, particularly those files on magnetic tape or magnetic disk. Processing these types of files requires a knowledge of the concepts involved in *sequential access* and in *direct access*. In both these access methods, we use the term *record* to describe a unit of information. In a card file, one card represents a record. In a data file, one line represents a record. Sequential access of a file specifies that we process records from the physical beginning of the file. This is the type of access we have used throughout the text. We read the first data line, then the second data line, and so on. In *direct access*, information is not necessarily accessed in its physical order. We may reference the tenth record, then the first record, and so on.

OPEN STATEMENT

The purpose of the OPEN statement is to connect an external file to a program. The OPEN statement is executable but is typically placed at the beginning of the program because it should only be executed once. The complete form of the OPEN statement is:

```
OPEN(UNIT = integer expression,
     FILE = character expression,
     ACCESS = character expression,
     STATUS = character expression,
     FORM = character expression,
     IOSTAT = integer variable,
     RECL = integer expression)
```

We now discuss each of the specifications in the OPEN statement.

Unit number: The integer expression in this specification is usually a constant. This value is used in READ or WRITE statements to specify the file to be used. The following example illustrates the use of a unit number to link together a file and the statements specifying that file:

```
        .
        .
        .
        OPEN(UNIT=23, FILE='DIST', STATUS='NEW')
        .
        .
        .
        WRITE(23,10)X, Y
 10     FORMAT(2F8.3)
        .
        .
        .
```

Note that there is no carriage control used in the FORMAT because the output file is not a print file.

File: The character expression in this file specification must be the name of the file. All references to a file must use the same name used when the file was originally created. The file names typically consist of 1–6 alphabetic letters or numbers, with an alphabetic letter as the first character.

Access: The character string in this specification must be either 'SEQUENTIAL' or 'DIRECT'. If this specification is omitted, 'SEQUENTIAL' is assumed.

Status: The character string in this specification must be 'NEW', 'OLD', or 'SCRATCH'. 'NEW' is used to specify that the file is being created, through WRITE statements. 'OLD' specifies that the file is already built, and its records are accessed with READ statements. 'SCRATCH' specifies that the file is an output file that is not being used after the program, and hence it will be deleted.

Form: The character string in this specification must be either 'FORMATTED' or 'UNFORMATTED'. A FORMATTED file uses either formatted READ and WRITE statements or list-directed input/output statements. All examples used in this text have been formatted examples. UNFORMATTED input/output is used for transfer of data with no conversion of the data. The data is transferred as binary strings, not numbers or characters. One of the main uses of UNFORMATTED input/output is to transfer tape or disk data to another tape or disk file. If this specification is omitted, the default is 'FORMATTED' for sequential files and 'UNFORMATTED' for direct files.

IOSTAT: The IOSTAT specification is not required but can be used to provide error-recovery. If no errors occur in attaching the specified file to the program, the value of the integer variable will be zero. If an error occurs, such as an input file with the proper name is not found, a value specified by the computer system will be stored in the variable. In your program, you can test this variable, and if it is nonzero, you can specify what action is to be taken. In this next example, an error in opening the file will cause IERR to be nonzero. An error message can be printed, and execution will continue. If the IOSTAT specification had not been used and an error had occurred in opening the file, execution would be terminated with an execution error.

```
      .
      .
      .
   OPEN(UNIT=15, FILE='XYDATA', STATUS='OLD',
 +      IOSTAT=IERR)
   IF(IERR.NE.0)WRITE(6,5)IERR
      .
      .
      .
```

RECL: The RECL specification is required for direct access files and specifies the record length. It is not used with sequential access files.

CLOSE STATEMENT

The CLOSE statement is an executable statement that disconnects a file from a program. Its general form is:

```
CLOSE(UNIT=integer expression,    STATUS=character expression,
      IOSTAT=integer variable)
```

The CLOSE statement is optional because all files will automatically be closed upon termination of the program's execution. Within the CLOSE statement itself, the STATUS and IOSTAT specifications are also optional. If a file has been used and the determination has been made that it will not be needed for any more processing, the file can be deleted with the instruction:

```
CLOSE(UNIT=10, STATUS='DELETE')
```

If an error-recovery is desired from the CLOSE statement, the IOSTAT specification can be used to detect an error.

REWIND STATEMENT

The REWIND statement is an executable statement that repositions a sequential file at the first record of the file. Its general form is:

```
REWIND    (UNIT=integer expression)
```

Some systems require a REWIND statement before reading an input file.

BACKSPACE STATEMENT

The BACKSPACE statement is an executable statement that repositions a sequential file to the last record read. Thus, it *backs up* one record in the file. Its general form is:

```
BACKSPACE    (UNIT=integer expression)
```

ENDFILE STATEMENT

When a sequential file is being built, a special *end-of-file* record must be written to specify the end of the file. This special record is written when the ENDFILE statement is executed. The general form of the executable ENDFILE statement is:

```
ENDFILE    (UNIT=integer expression)
```

The CLOSE statement automatically performs this function on some systems.

DIRECT ACCESS I/O

To read or write from a sequential access file, the READ, WRITE, and OPEN statements presented in Chapter 3 are used. A new form for the READ and WRITE statements is needed for direct access files. The general form is:

```
READ(unit number, format reference,
        REC=integer expression)    variable list
```

```
WRITE(unit number, format reference,
        REC=integer expression)    variable list
```

The integer expression on the REC specification is evaluated to give the record number that is to be accessed.

INQUIRE STATEMENT

The final new statement that is used with files is the INQUIRE statement. It has two general forms, which are given below:

> INQUIRE(FILE=*character expression, inquiry specifier list*)

> INQUIRE(UNIT=*integer expression, inquiry specifier list*)

The purpose of this executable statement is to gain information about a file or a unit number. For instance, by using the inquiry specifier OPENED, the following statement can be used to determine whether or not a file has been opened.

> INQUIRE(FILE=*file name,* OPENED=*logical variable*)

The logical variable is .TRUE. if the file has been opened; otherwise, it is .FALSE.. A specific example is:

```
LOGICAL   USED
     .
     .
     .
INQUIRE(FILE='TEMP', OPENED=USED)
IF(.NOT.USED)OPEN(UNIT=20, FILE='TEMP',
+    STATUS='NEW')
     .
     .
     .
```

Table 9-1 contains a complete list of the INQUIRY specifiers.

TABLE 9-1 Inquiry Specifiers

Inquiry Specifier	Variable Type	Value for File Inquiry	Value for Unit Inquiry
ACCESS =	character	'SEQUENTIAL' 'DIRECT'	'SEQUENTIAL' 'DIRECT'
BLANK =	character	'NULL' 'ZERO'	'NULL' 'ZERO'
DIRECT =	character	'YES' 'NO' 'UNKNOWN'	—
ERR =	integer	statement number of error routine	statement number of error routine
EXIST =	logical	.TRUE. .FALSE.	.TRUE. .FALSE.
FORM =	character	'FORMATTED' 'UNFORMATTED'	'FORMATTED' 'UNFORMATTED'
FORMATTED =	character	'YES' 'NO' 'UNKNOWN'	—
IOSTAT =	integer	error code	error code
NAME =	character	—	name of the file if it is not a scratch file
NAMED[†] =	logical	—	.TRUE. .FALSE.
NEXTREC =	integer	next record number in direct access file	next record number in direct access file
NUMBER[†] =	integer	unit number	—
OPENED =	logical	.TRUE. .FALSE.	.TRUE. .FALSE.
RECL =	integer	record length	record length
SEQUENTIAL =	character	'YES' 'NO' 'UNKNOWN'	—
UNFORMATTED =	character	'YES' 'NO' 'UNKNOWN'	—

[†]These specifiers do not refer to scratch files.

INTERNAL FILES

When the unit number of an input or output statement is the name of a character variable, the statement transfers data from one internal storage area to another internal storage area. These internal storage areas are called *internal files*. For instance, we can read data from a character string instead of a data line or data card. The input and output statements function exactly as if the contents of the character string were actually punched in a data card or entered in a data line, as shown in the following example.

```
CHARACTER*10   DATA
DATA = '12.7654217'
       .
       .
       .
READ(DATA, 5)A, B
5   FORMAT(2F4.1)
```

After execution of these statements, the value of A is 12.7 and the value of B is 654.2.

 ## 9-9   APPLICATION – Cryptography

Computers are widely used in *cryptography*, the encoding and decoding of information to prevent unauthorized use. There are many types of codes, ranging from simple codes in which one character is used to represent another character, to complicated codes where multiple character substitutions are used. When information is encoded, a *key* is required that specifies the substitutions being used. This key is also required to decode the encoded information.

EXAMPLE 9-3   Cryptography

A secret numeric message had been converted to characters with the following code:

$$
\begin{aligned}
0 &\longrightarrow T \\
1 &\longrightarrow A \\
2 &\longrightarrow + \\
3 &\longrightarrow \text{\small b, the blank character} \\
4 &\longrightarrow Z \\
5 &\longrightarrow K \\
6 &\longrightarrow \$ \\
7 &\longrightarrow * \\
8 &\longrightarrow / \\
9 &\longrightarrow B
\end{aligned}
$$

In addition, the secret message may include other characters that are to be ignored. For instance, the secret message,

'KSA$ /V/B TT'

should be decoded to the numeric message

'5163889300'

Write a program that will read a file SECRET, which contains records composed of character strings, each containing 30 characters. Create a new file, MESSGE, which will contain the decoded numeric messages. If the file SECRET does not exist, print an error message. If the file SECRET does exist, print a message that tells how many lines were decoded.

Solution

In the refined pseudocode and FORTRAN solution, two character strings are used to decode the secret message IN to the decoded message OUT. One character string CHAR contains the 10 characters that are in the secret message and the other character string NUM contains the key—the 10 numeric decoded characters in corresponding positions. Thus, we use the function INDEX with the string CHAR to give the position in CHAR of the secret message character to be decoded. We then move the character from the same position of NUM to form the decoded message.

General Pseudocode	Refined Pseudocode
PROGRAM DECODE	PROGRAM DECODE
	CHARACTER*10 NUM, CHAR
	CHARACTER*30 IN, OUT
COUNT ← 0	COUNT ← 0
IF no secret file THEN	IF no secret file THEN
PRINT error message	PRINT error message
STOP	STOP
ENDIF	ENDFILE
	OPEN secret file, message file
	NUM ← '0123456789'
	CHAR ← ' TA+ ZK$*/B'
Initialize decoded key	WHILE more messages DO
	READ IN
	OUT ← ' '
	PTROUT ← 1
	DO I = 1,30
	PTRIN ←
	INDEX(CHAR,IN(I,I))
WHILE more messages DO	IF PTRIN ≠ 0 THEN
READ message	OUT(PTROUT:
Decode message	PTROUT) ←
PRINT decoded message	NUM(PTRIN:
COUNT ← COUNT + 1	PTRIN)
ENDWHILE	PTROUT ←
	PTROUT + 1
	ENDIF
	ENDDO
PRINT COUNT	PRINT OUT
	COUNT ← COUNT + 1
	ENDWHILE
	PRINT COUNT
STOP	STOP

FORTRAN Program

```
C        PROGRAM   DECODE
C   THIS PROGRAM DECODES SECRET NUMERIC MESSAGES
C
         INTEGER   COUNT, PTRIN, PTROUT
         LOGICAL   FILE
         CHARACTER*10  NUM, CHAR
         CHARACTER*30  IN, OUT
         DATA   COUNT /0/
C
C   IF SECRET FILE DOES NOT EXIST,
C   PRINT ERROR MESSAGE AND STOP
C
         INQUIRE(FILE='SECRET',EXIST=FILE)
         IF(.NOT.FILE)THEN
            WRITE(6,5)
     5      FORMAT(1X,'SECRET FILE DOES NOT EXIST')
            STOP
         ENDIF
C
C   OPEN INPUT SECRET FILE AND OUTPUT MESSAGE FILE
C
         OPEN(UNIT=11, FILE='SECRET', STATUS='OLD')
         OPEN(UNIT=12, FILE='MESSGE', STATUS='NEW')
C
C   SPECIFY DECODER KEY
C
         NUM='0123456789'
         CHAR='TA+ ZK$*/B'
C
C   READ AND DECODE SECRET MESSAGE
C
     10  READ(11,15,END=990)IN
     15  FORMAT(A)
C
         OUT = ' '
C
         PTROUT = 1
         DO 20 I=1,30
            PTRIN = INDEX(CHAR,IN(I:I))
            IF(PTRIN.NE.0)THEN
               OUT(PTROUT:PTROUT) = NUM(PTRIN:PTRIN)
               PTROUT = PTROUT + 1
            ENDIF
     20     CONTINUE
         WRITE(12,15)OUT
         COUNT = COUNT + 1
C
     GO TO 10
C
C   PRINT FINAL MESSAGE
C
     990 ENDFILE (UNIT=12)
C
         WRITE(6,995)COUNT
     995 FORMAT(1X,I4,' CODE LINES DECODED')
C
         STOP
         END
```

◇

SUMMARY

The various new features of this section complete the set of statements available in the FORTRAN 77 language. Most compilers will add slight modifications to the language, but these modifications usually enhance the language and should be worth the effort to learn. As you use FORTRAN, and particularly the features presented in this chapter, follow the general guidelines of structured programming. Your programs will appear simpler and will be easier to use, even though they may contain some of the more complex techniques.

KEY WORDS

alternate RETURN
BACKSPACE statement
CLOSE statement
COMPLEX statement
complex value
direct access
DOUBLE PRECISION
    statement
double precision value
ENDFILE statement
ENTRY statement
external file
EXTERNAL statement

IMPLICIT statement
INQUIRY statement
internal file
INTRINSIC statement
local variable
LOGICAL statement
logical value
PARAMETER statement
record
REWIND statement
SAVE statement
sequential access
variable formatting

DEBUGGING AIDS

The primary debugging tool that will be discussed in this section is the WRITE statement. The usefulness of this statement cannot be over-emphasized. Since several different topics were discussed in this chapter, we shall address them separately.

Double precision: If an error is related to a double precision value, print it out with an E21.14 format (assumes 14 digits of accuracy) each time it is used to be sure that you are not losing the extra accuracy. Also, be sure that you are not moving the value into a single precision variable in an intermediate step in your program.

Complex: If your program errors relate to complex values, write the values of the complex numbers as soon as they are initialized and after each modification. Remember that if you move a complex value into a real variable, the imaginary part is lost.

Logical: Since there are many possible ways to read logical values (T, F, TRUE, FALSE, etc.), you should write the values of logical variables as soon as they are initialized, unless they are initialized with an assignment statement.

Implicit: When a program is not giving the desired results, carefully check the type of your variables. Remember that if a variable is not listed in a type statement or an IMPLICIT statement, the default typing of real and integer variables occurs.

Parameter: Remember that a variable initialized with a PARAMETER statement cannot have its value modified. The variable must be considered to be a constant throughout the program.

Subprograms: If your subprograms are not working correctly, minimize the interaction of different modules. Specifically, do not use multiple entry points and multiple returns in a program that you are having problems with because tracking all possible entries and exits becomes very complex. Another suggestion to help debug modules again uses the WRITE statement. Write the values of all variables used as you come into the module and again as you leave the module.

Files: As you debug a program with files, follow the READ statement with a WRITE statement that immediately prints the values read. If you are writing information to a file, follow the WRITE statement to the file with a WRITE statement to the terminal or line printer.

STYLE/TECHNIQUE GUIDES

When you use a feature of FORTRAN that is not commonly used, good documentation is very important. More comment lines may be necessary to clarify your code. If a computation uses complex numbers, explain the computations in more detail than in regular arithmetic computations. Part of good documentation also includes choosing descriptive names. This is particularly helpful when using logical variables. For instance, if a logical variable is used to flag errors, use statements like:

IF(ERROR) . . .

IF(.NOT.ERROR) . . . .

Since this is the last style/technique guide, it is important to emphasize two guidelines that have been stressed throughout the text. First, if there are several ways to solve the same problem, choose the simplest solution. Second, use structured techniques that lend themselves to a top-down set of instructions. This involves minimizing branching and using the one-way-in, one-way-out linkage with subprograms. These rules will become more important as your programs become longer, solve more complicated problems, and use more files.

PROBLEMS

In problems 1 through 6, show how to represent the following constants as double precision constants.

1   .25   2   .58   3   1/3

4   1/13   5   108.3   6   2.0

In problems 7 through 12, compute the value stored in CX if CY = 1.0 + i3.0 and CZ = 0.5 − i1.0. Assume CX, CY, and CZ are complex variables.

```
7   CX = CY + CZ

8   CX = CY - CZ

9   CX = CONJ(CZ)

10  CX = REAL(CY) + AIMAG(CZ)

11  CX = CMPLX(5.0,0.2)

12  CX = SQRT(CY)
```

In problems 13 through 18, determine the value of LX if LY = .TRUE., A = 4.0, and B = −1.5. Assume LX and LY are logical variables.

```
13  LX = .NOT.LY

14  LX = A.LT.B

15  LX = B.GE.A - 5.0

16  LX = LY.OR.A.EQ.B

17  LX = LY.AND.A.GT.B**2

18  LX = .NOT.LY.EQV.B.GT.0.0
```

In problems 19 through 24, show the output of the following WRITE statements. Assume that DX = 14.17862459, LX = .FALSE., and CX = 2.3 + 0.2.

```
19      WRITE(6,4)DX           20      WRITE(6,4)DX
     4 FORMAT(1X,D14.6)              4 FORMAT(1X,D19.12)


21      WRITE(6,5)LX           22      WRITE(6,5)LX
     5 FORMAT(1X,L1)                 5 FORMAT(1X,L5)


23      WRITE(6,6)CX           24      WRITE(6,6)CX
     6 FORMAT(1X,2F4.1)             6 FORMAT(1X,F4.1)
```

25 Write a complete program to read a double precision value from a data line with a D21.14 format. Compute the sine of the value using the following series:

$$\sin X = X - \frac{X^3}{3!} + \frac{X^5}{5!} - \frac{X^7}{7!} + \cdots$$

Continue using terms until the absolute value of a term is less than 1.0D−09. Print the computed sine and the value obtained from the function DSIN for comparison.

26 Write a complete program to compute π using double precision variables. The algorithm to be used should compute the area of a quarter circle with a radius of 1 and multiply that area by 4 to get an approximation to π. To compute the area of a quarter circle, called AREAQ, we sum the areas of 2000 subsections of the quarter circle. The area of a subsection is approximately the area of a trapezoid and will be called SUB. The basic relationships needed and a diagram are shown below:

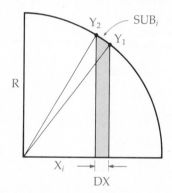

$$AREAQ = \sum_{i=1}^{2000} SUB_i$$

$$SUB_i = \frac{Y_2 + Y_1}{2} \cdot DX$$

$$Y_2 = \sqrt{R^2 - X_i^2}$$
$$Y_1 = \sqrt{R^2 - (X_i + DX)^2}$$
$$X_i = R - i \cdot DX$$
$$DX = R/2000$$

No arrays are needed. Print the value of π with an F16.13 format. Compare your value to the real value of π, which is 3.14159265358979.

27 Write a complete program that will read the coefficients A, B, and C of a quadratic equation from a data line in a 3F6.1 format. The variables A, B, and C represent the coefficients of the equation below:

$$AX^2 + BX + C = 0$$

Write a program to print the variables in an equation form, as above. Then print the two roots, X_1 and X_2, of the equation, where:

$$X_1 = \frac{-B + \sqrt{B^2 - 4AC}}{2A} \qquad X_2 = \frac{-B - \sqrt{B^2 - 4AC}}{2A}$$

Remember that the roots may be complex variables. If the value of A is zero, print an error message.

28 A class of 25 students has taken a true or false exam with 30 questions. The student responses have been stored in a file EXAM, each line of which contains a student's 6-digit identification number, followed by a blank and the 30 responses, where a T represents a true response and an F represents a false response. Write a complete program that will read the correct response key from a data card. Then read and score each student's responses. The output should be in the following form:

STUDENT ID	NUMBER CORRECT	PERCENT CORRECT
XXXXXX	XX	XXX.X
.	.	.
.	.	.
.	.	.

*29 Write a subroutine DECODE that receives a character string KEY containing 26 characters, and a character string TEXT containing 50 characters. The subroutine should decode TEXT, which has been encoded with a substitution key where the first letter in KEY was substituted for the letter A, the second letter in KEY was substituted for the letter B, and so on. Blanks were not changed in the coding process. Thus, if KEY contains the following character string

'YXAZKLMBJOCFDVSWTREGHNIPUQ'

and TEXT contained the character string

'DKKG YG YJRWSRG EYGHRZYU'

then the decoded character string would be,

'MEET AT AIRPORT SATURDAY'

The decoded character string should be written into a file whose name is stored in the character string NFILE. The subroutine will be called by the statement,

```
CALL DECODE(KEY, TEXT, NFILE)
```

Use the INQUIRE statement to determine if the file has been opened. If it has, then determine the appropriate unit number to use. If it has not been opened, then use the OPEN statement to open it.

*30 Write a subroutine ENCODE that receives a character string KEY containing 26 characters, and a character string TEXT containing 50 characters. The subroutine should encode TEXT, using a substitution code where the first letter in KEY is substituted for the letter A in TEXT, and the second letter in KEY is substituted for the letter B in TEXT, and so on.

Thus, if KEY contains the following character string,

'YXAZKLMBJOCFDVSWTREGHNIPUQ'

and TEXT contained the character string

'MEET AT AIRPORT SATURDAY'

then the encoded character string would be,

'DKKG YG YJRWSRG EYGHRZYU'

The encoded character string should be written into a file whose name is stored in the character string NFILE. Use the INQUIRE statement to determine if the file has been opened. If it has, then determine the appropriate unit number to use. If it has not been opened, then use the OPEN statement to open it. The subroutine will be called by the statement,

```
CALL ENCODE(KEY, TEXT, NFILE)
```

*31 Write a main program that will read a character string KEY of 26 characters from columns 1–26 of a data card. From the next data card, read two file names, FILE1 and FILE2, from columns 1–6 and columns 11–16 and a character called CONVRT from column 20. The main program should read records from FILE1, where each record is a character string of 50 characters. If CONVRT contains the letter E, the main program should call the subroutine ENCODE from problem 30. If CONVRT contains the letter D, the main program should call the subroutine DECODE from problem 29. In either case, the subroutine should write its output on FILE2. Thus, the main program will either encode all the messages in FILE1 and write them in FILE2, or it will decode all the messages in FILE1 and write them in FILE2.

APPENDIX A

SUMMARY OF FORTRAN 77 STATEMENTS

NONEXECUTABLE STATEMENTS

†These statements must have a statement number.

EXECUTABLE STATEMENTS

APPENDIX B

FORTRAN 77 INTRINSIC FUNCTIONS

In the following table of intrinsic functions, the names of the arguments specify their type as indicated below:

ARGUMENT	TYPE
X $\longrightarrow$	real
CHX $\longrightarrow$	character
DX $\longrightarrow$	double precision
CX $\longrightarrow$	complex, $a + ib$
LX $\longrightarrow$	logical
IX $\longrightarrow$	integer
GX $\longrightarrow$	generic

Function type, the second column of the table of intrinsic functions, specifies the type of value returned by the function.

Generic function names will be preceded by the dagger sign, †. Any type argument that is applicable can be used with generic functions, and the function value returned will be the same type as the input arguments, except for type conversion functions such as REAL and INT.

Function Name	Function Type	Definition
†SQRT(X)	Real	$\sqrt{X}$
DSQRT(DX)	Double precision	$\sqrt{DX}$
CSQRT(CX)	Complex	$\sqrt{CX}$
†ABS(X)	Real	$|X|$
IABS(IX)	Integer	$|IX|$
DABS(DX)	Double precision	$|DX|$
CABS(CX)	Complex	$|CX|$
†EXP(X)	Real	e^X
DEXP(DX)	Double precision	e^{DX}
CEXP(CX)	Complex	e^{CX}
†LOG(GX)	Same as GX	$\log_e GX$
ALOG(X)	Real	$\log_e X$
DLOG(DX)	Double precision	$\log_e DX$
CLOG(CX)	Complex	$\log_e CX$
†ALOG10(X)	Real	$\log_{10} X$
DLOG10(DX)	Double precision	$\log_{10} DX$
†REAL(GX)	Real	Convert GX to real value
FLOAT(IX)	Real	Convert IX to real value
SNGL(DX)	Real	Convert DX to single precision
†ANINT(X)	Real	Round to nearest whole number
DNINT(DX)	Double precision	Round to nearest whole number
†NINT(X)	Integer	Round to nearest integer
IDNINT(DX)	Integer	Round to nearest integer
†AINT(X)	Real	Truncate X to whole number
DINT(DX)	Double precision	Truncate DX to whole number
†INT(GX)	Integer	Truncate GX to an integer
IFIX(X)	Integer	Truncate X to an integer
IDINT(DX)	Integer	Truncate DX to an integer
†SIGN(X, Y)	Real	Transfer sign of Y to $|X|$
ISIGN(IX, IY)	Integer	Transfer sign of IY to $|IX|$
DSIGN(DX, DY)	Double precision	Transfer sign of DY to $|DX|$
†MOD(IX, IY)	Integer	Remainder from IX/IY
AMOD(X, Y)	Real	Remainder from X/Y
DMOD(DX, DY)	Double precision	Remainder from DX/DY

Function Name	Function Type	Definition
†DIM(X, Y)	Real	X − (minimum of X and Y)
IDIM(IX, IY)	Integer	IX − (minimum of IX and IY)
DDIM(DX, DY)	Double precision	DX − (minimum of DX and DY)
†MAX(GX,GY,...)	Same as GX, GY,...	Maximum of (GX,GY,...)
MAX0(IX,IY,...)	Integer	Maximum of (IX,IY,...)
AMAX1(X,Y,...)	Real	Maximum of (X,Y,...)
DMAX1(DX,DY,...)	Double precision	Maximum of (DX,DY,...)
AMAX0(IX,IY,...)	Real	Maximum of (IX,IY,...)
MAX1(X,Y,...)	Integer	Maximum of (X,Y,...)
†MIN(GX,GY,...)	Same as GX, GY,...	Minimum of (GX,GY,...)
MIN0(IX,IY,...)	Integer	Minimum of (IX,IY,...)
AMIN1(X,Y,...)	Real	Minimum of (X,Y,...)
DMIN1(DX,DY,...)	Double precision	Minimum of (DX,DY,...)
AMIN0(IX,IY,...)	Real	Minimum of (IX,IY,...)
MIN1(X,Y,...)	Integer	Minimum of (X,Y,...)
†SIN(X)	Real	Sine of X, assumes radians
DSIN(DX)	Double precision	Sine of DX, assumes radians
CSIN(CX)	Complex	Sine of CX
†COS(X)	Real	Cosine of X, assumes radians
DCOS(DX)	Double precision	Cosine of DX, assumes radians
CCOS(CX)	Complex	Cosine of CX
†TAN(X)	Real	Tangent of X, assumes radians
DTAN(DX)	Double precision	Tangent of DX, assumes radians
†ASIN(X)	Real	Arcsine of X
DASIN(DX)	Double precision	Arcsine of DX
†ACOS(X)	Real	Arccosine of X
DACOS(DX)	Double precision	Arccosine of DX
†ATAN(X)	Real	Arctangent of X
DATAN(DX)	Double precision	Arctangent of DX
†ATAN2(X,Y)	Real	Arctangent of X/Y
DATAN2(DX,DY)	Double precision	Arctangent of DX/DY
†SINH(X)	Real	Hyperbolic sine of X
DSINH(DX)	Double precision	Hyperbolic sine of DX
†COSH(X)	Real	Hyperbolic cosine of X
DCOSH(DX)	Double precision	Hyperbolic cosine of DX

Function Name	Function Type	Definition
†TANH(X)	Real	Hyperbolic tangent of X
DTANH(DX)	Double precision	Hyperbolic tangent of DX
DPROD(X,Y)	Double precision	Product of X and Y
†DBLE(X)	Double precision	Convert X to double precision
†CMPLX(X)	Complex	$X + i \cdot 0$
†CMPLX(X,Y)	Complex	$X + i \cdot Y$
AIMAG(CX)	Real	Imaginary part of CX
†REAL(CX)	Real	Real part of CX
CONJ(CX)	Complex	Conjugate of CX, $a - ib$
LEN(CHX)	Integer	Length of character string CHX
INDEX(CHX,CHY)	Integer	Position of substring CHY in string CHX
CHAR(IX)	Character string	Character in the IXth position of collating sequence
ICHAR(CHX)	Integer	Position of the character CHX in the collating sequence
LGE(CHX,CHY)	Logical	Value of (CHX is lexically greater than or equal to CHY)
LGT(CHX,CHY)	Logical	Value of (CHX is lexically greater than CHY)
LLE(CHX,CHY)	Logical	Value of (CHX is lexically less than or equal to CHY)
LLT(CHX,CHY)	Logical	Value of (CHX is lexically less than CHY)

GLOSSARY OF KEY WORDS

algorithm   a stepwise procedure for solving a problem

argument   a variable or constant used in a function or subroutine reference

arithmetic expression   an expression of variables, constants, and arithmetic operations that can be evaluated as a single numerical value

arithmetic logic unit (ALU)   a fundamental computer component that performs all the arithmetic and logic operations

arithmetic statement function   a function that can be defined in a single arithmetic statement that is placed before any executable statement in a program

array   a group of variables that share a common name and are specified individually with subscripts

ascending order   an order from lowest to highest

ASCII code   a binary code (American Standard Code for Information Interchange) commonly used by computers to store information

assembler   a program that converts an assembly language program into machine language

assembly language   a programming language that is unique to an individual computer system

assignment statement   a FORTRAN statement that assigns a value to a variable

batch processing a method of interacting with the computer in which programs are executed in generally the same order in which they are submitted

binary a term used to describe something that has two values, such as a binary digit which can be 0 or 1

binary string a string or group of binary values, such as 11011000

blank common a single group of storage locations that is accessible to subprograms without being specified as subprogram arguments

branch a change in the flow of a program such that the steps are not executed in the sequential order in which they are written

buffer an internal storage area used to store input and output information

bug an error in a computer program

carriage control a character used at the beginning of a line of printed output that specifies the page spacing desired before the line is printed

cathode ray tube (CRT) terminal a terminal that uses a video screen for its input and output

central processing unit (CPU) the combination of the processor unit, the ALU, and the internal memory that forms the basis of a computer

character string a string or group of characters that contains numerical digits, alphabetical letters, or special characters

checkpoint a strategic location in a program for printing the values of important variables when debugging the program

collating sequence the ascending order of characters specified by a particular code

comment statement a statement included in FORTRAN programs to document the program but not translated into machine language

common block a block or group of storage locations that is accessible to subprograms without being specified as subprogram arguments

compilation the process of converting a program written in a high-level language into machine language

compiler the program that converts a program written in a high-level language into machine language

complex value a numerical value that is of the form $a + ib$; where $i = \sqrt{-1}$

compound logical expression a logical expression formed by combining two single logical expressions with the connectors .AND. or .OR.

concatenation an operation that connects two strings together to form one string

connector the operators .NOT., .AND., and .OR. that are used with logical expressions

constant a specific value used in arithmetic or logical expressions

control structure a structure that controls the order of execution of a series of steps

conversational computing   a method of interacting with the computer in which the computer seems to converse with the user in an English-like manner

counter   a variable used in a program to store the count of some occurrence

data   the information used by a program or generated by a program

data file   a file used to store information used by a program or generated by a program

debugging   the process of eliminating bugs or errors from a program

descending order   an order from highest to lowest

diagnostic   a message that describes an error in a program that has been located in either the compilation or execution step

direct access file   a file whose information can be accessed in nonsequential order

DO loop   an iteration loop specified in FORTRAN with the DO statement

double precision value   a real value that has been specified to have more precision than the standard real value

driver   a main program written specifically to test a subprogram

dummy variable   a variable whose value will not be used in a program but that was necessary to use in order to read desired data values

EBCDIC code   a binary code (Extended Binary-Coded-Decimal Interchange Code) commonly used by computers to store information

echo   a debugging aid in which the values of variables are printed immediately after being read

editor   a program in a time-sharing system that allows you to modify programs entered into the system

element   a specific storage location in an array

executable statement   a statement specifying action to be taken in a program that is translated into machine language by the compiler

execution   the process of executing the steps specified by a program

explicit typing   a specification of the type of information to be stored in a variable with a REAL or INTEGER statement

exponential notation   a notation for real values that uses an E to separate the mantissa and the exponent

external file   a file that is available to a program through an external device such as a card reader or tape drive

fixed-point value   a numerical value that may represent only integers

floating-point value   a numerical value that may contain decimal positions

flowchart   a graphical diagram used to describe the steps in an algorithm

formatted I/O   the input or output statements that use FORMAT statements to describe the spacing

FORTRAN character set the set of characters accepted by FORTRAN compilers

FORTRAN 77 the version of FORTRAN established in 1977 that includes a number of new features, such as the IF-THEN-ELSE-ENDIF structure

function a subprogram that returns a single value to the main program

generic function a function that returns a value of the same type as its input argument

hard-copy terminal a terminal whose output is printed on paper

hardware the physical components of a computer

high-level language an English-like language that has to be converted into machine language before it can be executed

implicit typing the specification of the type of information (real or integer) to be stored in a variable by the beginning letter of the variable name

implied DO loop a DO loop that can be specified completely on an I/O statement or a DATA statement

increment value the parameter in a DO loop that specifies the increment to be added to the index each time the loop is executed

index the variable used as a loop counter in a DO loop

initial value the parameter in a DO loop that specifies the initial value of the index

initialize give an initial value to a variable

input/output (I/O) the information that a program reads or writes

integer value a value that contains no fractional portion

interface a connection between two devices

intermediate result a result used in evaluating an expression to get the final result

internal file a file defined on information stored in the internal memory of the computer

intrinsic function a function used so frequently that its code is included in a library available to the compiler

iteration loop a loop that is controlled by the value of a variable called the index of the loop or the loop counter

job control information the information that must accompany a program submitted to a batch-processing system

left-justified no blanks on the left side

lexicographic order dictionary order

library function a function used so frequently that its code is available in a library available to the compiler

library subroutine a subroutine whose code is included in a library available to the compiler

limit value the parameter in a DO loop that specifies the value used to determine completion of the DO loop

list-directed I/O the input or output statements that do not use FORMAT statements to describe the spacing

literal a character string

local variable a variable used in a subprogram that is not an argument or a variable in common

logic error an error in the logic used to define an algorithm

logical expression an expression of variables, constants, and operations that can be evaluated as a single logical value

logical value a value that is either "true" or "false"

loop a group of statements that are executed repeatedly

machine language the binary language understood by computers

main program a complete program that may access functions and sub-routines

memory the storage available for the variables and constants needed in a program

microprocessor a small computer usually contained in one or more integrated-circuit chips

minicomputer a small computer system that is usually contained in small, portable consoles

mixed-mode operation an operation between values that are not of the same type

module a function or a subroutine

multi-dimensional array a group of variables that share the same name and whose elements are specified by more than one subscript

named common a group of storage locations that is accessible to sub-programs by name without being specified as subprogram arguments

nested DO loop a DO loop that is completely contained within another DO loop

nested function a function argument that is the value of another function

nonexecutable statement a statement that affects the way memory is used by a program although it is not converted into machine language by the compiler

object program a program in machine-language form

one-dimensional array a group of variables that share the same name and whose elements are specified by one subscript

overprinting printing a new line of information over a line of information that has already been printed

parameter a value or variable used in the DO statement to specify the DO loop

pen plotting plotting that uses a pen that can move in more than one direction to generate plots

permanent workspace the workspace available in a time-sharing system that is not erased each time you log off the system

printer plotting plotting that uses print characters to generate plots

processor a fundamental computer component that controls the operation of the other parts of the computer

program a set of statements that specify a complete algorithm in a computer language

pseudocode the English-like statements used to describe the steps in an algorithm

real value a value that may contain a fractional or decimal portion

record the basic unit of information related to a data file

relational operator an operator used to compare two arithmetic expressions

right-justified no blanks on the right side

rounding a technique that approximates a value

scientific notation a notation for real values that expresses the value as a number between 1 and 10 multiplied by a power of 10

sequential access file a file whose information can be accessed only in a sequential order

software the programs used to specify the operations in a computer

sort put in a specific order

source program a program in a high-level language form

specification statement a statement that specifies the nature of the values to be stored in a variable

stepwise refinement a process for converting a general algorithm to one that is detailed enough to be converted into a computer language

structured programming programming with a top-down flow that is easy to follow and modify because of its structure

style a manner of defining procedures used in computer programs that enhances their simplicity and readability

subprogram a function or subroutine

subroutine a subprogram that may return many values, a single value, or no value to the main program

subscript an integer variable or constant used to specify a unique element in an array

substring a string that is a subset of another string and maintains the original order of characters

syntax error an error in a FORTRAN statement

technique   the type of procedures used in computer programs that enhances their simplicity and readability

temporary workspace   the workspace available in a time-sharing system that is erased each time you log off the system

text processing   processing of character information

time-sharing   a method of interacting with the computer in which a number of programs are being executed at the same time although the user appears to have the complete attention of the computer

top-down code   program statements in which the statements are executed in a flow that goes from the top to the bottom, although the statements are not necessarily executed sequentially

trailer signal   a signal at the end of a data file that indicates that no more data follows

truncation   a technique which approximates a value by dropping its fractional value and using only the integer portion

two-dimensional array   a group of variables that share the same name and whose elements are specified by two subscripts

variable   a memory location referenced with a name whose value can be changed within a program

variable dimensioning   a technique that permits the size of an array in a subprogram to be specified by an argument to the subprogram

variable formatting   a technique that permits the format for a formatted I/O statement to be specified by a character string

WHILE loop   a loop that is executed as long as a specified condition is "true"

word processing   processing of character information

ANSWERS TO SELECTED PROBLEMS

Answers that contain FORTRAN statements are not always unique. Although these answers represent good solutions to the problems, they are not necessarily the only valid solutions.

Chapter 2

1 valid—real variable name

3 valid—real variable name

5 invalid—illegal character (dash)

7 invalid—illegal characters (parentheses)

9 valid—real variable name

11 Since 2.3E4 is equivalent to 23000, the two values are not equal.

13 same value

15 Since $-0.34E02$ is equivalent to -34.0, the two values are not equal.

17 `SL = (Y2 - Y1)/(X2 - X1)`

19 `FR = V**2/(30.0*S)`

21 `P = F*P*(L/D)*(V**2/2.0)` or `P = F*P*L/D*V**2/2.0`

23 `AMU = 0.023*X**8*Y**(1.0/3.0)`

25 $V = \sqrt{(VI)^2 + 2A \cdot X}$

27 $R = \dfrac{2(VI)^2 \cdot \sin B \cdot \cos B}{G}$

29 $L = LI \cdot \sqrt{1 - \left(\dfrac{V}{C}\right)^2}$

31 $F = (0.35 \times 10^{-4})\left(\dfrac{X}{Y}\right) \cdot \sqrt{2G} \cdot (Y2 - Y)^{2.5}$

33 K $\boxed{\quad 1 \quad}$

35 T $\boxed{\ 5.0\ }$

37 MASS $\boxed{\quad 2 \quad}$

39 VOL $\boxed{16.6}$

41 IBASE $\boxed{\quad 14 \quad}$

43 The contents of A and B are switched. The original value of C is lost, and it now contains the original value of A.

45 `X = (Y**2 + 1.0)**2*X`

47 `Y = (2.0*Y + 2.5)/Y`

49 `HOURS = 24.0*DAYS`

Chapter 3

1 $_b$0.40E−03

3 **

5 ****

7 single space from previous line

$\begin{aligned}\text{single} & \quad \text{TIME}_b = {}_{bb}4.55_{bb}\text{RESPONSE}_b1_b = {}_{bb}0.00074 \\ \text{space} & \quad \text{TIME}_b = {}_{bb}4.55_{bb}\text{RESPONSE}_b2_b = {}_b56.83000\end{aligned}$

9 ID $\boxed{1456}$

HT $\boxed{14.6}$

WIDTH $\boxed{0.7}$

11 line or card 1: col 1–6 TIME F6.3
col 7–12 DIST F6.3
col 13–18 VEL F6.3
col 19–24 ACCEL F6.3

13 line or card 1: col 1–3 TIME F3.2
line or card 2: col 1–4 DIST F4.1
line or card 3: col 1–3 VEL F3.2
line or card 4: col 1–4 ACCEL F4.1

15
```
      PROGRAM  CIRCLE
C
C  THIS PROGRAM READS THE DIAMETER OF A CIRCLE AND COMPUTES
C  THE CORRESPONDING RADIUS, CIRCUMFERENCE, AND AREA.
C
      READ(5,1)DIAMTR
    1 FORMAT(F5.2)
C
      PI = 3.141593
      RADIUS = DIAMTR/2.0
      CIRCUM = PI*DIAMTR
      AREA = PI*RADIUS**2
C
      WRITE(6,5)DIAMTR, RADIUS, CIRCUM, AREA
    5 FORMAT('1','PROPERTIES OF A CIRCLE WITH DIAMETER ',
     +          F5.2/1X,5X,'(1)  RADIUS = ',F5.2/
     +          1X,5X,'(2)  CIRCUMFERENCE = ',F6.2/
     +          1X,5X,'(3)  AREA = ',F9.4)
C
      STOP
      END
```

Chapter 4

1 true

3 true

5 true

7 true

9 false

11 `IF(TIME.GT.15.0)TIME = TIME + 1.0`

13 `IF(ABS(VOLT1 - VOLT2).GT.10.0)STOP`

15 `IF(ALOG10(A).GE.ALOG10(Q))TIME = 0.0`

17 `3    IF(CTR.LE.200)THEN`

19 The statements put the minimum value of I, J, and K into M and print it.

21 `IF(I.GT.M - N.OR.I.EQ.6)K = L + 1`

23
```
IF(HOURS.LE.40)THEN
    SALARY = HOURS*RATE
ELSE
    IF(HOURS.LE.50)THEN
        SALARY = 40.0*RATE + (HOURS - 40.0)*RATE*1.5
    ELSE
        SALARY = 40.0*RATE + 10.0*RATE*1.5 + (HOURS - 50.0)*RATE*2.0
    ENDIF
ENDIF
```

Chapter 5

1 21 times

3 391 times

5 1 time

7 41 times

9 COUNTR ☐ 10

11 COUNTR ☐ 7

13 COUNTR ☐ 51

15
```
        .
        .
        .
    SUM = 0
    DO 5 COUNTR=0,49
        SUM = SUM + COUNTR
 5  CONTINUE
        .
        .
        .
```
or
```
        .
        .
        .
    SUM = 0
    DO 5 COUNTR=1,49
        SUM = SUM + COUNTR
 5  CONTINUE
        .
        .
        .
```

17
```
        .
        .
        .
     SUM = 0
     READ(5,1)NUM
 1   FORMAT(I2)
     DO 10 COUNTR=1,NUM
         SUM = SUM + COUNTR
10   CONTINUE
        .
        .
        .
```

19 I ☐ 51

SUM ☐ 5

CALC ☐ 1681

21 KT ⬚ 7

23
```
   DO 5 X=1,5,9,0,5
      Y = (X*X - 9,0)/(X*X + 2,0)
      WRITE(6,3)X, Y
 3    FORMAT(1X,F3,1,2X,F6,2)
 5 CONTINUE
```

25
```
      PROGRAM  SQUARE
C
C  THIS PROGRAM SQUARES THE CONSECUTIVE
C  EVEN INTEGERS FROM 2 THROUGH 200,
C
      WRITE(6,1)
    1 FORMAT('1',' I',13X,'I*I'/
      +        '+',' -',13X,'---')
C
      DO 10 I=2,200,2
         WRITE(6,5)I, I*I
    5    FORMAT('0',I3,10X,I6)
   10 CONTINUE
C
      STOP
      END
```

Chapter 6

1 M

2	3	4	5	6	7	8	9	10	11

3 R

9.0	8.0	7.0	6.0	5.0	4.0	3.0	2.0

5 R

2.5	2.5	2.5	−2.5	−2.5	−2.5	−2.5	−2.5

7 CH

1.0	2.0	3.0	4.0
2.0	4.0	6.0	8.0
3.0	6.0	9.0	12.0
4.0	8.0	12.0	16.0
5.0	10.0	15.0	20.0

9 I

2	3
2	3
2	3
2	3
2	3
2	3
2	3
4	5

11
```
      DIMENSION  K(50)
         .
         .
         .
      MINSUB = 1
      DO 10 I=2,50
         IF(K(I),LT,K(MINSUB))MINSUB = I
   10 CONTINUE
      WRITE(6,20)MINSUB, K(MINSUB)
   20 FORMAT(1X,'MINIMUM VALUE OF K IS'/
      +        1X,5X,'K(',I2,') = ',I5)
         .
         .
         .
```

```
13      DIMENSION  K(50)
            .
            .
            .
        DO 10 I=1,50
            K(I) = ABS(K(I))
     10 CONTINUE
        WRITE(6,20)K
     20 FORMAT(1X,10I6)
            .
            .
            .

15      INTEGER  WIND(10,7)
            .
            .
            .
        WRITE(6,5)
      5 FORMAT(1X,'CHICAGO WIND VELOCITY (MILES/HOUR)')
        WRITE(6,10)((WIND(I,J), J=1,7), I=1,10)
     10 FORMAT(1X,7I10)
            .
            .
            .

17      DIMENSION  NUM(100)
            .
            .
            .
        DO 10 I=1,50
            K = NUM(I)
            NUM(I) = NUM(101-I)
            NUM(101-I) = K
     10 CONTINUE
            .
            .
            .

19      DIMENSION  TEST(100)
            .
            .
            .
        SUM1 = 0.0
        SUM2 = 0.0
        DO 10 I=1,100
            IF(I.LE.50)THEN
                SUM1 = SUM1 + TEST(I)
            ELSE
                SUM2 = SUM2 + TEST(I)
            ENDIF
     10 CONTINUE
        WRITE(6,20)SUM1/50.0, SUM2/50.0
     20 FORMAT(1X,10X,'AVERAGES'/
      +        1X,'1ST 50 EXAMS',4X,'2ND 50 EXAMS'/
      +        1X,2X,F6.2,10X,F6.2)
            .
            .
            .
```

Chapter 7

1 −0.5   **3** 0.5

```
5      PROGRAM  CALC5
          .
          .
          .
       ALPHA = (6.9 + Y)/DENOM(Y)
       WRITE(6,10)ALPHA
    10 FORMAT(1X,F8.2)
          .
          .
          .

7      PROGRAM  CALC7
          .
          .
          .
       GAMMA = SIN(Y)/DENOM(Y*Y)
       WRITE(6,10)GAMMA
    10 FORMAT(1X,F8.2)
          .
          .
          .

9      FUNCTION  MAXA(K)
   C
   C   THIS FUNCTION RETURNS THE MAXIMUM VALUE
   C   OF AN INTEGER ARRAY WITH 100 ELEMENTS.
   C
       DIMENSION  K(100)
   C
       MAXA = K(1)
       DO 5 I=2,100
          IF(K(I).GT.MAXA)MAXA = K(I)
     5 CONTINUE
   C
       RETURN
       END

11     FUNCTION  NPOS(K)
   C
   C   THIS FUNCTION COUNTS THE NUMBER OF VALUES GREATER
   C   THAN OR EQUAL TO ZERO IN AN ARRAY OF 100 ELEMENTS.
   C
       DIMENSION  K(100)
   C
       NPOS = 0
       DO 10 I=1,100
          IF(K(I).GE.0)NPOS = NPOS + 1
    10 CONTINUE
   C
       RETURN
       END

13     FUNCTION  NZERO(K)
   C
   C   THIS FUNCTION COUNTS THE NUMBER OF ZEROS
   C   IN AN ARRAY OF 100 ELEMENTS.
   C
       DIMENSION  K(100)
   C
       NZERO = 0
       DO 10 I=1,100
          IF(K(I).EQ.0)NZERO = NZERO + 1
    10 CONTINUE
   C
       RETURN
       END
```

15 `RADIAN(DEGREE)=(180.0/3.141593)*DEGREE`

17 `T(M,W,A,S)=M*W*W*A*A*S/4.0`

19 N | 5 | 4 | 1 |

L | 10 |

21 N | 5 | 4 | 1 |

L | −2 |

23
```
      SUBROUTINE   ABSOL(Z, W)
C
C THIS SUBROUTINE PUTS THE ABSOLUTE VALUE OF
C EACH ELEMENT OF Z INTO THE CORRESPONDING
C POSITION OF W.
C
      DIMENSION   Z(5,4), W(5,4)
C
      DO 10 I=1,5
         DO 5 J=1,4
            W(I,J) = ABS(Z(I,J))
  5      CONTINUE
 10 CONTINUE
C
      RETURN
      END
```

25
```
      SUBROUTINE   GREAT(Z, W)
C
C THIS SUBROUTINE MOVES CORRESPONDING VALUES OF
C Z INTO W UNLESS THE VALUE IS LESS THAN
C THE AVERAGE OF ALL VALUES IN Z. IN THESE
C CASES, THE AVERAGE VALUE OF Z IS USED IN W.
C
      DIMENSION   Z(5,4), W(5,4)
C
      SUM = 0.0
      DO 10 I=1,5
         DO 5 J=1,4
            SUM = SUM + Z(I,J)
  5      CONTINUE
 10 CONTINUE
C
      AVE = SUM/20.0
      DO 20 I=1,5
         DO 15 J=1,4
            IF(Z(I,J).GT.AVE)THEN
               W(I,J) = Z(I,J)
            ELSE
               W(I,J) = AVE
            ENDIF
 15      CONTINUE
 20 CONTINUE
C
      RETURN
      END
```

```
27        FUNCTION  INVRT(NUMIN, NUMOUT)
     C
     C  THIS FUNCTION REVERSES THE DIGITS IN A TWO-DIGIT NUMBER,
     C
          INTEGER  DIGIT1, DIGIT2
     C
          IF(NUMIN,LT,10,OR,NUMIN,GT,99)THEN
             NUMOUT = 0
             RETURN
          ENDIF
     C
          DIGIT1 = NUMIN/10
          DIGIT2 = MOD(NUMIN,10)
          NUMOUT = DIGIT2*10 + DIGIT1
     C
          RETURN
          END
```

Chapter 8

1 CONSERVATION OF ENERGY$_{bbb}$

3 $_b$OF ENERGY$_b$

5 A

7 CONSERVATION

9 CONSERVATION OF ENERGY$_{bbb}$LAW

11 CONSERVE ENERGY$_{bbb}$

13 WORD ENDISIT ...

13 WORD | DENSIT |

15 WORD | CAN'T$_b$ |

17 WORD | FT/SEC |

19 true

21 false

23 true

25 40

27 7

29 0

31 TITLE | ENERGY ALTERNATIVE A |

33 TITLE | ENERG$_{bbbbbbbbbbbbbbb}$ |

35 single spacing METERS$_{bbbb}$

37 single spacing $_{bbbbb}$METERS$_{bbbb}$

Chapter 9

1 0.25D+00

3 1.0D+00/3.0D+00

5 10.83D+00

7 CX | $1.5 + i2.0$ |

9 CX | $0.5 + i1.0$ |

11 CX | $5.0 + i0.2$ |

13 LX | .FALSE. |

15 LX | .FALSE. |

17 LX | .TRUE. |

19 single spacing $_{bb}$0.141786D$_b$02

21 single spacing F

23 single spacing $_b$2.3$_b$0.2

INDEX

.GE., 90
.GT., 90
G format specification, 308–309
Generic function, 216, 331–334
GO TO statement
  assigned, 124–125
  computed, 123–124
  unconditional, 99

H format specification, 309
Hardcopy terminal, 11
Hardware, 5
Hierarchy
  arithmetic operations, 27
  combined operations, 294
  logical operations, 90–91
High-level language, 6–8
Hollerith format specification, 309
Horizontal spacing, 57

I format specification, 61, 69
IF statement
  arithmetic, 122–123
  logical, 90
IF-THEN-ELSE-ENDIF structure, 102–103
IF-THEN-ELSEIF-ENDIF structure, 105–107
IF-THEN-ENDIF structure, 91
Implicit
  statement, 295
  typing, 22–23, 295
Implied DO loop, 174
Increment value, 136
Index of a DO loop, 136
Initial value, 136
Initialize, 25
Input
  device, 9–12
  formatted, 68–72
  list-directed, 50–56
Input/output, 4, 9–12, 45
INQUIRE statement, 316–317
Inquiry specifier
  ACCESS, 313, 317
  BLANK, 317

Inquiry specifier *(continued)*
  DIRECT, 317
  ERR, 317
  EXIST, 317
  FORM, 313, 317
  FORMATTED, 317
  IOSTAT, 314, 317
  NAME, 317
  NAMED, 317
  NEXTREC, 317
  NUMBER, 317
  OPENED, 316–317
  RECL, 314, 317
  SEQUENTIAL, 317
  UNFORMATTED, 317
Integer
  constant, 21
  input and output, 61, 69
  specification, 23
  variable, 22–23
INTEGER statement, 23
Interface, 5
Intermediate result, 29
Internal file, 318
Intrinsic function, 32–33, 215–216, 331–334
INTRINSIC statement, 305–306
I/O. *See* Input/output
IOSTAT specifier, 314, 317
Iteration loop, 135

Job control statements, 50–53

Keypunch
  guide, 12
  machine, 10–11

.LE., 90
.LT., 90
L format specification, 293
Labelled COMMON statement, 239
Language
  assembly, 7
  high-level, 6–8

String
  binary, 6, 250
  character, 249–251
Structured programming, 97, 211–212, 304
Style/technique guides, 38–39, 82–83, 127,
    159–160, 201, 242, 279–280, 323
Subprogram, 211
  block data, 239–240
  function, 215–220
  subroutine, 222, 226
Subroutine
  alternate entry, 306–307
  alternate return, 307–308
  argument, 222
  call, 222
  library, 222
  name, 222
  user-written, 226
SUBROUTINE statement, 226
Subscript, 169–172, 187–188
Substring, 254–255
Syntax error, 9

.TRUE., 90
Tab specification, 80
Temporary workspace, 13
Terminals, 10–11
Text processing, 249
THEN, 91
Time-sharing, 13
TLn format specification, 309
Tn format specification, 80
Top-down code, 97. *See* Structured
    programming
Trailer signal, 117
Transfer statement, 99, 122–124
TRn format specification, 309
Truncation, 30
Two-dimensional array
  initialization, 187–190
  input and output, 191–193
  specification, 188
  storage, 187–188
Type
  character, 249–251
  complex, 290–291
  double precision, 288
  explicit, 22
  implicit, 22

Type *(continued)*
  integer, 23
  logical, 292–293
  real, 23
  statement, 23

Unconditional GO TO statement, 99
Unformatted file, 313
UNFORMATTED specifier, 317
Unit number, 47, 74, 313
UNIT specifier, 74, 313
User-written
  function, 216–222
  subroutine, 226

Variable
  character, 250–251
  complex, 290–291
  dimensioning, 220
  double precision, 289
  formatting, 311–312
  integer, 21–23
  local, 304–305
  logical, 292–293
  name, 22
  real, 21–23
Vertical spacing, 57

WHILE loop, 89, 97–99
Width of format specification, 61
Word processing, 249
Workspace, 13
WRITE statement
  formatted, 56–68
  list-directed, 45–48

X format specification, 60